750

D0985026

A
Dialogue between a
Philosopher & a Student
of the
Common Laws of England

Compositum jus, fasque, animi, sanctosque recessus.
Mentis, & incoctum generoso pectus honesto.
Hæc cedo, ut admoveam templis, & farre litabo.

Pers. Sat. 2.

Thomas Hobbes of Malmesbury

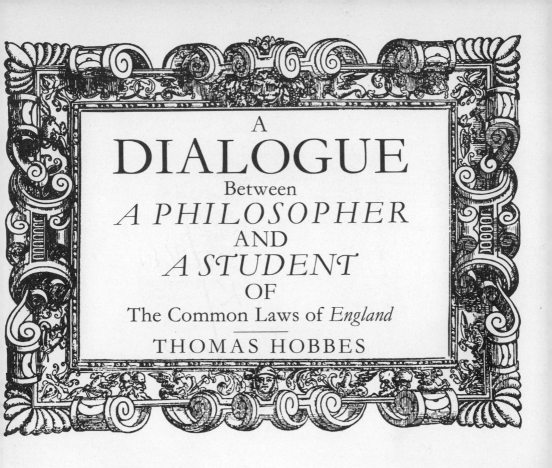

A
DIALOGUE
Between
A PHILOSOPHER
AND
A STUDENT
OF
The Common Laws of *England*

THOMAS HOBBES

Edited and with an Introduction by
Joseph Cropsey

THE UNIVERSITY OF CHICAGO PRESS
CHICAGO AND LONDON

International Standard Book Number: 0-226-34540-8
Library of Congress Catalog Card Number: 76-120008
The University of Chicago Press, Chicago 60637
The University of Chicago Press, Ltd., London

Printed in the United States of America

CONTENTS

NOTE: Numbers in parentheses refer to the pagination of the first edition; italic numbers, to the pagination of the present volume.

ACKNOWLEDGMENTS

I am grateful to Dean D. Gale Johnson and to the Research Committee of the Division of the Social Sciences at the University of Chicago for their support of my work on this volume. My research assistant, Diane E. Cole, was a faithful collaborator whose unstinting help was of great value to me. Librarians of the British Museum, the Bodleian, and Christ Church and Worcester Colleges, Oxford, obliged me by responding to inquiries about materials in their custody, as did Mr. T. S. Wragg, Librarian of the Devonshire Collections. Professor Benedict Einarson of the University of Chicago generously answered questions out of the great store of his knowledge. It is a pleasure to express my thanks for their help.

The frontispiece from *The Moral and Political Works of Thomas Hobbes of Malmesbury* (London, 1750) and the facsimile title and half-titles pages from the first edition of the present *Dialogue* (London, 1681) are reproduced through the courtesy of the Department of Special Collections of the University of Chicago Library, Robert Rosenthal, Curator.

INTRODUCTION

THE TEXT

Thomas Hobbes (1588–1679) is, to the best of our knowledge, the author of *A Dialogue between a Philosopher and a Student, of the Common Laws of England*, which was published for the first time in 1681, two years after the author's death.[1] The *Dialogue* was published in two different volumes by the same publisher in 1681: as the second piece in a volume containing *The Art of Rhetoric* and as one of a number of Hobbes's writings collected in *Tracts of Thomas Hobb's Containing I. His Life in Latine*, etc.[2] The *Dialogue* has been reprinted with editorial attention to the text twice: first in 1750 in *The Moral and Political Works of Thomas*

---

1. In the "Life" prefixed to *The Moral and Political Works of Thomas Hobbes of Malmesbury* (London, 1750), the following is said: "In 1678, appeared his *Decameron Physiologicum*, or *ten Dialogues of Natural Philosophy*, to which he added a Book composed some Years before, at the Request of a Person of great Distinction, entituled, *A Dialogue between a Philosopher and a Student of the Common Law of England*. . . ." This "Life" is attributed to John Campbell (see Leslie Stephen's article "Hobbes" in *The Dictionary of National Biography*) and is said to be simply Campbell's biography of Hobbes in *Biographia Britannica*. The sentence in the *Biographia* corresponding to the one quoted reads: "In 1678, appeared his *Decameron Physiologicum*: or, *Ten Dialogues of Natural Philosophy*; about the same time he revised and put the last hand to a work formerly published, though without his name, the Art of Rhetoric, collected from Aristotle and Ramus; to which he added a book, composed some years before at the request of a person of great distinction, entituled, A *Dialogue* between a *Philosopher* and a *Student* of the *Common-Law* of England . . ." (4:2613). To this sentence there is a note: "These two pieces of our author, which did not appear together 'till after his death, are in effect but detached branches of his general philosophy." The statement in *Biographia Britannica* (whether it be an earlier or a later version of the sentence than the one in the 1750 *Works* we cannot now take up) is not entirely unambiguous; but it comes much closer to conveying that the *Dialogue between a Philosopher and a Student* was not published during Hobbes's lifetime. Being unable to find any other indication that this *Dialogue* was published in 1678, that is, during Hobbes's lifetime, I shall concur in the general understanding that the 1681 edition is the first and that the author never saw the disfigurement that his text suffered at the hands of the compositor.
2. *Tracts of Thomas Hobb's* is the first of two volumes of Hobbes's "Tracts" published by Crooke in 1681 and 1682 respectively. These two volumes comprise, apparently, the publication entitled *Tracts Written by Thomas Hobbes of Malmesbury; in Two Volumes in Octavo* referred to by Edward Arber, *The Term Catalogues* (London, 1903, privately printed), 1:463.

Hobbes of Malmesbury, a volume of which neither the editor nor the publisher is named on the title page, and again in 1840 in volume 6 of *The English Works of Thomas Hobbes of Malmesbury*, edited by Sir William Molesworth and published in London by John Bohn. The 1750 editor has made useful corrections of the text, and so has Molesworth; but each has left difficulties unresolved and errors undetected. Molesworth appears to have consulted the 1750 edition but has not profited from some of its obviously valid emendations. Neither editor gives the reader notice when an alteration of the 1681 edition is being introduced. In correcting the text, the 1750 editor had a material advantage in being bred to a state of the English language disparate to that prevalent in Hobbes's latter years by the evolution of mere decades. Molesworth had the merit of being sensitive to errors in the legal citations as misprinted by Hobbes's unworthy publisher, William Crooke. Neither editor succeeded in producing a text that is clear and dependable throughout, and it is in the hope of progressing toward the provision of such a text that the present work is offered.

I am unable to determine with any accuracy the date of composition of the *Dialogue*. The latest specific event referred to in the text is, I believe, an act of legislation in the thirteenth year of Charles II. That monarch dated his reign from his father's execution in 1649. The thirteenth of Charles II is therefore the year 1662, before which this *Dialogue* cannot have been written or at any rate completed. (Whether it can be said to have been completed at all will be argued below.) There is reason to believe that the manuscript was in existence by the middle or late 1670s. First, the sentence from "Hobbes" in *Biographia Britannica* (quoted in n. 1 above) describes the *Dialogue* as having been composed "some years before" the period just prior to his death. Second, there is an illuminating entry in *Thomas Hobbes: A Bibliography* by Hugh Macdonald and Mary Hargreaves. In an addendum to their entry for the 1675 print of Hobbes's poem "De Mirabilibus Pecci" ("The Wonders of the Peak," referring to a mountain in Derbyshire), the authors show that Christ Church College and Worcester College, Oxford, possess copies of the printed poem to which the publisher, W. Crooke, appended the announcement:
"There are these following Manuscripts of M$^{r.}$ *Hobbes's*

. . . .

> 2. A Dialogue betwixt a Student in the Common Laws of *Eng-land*, and a Philosopher.
>
> ....
>
> *Which Manuscripts are delivered by the Author into the hands of* W. Crooke."[3]

Not because Crooke is to be trusted implicitly but because Hobbes was very much alive in 1675 and capable of troubling Crooke for exceeding the truth, this announcement by Crooke carries a certain presumption of verity. It follows that most likely the work was composed, in some loose sense that abstracts from "completion," no earlier than 1662 and no later than 1675. The latter date could be upset by a showing that Crooke wrongly dated the reprint as 1675 although in fact it was later than 1679—which I have not seen intimated anywhere—or that the poem was indeed printed in 1675 but that, after Hobbes's death, Crooke added the crucial catalogue of manuscripts to some unbound copies of the poem, the date of the reprint thus not applying to the catalogue. In support of this possibility is the fact noted by Macdonald and Hargreaves that among the copies of the poem they examined, the catalogue appears only in those possessed by Christ Church and Worcester. Macdonald and Hargreaves do not mention that the catalogue in the Christ Church copy comes at the end of the poem (C4 verso) while the catalogue in the Worcester copy comes at the beginning (A1 verso). All these facts tend to weaken the conclusion that the stated date of the reprint of "De Mirabilibus Pecci," namely, 1675, is the date of the catalogue, seemingly joined to the poem adventitiously and thus perhaps at odd times. The collation of the Christ Church and Worcester copies does, at least, cause it to appear most probable that the catalogues, although in different positions in the two volumes, are on leaves that are conjugate with leaves on which the poem itself is printed. I cannot explain why the printing should have been executed in that way; what follows might, however, shed some light. Macdonald and Hargreaves give, as entry number 106 in their book, a collection of Hobbes's writings published by Crooke in 1675 and containing as the first work "De Mirabilibus Pecci." The authors write "The title-page [of the volume as a whole?], *De Mirabilibus Pecci*, and the catalogue at the end, were printed

---

3. *Thomas Hobbes: A Bibliography* (London: Bibliographical Society, 1952), p. xv.

together (forming A–C4) and are the only parts of this work printed especially for it."[4] One can therefore guess that Crooke bound separately some of the copies of the poem printed for inclusion in this collection, the catalogue coming at the end and being conjugate with a leaf of the poem itself. This is Macdonald and Hargreaves's thought expressed in their notes to entry number 9.[5] The description fits the Christ Church copy. Item number 8 in Macdonald and Hargreaves is an issue of "De Mirabilibus Pecci" without a title page and without a printed date, but with "1666" handwritten in the Bodleian's copy belonging to the Anthony Wood collection. The collation shows that "A1 was probably a blank leaf." If Crooke, in 1675, reworked sheets of this earlier edition and used A1^v for printing the catalogue, he would have produced a copy with the characteristics of the copy now owned by Worcester College, that is, with the catalogue at the front of the volume. In both cases the date 1675 would apply to the catalogue, and the manuscript of this *Dialogue* would in truth have been in Crooke's possession four years before Hobbes's death.

Crooke's announcement is significant not primarily because of the help it gives in determining the period of the composition of the *Dialogue*, for that is not of supreme interest. What is more important is that Hobbes apparently transmitted to his publisher, presumably for publication, a work that, as we now possess it, seems to be incomplete. If Hobbes had done this on his death bed, or when he no longer felt capable of working, there would be a question, namely, why did he not simply suppress an imperfect production. But Hobbes appears to have transmitted this manuscript to the publisher at a time when his death was at least four years off, when he was in full possession of his mental faculties and still at work. His only disability appears to have been an unsteadiness of the hand that made him depend on an amanuensis. The question that arises is not, why did he not destroy this incomplete work, but rather, is this work in fact incomplete, and if it is, why then did he not destroy it; but if it is complete, why did he leave it appearing as if it were not?

The *Dialogue* ends abruptly, without any doubt. Sir Leslie Stephen says it was "not finished."[6] Tönnies considers it incom-

---

4. *Hobbes: Bibliography,* p. 79.   5. Ibid, p. 5.
6. *Hobbes* (London: Macmillan, 1928), p. 61.

plete.[7] Croom Robertson also considers it unfinished, and to support his judgment refers to a place in John Aubrey's "The Life of Mr. Thomas Hobbes of Malmesburie."[8] This "Life" is not that which appears in the collection entitled *Brief Lives* but runs to about forty-five pages, with addenda, including Hobbes's will, appended at uncertain times. The "Life" proper was written or at least begun shortly after Hobbes's death, which occurred on 4 December 1679. This dating of the composition can be deduced from Aubrey's reference, early in the "Life," to Hobbes's brother Edmund: Edmund was "about" two years older than Thomas, thus born in 1586. He died at the age of "about" eighty—"about" thirteen years before the words were written. The writing therefore took place in "about" 1679, presumably in the last weeks of December or in January, at the earliest. This "Life" was printed in 1813 in the edition[9] referred to by Robertson, who draws attention to certain matter on pages 613 and 614. After speaking of his attempt, in 1664, to stimulate Hobbes to make a study of the law, going so far as to give him a copy of Bacon's "Elements of the Law" to read, Aubrey writes, "I desponded that he should make any attempt (*tentamen*) towards this designe. But afterwards, it seems, in the country, he writt his treatise 'De Legibus,' (unprinted) of which Sir J. Vaughan, L[d] Chief Justice of the Common Pleas, had a transcript, and I doe affirm that he much admired it." At this point Aubrey introduces the following note: "In a letter to me, dated Aug. 18, 1679, among other things, he writes, 'The treatise De Legibus, at the end of it is imperfect. I desire Mr. Horne to pardon me that I cannot consent to his motion; nor shall Mr. Crooke himselfe get my consent to print it. . . . I am, Sir, your very humble servt. TH. HOBBES.' " It is to this passage that Robertson apparently refers in saying of the *Dialogue* that it is, "according to Hobbes himself . . . unfinished."[10]

In considering whether the present *Dialogue* is in fact incomplete, or in what sense it is so, the following should be kept in view. In the first place, there is the question whether the "treatise

---

7. Ferdinand Tönnies, *Thomas Hobbes: der Mann und der Denker* (Leipzig: Zick-feldt, 1912), p. 49.

8. George Croom Robertson, *Hobbes* (London and Edinburgh: Blackwood, 1886), pp. 2, 199.

9. *Letters Written by Eminent Persons in the Seventeenth and Eighteenth Centuries: to which are added, . . . Lives of Eminent Men, by John Aubrey, Esq.* (London: 1813), 2:593 ff.   10. Robertson, *Hobbes*, p. 199, n. 1.

de legibus" is this *Dialogue*. Let it be assumed that no important difficulty is raised by the designation of a dialogue as a treatise, and therefore that the remarks of Hobbes and Aubrey point to the present work. Next, it is to be noted that Aubrey says of it not that it is unfinished but that it is unprinted (as of course this work was in 1679 or 1680); while Hobbes says of it not that the work is unfinished but that "at the end it is imperfect." One does not know how literally to read this expression, but what it means most precisely is that the work is ended but the end is imperfect. Whether perfecting the end would have led Hobbes to augment it or to refine it by shortening it is more than we know or perhaps will ever know. Whatever the character of the imperfection, Hobbes seems to have found it a sufficient reason for desiring that the work remain unpublished.

In the third place, in order to strengthen the case for incompleteness, I shall suppose that Aubrey wrote the "Life" in the last weeks of 1679 and in 1680 and certainly finished the body of it before that date in 1681 (not known to me) on which the present *Dialogue* was published by Crooke. Then there is no difficulty in understanding how Aubrey[11] can say of Hobbes's "treatise 'De Legibus'" that it is "unprinted" without implying that the "treatise" is not the *Dialogue*: before the *Dialogue* was printed, any work on the law by Hobbes described as unprinted might have been this *Dialogue*; and if such a work were said by Hobbes to be unfinished (or words to that effect), then this *Dialogue* might be the very work described by Hobbes as unfinished. But Aubrey lived until 1697, and was improving the "Life" to about 1688 at least. He appended to the "Life" proper a "Catalogue of his [Hobbes's] Learned Familiar Friends and Acquaintance, besides those already mentioned, that I remember him to have spoken of."[12] On page 631 (edition of 1813), moreover, Aubrey writes, "In May, 1688, his [Hobbes's] 'Ecclesiastica Historia Carmine Elegiaco conscripta,' was printed at . . . London." Yet Aubrey never altered the remark that Hobbes's treatise "De Legibus" was unprinted, although the *Dialogue* was published in 1681—once with the *Rhetoric* and once in the *Tracts*. We observe, therefore, a faint revival of the question of whether the *Dialogue* is the treatise, and thus whether the *Dialogue* is incomplete. In fact, however, a somewhat different question may now be seen to arise, for

---

11. *Letters written by Eminent Persons*, 2:614.   12. Ibid., pp. 625 ff.

Aubrey's silence on the publication of this work, one which he himself might have urged Hobbes to write, includes his failure to accuse Crooke of violating Hobbes's injunction against publishing it.

I have sought but have been unable to find any animadversion on W. Crooke for what would have been his breach of faith in publishing the *Dialogue* against the wishes of Hobbes, as those wishes were perfectly known to Aubrey through the letter of Hobbes's quoted above, if indeed Hobbes was expressing the wish that this *Dialogue* be suppressed. Not only is there no remonstrance with Crooke by Aubrey, but there is none by Anthony Wood, whose *Athenae Oxonienses* includes, as part of the article on Hobbes, a bibliography that contains an entry for the present *Dialogue*.[13] Wood's record reaches to the year 1690 and includes reference to the publication of Hobbes's history of the Roman Church in 1688. The state of Wood's communication with Aubrey makes it more than unlikely that Wood was unaware of the contents of Hobbes's letter of 18 August 1679 to Aubrey. I consider the absence (to the best of my present knowledge) of any sign of a protest against Crooke's publication of this *Dialogue* as evidence against the view that this is a work desired by Hobbes to be suppressed. Implicit in this inference is the question whether the treatise is the *Dialogue*, and whether the *Dialogue* is unfinished. Also implicit, however, is the question whether the treatise-*Dialogue*, supposed one and the same, was meant by Hobbes to be suppressed. The remainder of this discussion of the completedness of the *Dialogue* is influenced by the fact that if the question of completedness is to any extent open, that question transforms itself into a very different one, namely, did Hobbes seriously forbid the publication of this work.

When Crooke published this *Dialogue* in 1681, he issued it, as has been said, in two different collections of Hobbes's works. In the smaller, it appears with *The Art of Rhetoric*, which filled the first part of the volume. Prefixed to the book was a statement "To the Reader" in which someone, perhaps or presumably Crooke, writes: "The other piece is a Discourse concerning the Laws of England, and has been finish'd many years. . . ." Robertson[14] draws attention to the fact that this assertion was made when Hobbes (two years dead) could no longer contradict it. This,

13. Anthony Wood (or à Wood), *Athenae Oxonienses*, 3d ed. (London, 1817), column 1215, vol. 3.   14. *Hobbes*, p. 199, n. 1.

while fair enough as far as it goes, loses weight, and the assertion
that the "Discourse" was finished many years earlier correspondingly gains, when it is remembered that Crooke announced in
1675 that he was in possession of this very work in manuscript;
and Hobbes was well situated to deny that, or to recover the
manuscript if it was unfinished (leaving aside the question of how
Crooke would have obtained an unfinished manuscript from
Hobbes against the author's wishes, and why he would then have
gone on to tell the world he possessed it with the implication that
he meant someday to publish it, precisely as he did).

I do not suppose the foregoing to prove that the *Dialogue* as we
have it is finished. I do believe that even on purely biographical
and bibliographical grounds, it is not certain that this *Dialogue* is
unfinished, as it has been hitherto somewhat uncritically considered. Furthermore, the fact that it ends so abruptly should be
taken in conjunction with the fact that it begins at least as abruptly.
Something has been passing between the interlocutors before the
first recorded speech by the Lawyer, as is self-evident. I believe
it would be well to leave open the possibility that, as the author
of a dialogue might wish to suggest speeches prior to those he
writes down, so he might also wish to suggest that there are
speeches posterior, both kinds to be imagined by the reader. In
brief, there is no reason in principle why abruptness at the end
should be more positive a sign of incompleteness in a dialogue
than abruptness at the opening. I wish, therefore, to suggest no
more than that readers study the present work without any pre-
judgment as to whether it is a finished or an unfinished writing,
notwithstanding the prevailing and by no means implausible view
of it as incomplete.

Biographical and bibliographical considerations seem to justify
leaving this question open; but such considerations, independent
of the substance of the book and its argument, cannot settle the
question or even endow it with great interest or importance. On
the other hand, if by examination of the course of argument it
appears that the termination of the work on the theme with which
it at present comes to a close brings the argument itself to an
intelligible period, the biographical and bibliographical considerations acquire a certain weight. In the section of this Introduction dealing with the argument proper, I shall try to give an
account of the doctrine that Hobbes's interlocutors generate
through the *Dialogue* as a whole; but for the present I wish to

sketch only so much of that argument as bears on the question, whether the present abrupt end is in any sense the end of an orderly construction that could have been intended to have the shape it now has.

In a manner of speaking, the *Dialogue* as a whole deals with the theme of law and reason. More specifically, the basis of law in one sense is authority alone; but although its reasonableness might not be, and is said not to be, the sufficient condition for the legality of a given command, Hobbes exhibits arguments tending to the thought that the authoritative law can conflict with right reason. The intelligence of the monarch is sufficient for legislation because the authority of the monarch is legally sufficient for legislation; but the intelligence of the monarch may be insufficient on other grounds, as is obvious. For this reason and for others, the monarch's "consultation" with Parliament and the "assent" of Parliament to the monarch's prescriptions become important. Moreover, as is made plain in the very concluding section that we now have in view, the collaboration of Parliament is a means to procure that assent of the multitude to their government which the late revolution had so abundantly shown to be of the essence of civil society. It is also a fact, and I believe a significant one, that Hobbes presents an account of the English Parliament that shows it to be precisely coeval with the English (or rather Saxon) monarchy, not a mere concession or contrivance; that in the modern world, the king cannot have troops except through Parliament; and that it is of the nature of the English Parliament to include a house composed of members elected by the people— not chosen by the crown—for their discretion. One of the chief questions arising out of Hobbes's constructions in this *Dialogue* is precisely whether he is presenting a novel doctrine—novel at least for him—as to Parliament and thus as to law and legislation. If it should prove to be the case that the theme of Parliament is of high importance for the *Dialogue* as a whole, and if what he has to say about Parliament constitutes a magnification of the place of the legislative that would be unpleasing to many ears, including the king's own and the bishops', then it would not be irrational in Hobbes to give his publisher (with a perfunctory instruction not to publish it) an "unfinished" work ending abruptly with a certain description of what constitutes a perfect English parliament. Whether any of these conjectures materialize cannot be seen until the argument is examined in detail; but I do wish to suggest provisionally that the substance of the *Dialogue* is not grossly incompatible with the termination of the work on the theme of Parliament, as it now in fact closes.

This book is in the form of a colloquy between a speaker called Philosopher (through the title of the work and through the abbreviations prefixed to his speeches) and a speaker called Lawyer in the text but Student of the Common Law on the title page. The seeming distinction between Lawyer and Student of the Law, drawing attention to a disparity between a qualified person and an apprentice, proves in the context of the *Dialogue* to indicate an identity: Hobbes considers the members of the legal profession, bench as well as bar, to be studiers of something that they do not make but in which it is their duty simply to become versed: lawyers are never rightly more than students of the law, a point that must be pressed emphatically in respect of the common law, which is thought by its hierophants to be generated by themselves out of their enriched reason.

There is one master of the common law whom Hobbes takes very particularly under consideration in the *Dialogue*, and that is Sir Edward Coke (1552–1634), who is made the spokesman for the doctrine of autonomous common lawyers and thus the antagonist of what is surely Hobbes's own explicit position that sovereignty is entire in the monarch. Rather generally, there is a correspondence between Hobbes's familiar teachings and the sayings of the Philosopher, while the Lawyer occasionally introduces the doctrines of Coke as being authoritative and is given the role of defending those doctrines, as well as of presenting the facts, often under questioning, as to statutes, texts, and so on. But the Lawyer is also the introducer of some of the most famous Hobbesian conceptions, especially the characterization of the pre-civil condition as one of mutual hostility and unlimited right. (It is remarkable that the expression "state of nature" never occurs in this *Dialogue*, although it would be appropriate in the context.) On the whole, it would be too simple to make the Lawyer into Coke; while in a sense that draws us back to the biographical and bibliographical considerations, it would be impossible to identify the Philosopher and Hobbes. The Philosopher at the outset declares that he read the laws of England only to obey and never to dispute them, nor to examine them with a view to their being more or less rational. This is compatible enough with the lifelong teaching of Hobbes the author of avowedly edifying exhortations to obedience; but it is incompatible with the behavior of Hobbes the author of a book (*Behemoth*) forbidden to be published by the king himself, a book which he handed in manuscript to his publisher directly upon receiving it back from the king with what is described by Hobbes as a flat prohibition to publish it. I cannot speculate, nor do I know whether anyone can be in a position fruitfully to speculate, on whether Charles II gave his injunction to Hobbes with a wink. It is true that the posthumous publication of *Behemoth* did not subject the publisher to prosecution. Without such speculation, one is disposed to think that Hobbes as philosopher, that is, as subject more rational than the sovereign monarch, disobeyed on behalf of the *salus populi* when death had put him beyond punishment. Ultimately, Hobbes did not put obedience above all. It cannot be said, however, that the circumstances of his disobedience, if that is indeed what it was, point to so elevated if unsettling a maxim as that freedom to philosophize and to utter the fruit of philosophy knows no legitimate restraint, the philosopher being thus as much above the law as is the sovereign. For Hobbes's "disobedience" was posthumous, and as such is open to imitation by every nonphilosopher in principle (if he can find an instrument of disobedience to operate after his death), showing that it is man's natural right to cheat not only the executioner but the grave itself, together with the king.

This *Dialogue* is to some extent a polemic against Coke. Coke was a man of great gifts in the law, who prospered early and almost continuously to a fullness of years and riches, and of honors reaching to the high places of the English judiciary. He was, of course, a renowned common-lawyer, sitting as chief justice of the Court of Common Pleas (from 1606) and then as chief justice of the King's Bench (beginning 1613). There was no controversy between Hobbes and Coke during the latter's lifetime, and a question arises as to why Hobbes saw fit, more than thirty years after Coke's death, to frame his reflections on the law as an assault on Sir Edward Coke. This is not to imply that Hobbes had not noticed Coke, and noticed him critically, much earlier, and with a view to some of the leading issues of the present *Dialogue*. Hobbes mentions Coke by name and also allusively in chapter 26 of *Leviathan*—"Of Civil Laws"—of which this work is in some respects an elaboration.

A convenient way of penetrating the question of Coke's signifi-
cance for the *Dialogue* is by going back to John Aubrey's intelligent contrivance for stimulating Hobbes's interest, in 1664, in
writing on the law. Aubrey recounts that he gave Hobbes Bacon's
"*Elements of the Law*," more accurately *The Elements of the Common
Laws of England*, to prime the pump of Hobbes's legal rumination.
If we ourselves turn to Bacon's legal writings, not only to the
brilliantly lucid *Elements* but to his abridgments of the law, his
sketches for the reformation of the law, and his masterly presenta-
tion of leading legal questions in letters to King James, we per-
ceive in its legal-political material the tension between Bacon and
Coke that strained their relation during the decades in which they
both labored in the English judiciary. Concretely, what we find
is that Coke on crucial occasions maintains a distinct judicial independence of the sovereign, under law. He further maintains the
autonomy of the common-law judiciary as against Chancery, the
great court of equity, in which aggrieved parties believed, contrary to the opinion of Coke, that they could obtain relief on
appeal from judgments given in the courts of Common Pleas and
King's Bench. These might look like two disjoint considerations,
but Bacon understood them as related or even identical. The
sovereign is master of the judiciary, whose officials are his magis-
trates, bound not only to cleave to the law but to sustain their
master's prerogative. And the Chancery was considered by Bacon
to be "the Court of [the king's] absolute power,"[15] presumably
because it was precisely in Chancery that equity rules, and every
ill must be subject to a right remedy, under the royal chancellor.
The cases at law in which these principles came forth are
Peacham's case and the great threat of premunire against the
chancellor. We cannot go into these. For the present, the point to
be made is that Hobbes seems to have appointed himself the heir
of his old master's law, and Hobbes's controversy with the dead
Coke is the continuation of Bacon's.

We can readily determine that important elements of Hobbes's
legal understanding correspond with conspicuous points of
Bacon's jurisprudence. In particular, the passages or sections of
this *Dialogue* on the supremacy of the king as judge, on the courts,
and on the writ of premunire suffice to make the relation clear.
But although we can say that in the main Hobbes's doctrine

15. Bacon's letter to James I, in *The Works of Francis Bacon* (London: A. Millar,
1740), 4:612.

follows Bacon's and that Hobbes's polemic against Coke is to that extent Bacon's, we still have not explained why Hobbes should have chosen to pursue in 1665 such issues as were agitating legal-political circles in 1615.

Any answer to this question must be compatible with the massive fact that, in this *Dialogue*, Hobbes is reflecting, as he does in *Behemoth*, on the grounds of the late Revolution. As will appear, he argues that certain legal constructions beginning with the premise that reason is the warrant of law conduce to the destruction of the sovereign power and hence to the ruin of the people. His emphasis is on the doings of the legal profession. In other writings his most renowned arguments are to the effect that it is the Universities, and their progeny the clergy, that are the wells and the spouts of ill doctrine. The emphasis on law rather than divinity cannot be satisfactorily explained by the fact that this *Dialogue* is a book on the law of England; for it is precisely Hobbes's intention in taking up the old polemic against Coke, i.e., his intention in writing about law and lawyers, that is to be explained. To imply on the basis of this *Dialogue* that Hobbes replaced divinity by law and divines by legists as crucial for understanding civil peace would go far beyond what can be maintained. On the contrary, this work contains an explicit repetition of Hobbes's familiar thought that the clergy are largely responsible for the state of the multitude's opinion;[16] although it is to be noticed that this thought is given to the Lawyer for expression and is waved away somewhat brusquely by the Philosopher as being beside his present purpose, which is to inquire into the laws of England. What I believe can be maintained is that there is a difference of emphasis between the teaching of *Leviathan* and the teaching of the *Dialogue*, a difference indicated by the fact, already mentioned, that Hobbes never once refers by name to the state of nature in the *Dialogue*. A merely prudential reason cannot cogently be assigned for this silence, for nothing that Hobbes could ever do by way of silence alone could withdraw that powerful conception from the crannies of the world into which it had long since penetrated. A more solid explanation of that silence and of the greater fact to which it points, namely, the difference in emphasis between the *Dialogue* and Hobbes's earlier writings, is

---

16. P. (8). References to the pages of the *Dialogue* are given as arabic numerals in parentheses, corresponding to the pagination of the first edition, which is also noted in the margins of this edition.

one that grows out of the substance of this book itself: the true rationality of law inheres not simply in the reason of the sovereign doctrinairely insisted upon but in the endurability of the laws as that is signified or imparted to them through the assent of the people in Parliament.[17] As I hope will appear, Hobbes maintains the king's prerogative, the need for the assent of Parliament, and the indispensability of subordinating the common law (thus the legal profession) to statute and Chancery, or equity. This is the paradigm of Bacon's practical politics. It is to be remembered that Bacon sought the chancellory above all posts, even reminding the king of the enormous sacrifices in money that he would make if he gained his suit to be appointed to that place. [18] Bacon favored the calling of Parliament,[19] with the thought expressed that his great influence with the Commons would prove beneficial to the crown and country. Bacon sought to reduce the pretension of the common-lawyers to make law by interpretation, popular men popularly legislating, free from the check of Chancery. And Bacon warned against the disruptive influence of Coke specifically, the chief of legal experts, upon a Parliament.[20] But Bacon fell upon hard times, and James perhaps sacrificed him to protect Buckingham. Within a few years, James had died, Bacon also, and Coke was agitating the Parliament sitting in 1628. Only twenty years later the king was executed. If this *Dialogue* is a true retrospect on the causes of the great dissolution of English civil society, it is so in a manner that skillfully combines the occasional and the enduring. In a sense, it teaches that the defeat of Bacon's conception was the source of the English disaster. It tries to revive Bacon's conception without accusing the father and grandfather of Charles II of obstinate folly, and without radical yet with genuine indications of the need for Parliamentary consent in government. It certainly does not obtrude on the reader the notion that supreme wisdom in the chancellor is indispensable to the success of the English monarchy or of a monarchy in general or of government in principle. Yet Bacon was, until the seventeenth century and down to our own, the only philosophic man of first rank to have come so close to regality as in fact to have sat vicegerent while the monarch was absent from the realm. Hobbes says nothing of all this. But he calls his interlocutors a "Lawyer," who speaks for Sir Edward Coke, and a "Philosopher" who is his adversary. The

---

17. P. (204).   18. Bacon, *Works*, 4:607.   19. Ibid., pp. 719-20.
20. Ibid., p. 670.

Lawyer speaks for Coke but also, as has been seen, for Hobbes too. The Philosopher is a composite of Bacon and Hobbes, and the dialectic of the work produces a teaching of moderateness in popular politics that is edifying in all times and places.

THE ARGUMENT

⚓ *Of the Law of Reason*

The *Dialogue* opens with a speech by the Lawyer which must be a response to a speech by the Philosopher that precedes the recorded conversation. The subject appears to have been the noetic basis of law or perhaps of justice, with the Philosopher arguing in such a sense that he could be misunderstood as meaning that the study of law is less rational than the study of mathematics. His correction of this misunderstanding with the notion that mathematicians err less often than legists is the beginning of his argument directed not against the intelligibility of law but against the claim by professional practitioners of the law to be the authentic declarers of what the law concretely is. Within the context of the *Dialogue*, it will prove to be the Philosopher and not the possessor of the legal art who is able to say what law is.

The Philosopher's first long statement makes broad concessions to the view that there is a rational basis of law, that is, to the view that law is informed by reason and cannot be law if it conflicts with reason. At least one of his specific concessions (that reason in the shape of equity amends the statute law) is explicitly rejected by him on page (87). For the present, however, and notwithstanding any provisional or superficial concessions, his point is simply that the reduction of law to reason opens the way to disobedience on the part of every man (and there can be many) who claims to be more fully reasonable than is the law itself. Thus the hard case is put: if law is reason and reason alone generates law, then law gains greatly in dignity but loses its own nature; for it is of the nature of law to command, and it is of the nature of command that it comport with obedience; but a command whose authoritativeness begins and ends with the reasonableness of the command will not, by its nature, procure obedience, for it is of the nature of reason to be always open to question. Therefore the dignity of law conflicts with the efficacy and therefore with the nature of law. Worse yet, if the reasonableness of law is in fact the justness of the law, then not merely its dignity but its justness is in conflict with its efficacy or its nature. But is not the justness of the law at least as much of the nature of law as is the efficacy of law or its capacity to perform its function of procuring obedience? If it is so, as it seems to be, then law itself is a paradox, for its nature to be just conflicts with its nature as a command. The resolution of this difficulty is one of the aims of the *Dialogue*.

The Philosopher requires the Lawyer to explain how Coke, speaking for the legists, can avoid the charge that in connecting the law so closely to reason he is destroying the law by encouraging disobedience. The Lawyer cites Coke's dictum that the law is not based upon what is reasonable according to the lights of any man as reasonable but only according to the reason of men possessing the legal art. This gives the Philosopher an occasion to depreciate art, in the context if not generally, by arguing that there is no art the possession of which entitles a man or men to make law: "It is not Wisdom, but Authority that makes a Law." So far as this formula reflects Hobbes's contentment with the disjunction of the excellence of the ruler from the power of the ruler, it reinforces the reader's impression that Hobbes's chief concern is with the virtue of subjects (namely, obedience) rather than with the virtue of rulers. He appears to think that it is more important for civil life that subjects be governable than that they be excellently governed, except so far as the latter is the condition for the former. It is as if the chief end of government is to guarantee government: civil life undominated by foreigners, later to be called the safety of the people, is the highest political good. That it is so will go far in enabling Hobbes to reconcile the justness and reasonableness of laws with their efficacy: what effectively promotes the civil good *is* the just and reasonable *eo ipso*.

The Lawyer now introduces the distinction between statute law and common law, supposing the Philosopher's disqualification of the legists' legislating art to apply to the making of statute but not common law. Of course the Philosopher's intention is precisely to make clear that there is no such thing as a common law that has been generated by the skill, wisdom, or experience of any body of essentially unauthorized men—as he takes lawyers and judges together to be. This being sufficiently intimated, the Lawyer makes a pregnant statement in reply. He supposes that there is such a thing as a law which is not statute law (i.e., human positive law), and that that law is the common law qua Divine and Eternal, the breaches of which are "not punished in this

World, yet they will be punished sufficiently in the World to come."[21] In this speech of the Lawyer's, with its Thomistic language of Divine and Eternal law and its reliance on judgment to be fulfilled in the life beyond, Hobbes shows or constructs the relation between the notion of a natural law accessible to the reason as such and the notion that such a natural law has a divine source. He thus succeeds in suggesting the congeniality of divines and legists, and gives an intimation of his plan in writing the *Dialogue*: the deflation of (essentially private) legists is the continuation of the deflation of the (essentially private) divines pursued in his other famous writings.[22] The deflation of clergy and legists constitutes the attempt to deprive private men of a politic function that they cannot exercise without a harmful usurpation. The harm, at least with reference to the legists, as this *Dialogue* will show, proceeds from the fact that the legists, while claiming to translate reason into law, must fail because they do not possess reason but a deceptive facsimile of it, namely, art. As will be seen, Hobbes proceeds to his end through an overstatement of the case against reason as the source of law.

The ground for the common deflation can be discerned even in the early passages of this work. Hobbes denies that reason as such, or art, or reason as informed by a divinity is sufficient for declaring law. All of these are incompetent whereas something called authority is competent to declare law. To deny that natural reason, art, and divinely informed reason are competent is to deny that nature, art, and divinity or the supplement of nature are competent whereas authority is competent. Mere reason, art, and divinely informed reason are the private possessions of individual human beings qua private. Authority is the possession and the sign of what is quintessentially public or politic. For Hobbes, the distinction between public and private or authorized and unauthorized takes precedence of the distinction between natural, artificial or conventional, and divine. It is not true that there are no natural standards known to Hobbes for the guidance of human affairs; but in the main those standards are conceived as directed to the support of authority. Thus the natural priority of preservation demands the clear demarcation between authority and nonauthority, or all falls into disorder. Hobbes's disjoining so emphatically the authorized and the unauthorized or the public and

---

21. P. (5).   22. See especially p. (22).

the private is his own version of the teaching of Plato to the effect that each man must do those things and only those things which are assigned to him: everyone must mind his own concerns. Plato accompanied this teaching with the supporting thought that men —as citizens surely—must be free to do only those things that authority assigns to them by law. Hobbes however has taught that men must be free to do all those things that are not expressly forbidden them by law. He is therefore to be understood as hoping that every man can be induced to do only what is appropriate to his private or public station although the spirit of the law is in an important or perhaps crucial sense libertarian, and must be so to the extent that the natural foundation for norms going significantly beyond preservation has been undermined. Hobbes expected that salutary indoctrination of subjects would cause them to observe the indispensable division of labor between authority and privacy. It may be noted incidentally that he did not solve perfectly the problem of who is to indoctrinate the indoctrinators, for at one and the same time he nominated the clergy to be the indoctrinators of the many and himself to be the indoctrinator of the clergy, while he instantly and violently alienated that order of men in ways and to a degree that the world knows well. The tension in modern life between idiosyncrasy and civil division of labor cannot be traced to this rhetorical blunder of Hobbes's, if it is a blunder, but rather to the more fundamental fact that Hobbes, while pointing the way to modernity, tried to restore the wholeness of authority, or of the public, or even as one might say of the polis, through dispensing with everything —reason, art, divinity—that might raise a claim threatening to the public; but he made little allowance for the fact that men's observance of the basic division of labor between the private and the public tasks is a species of moderation or self-restraint that is weakened by whatever compels men to conceive the norms of political existence as the creation of just such poor beings as they themselves are.

Towards the close of the first section, the Philosopher presses the Lawyer to say why, if the law of reason is the true rule for settling every dispute, there need be statute law at all. The Lawyer returns a curious answer.[23] He shows first that "an irregular Appetite to Riches, to Power, and to sensual Pleasures" over-

---

23. P. (7).

comes reason. That irregular appetite is next described as "the root of Disobedience, Slaughter, Fraud, Hypocrisie, and all manner of evil habits." Those in turn are said to have "fruits," which are "evil Actions." He thus portrays a tree of wickedness in preparation for the assertion that "the Laws of Man" (he uses this expression and, in the sequel, "human law," rather than the Philosopher's "Statute Law") can punish the fruits but cannot pluck up the roots. Human law can notice actions and can punish them; but "the root remaining, new fruit will come forth till you be weary of punishing, and at last destroy all Power that shall oppose it." This is, to say the least, an imperfect explanation of the usefulness of statute law as against the law of reason, for its concluding thought is not only that the laws of man are power-less against evil but that evil must eventually destroy the power (i.e., human power) that tries to oppose it through the statutes. Understandably, the Philosopher asks what hope there is then for peace. The Lawyer replies that fear—mutual fear—will be the basis for peace among nations; and of course, to be feared the nation itself must be at peace domestically, or in other words it must be obedient to the sovereign. That obedience is to be ob-tained through indoctrination of the people by divines using arguments drawn from reason and Scripture. For some reason the Philosopher brushes this all aside and repeats his question: what is the end of statute-laws? Since the conclusions from the previous line of argument do not conflict with conclusions to be reached subsequently, it is presumably the way to the conclusions rather than the conclusions themselves that is defective and must be repaired.

Of Sovereign Power

Having been asked again to say what purpose is served by statute law, the Lawyer responds by referring to "human law," saying that its "scope" is peace and justice domestically, and defense against foreign enemies. He thus tacitly gives as the end of law what Hobbes generally teaches to be the end of civil society altogether. It is therefore necessary for the Philosopher to point out that laws as such can do nothing and protect no one. This leads the Lawyer to explain that he meant laws "living and armed," that is, executed by a man or men in possession of money and in command of troops. The Lawyer has arrived at this point by passing through a description of a human condition, without human law, in which everything is everyone's. In this condition, the community of all things would be a cause of "Incroachment, Envy, Slaughter, and continual War of one upon another. . . ."[24] Human (statute) law dispels that community, replacing it with property and justice, and simultaneously puts down, if not perfectly at least very largely, the envy and slaughter which, a few pages earlier, the Lawyer was despairingly describing as likely to destroy all power that shall oppose them. At that place, the theme was the applicability of the law of reason to real controversies and the incapacity of reason to pluck up the roots of crime. Here, in the context of the coercive power of the sovereign, those "roots" are dealt with without having to be plucked up. The utility of a second posing of the question, Why statute law? begins to appear.

Here enters a thought of some importance: the laws in themselves being only words, a distinction must be made between who makes the laws in the sense of who "devises" or "pens" them and who makes them in the sense of who makes them effectual. In the spirit of this distinction, the Philosopher now asserts that "it is the King that makes the Laws, whosoever Pens them."[25] When making the Lawyer speak of the Athenian laws, Hobbes says that Solon "devised" them, while in the subsequent speech by the Philosopher, in which England and its laws are the theme, Hobbes tactfully refers to whosoever "pens" the laws; yet it is obvious that the penman is the deviser, and that the legislating intelligence is no more the king's in England than it was that of the populace in Athens. As the one who makes the laws in the sense of making them effectual, of raising the forces that make the laws real laws, the sovereign monarch is the servant of him or them by whom the laws were penned as well as of the people whose safety is procured through the enforcement of those laws. Certainly Hobbes did not have a naive conception of monarchy or of sovereignty, though he did not dwell on the conjoining of kingship and philosophy as one of the great subjects of political philosophy.

Following this tacit depreciation of the sovereign's legislative initiative, there is a lengthy passage consisting of a strong affirmation of the sovereign's executive independence, concretely, his prerogative freely to levy taxes and troops according to his own "conscience." It is in the course of this argument that the

---

24. P. (9).   25. P. (11).

Philosopher declares that "God made Kings for the People, and not People for Kings"[26]—a thought sometimes supposed to have been inaccessible to Hobbes.

The Philosopher having shown that the king's authority over money and soldiers, even against the judgment of Parliament on some occasions, is the dictate of reason, he would like the Lawyer now to admit that that authority is law according to the Lawyer's, or Coke's, formula that reason is law and law is reason. The Lawyer surprisingly responds with a word for word repetition of the passage from Coke that he had already recited in full early in the preceding section: the reason that underlies the law is the legal reason of generations of legists. What looks at first like a wooden and rather irrelevant repetition of an authoritative formula has in fact a somewhat subtle function. It is the Lawyer's immediate reaction against the Philosopher's having reasoned to the real meaning of the law from some considerations about civil life and the subservience of the king to the people's safety. In other words, the Philosopher has applied his entirely private reason to the public's difficulties and has emerged with an interpretation of the law (25 Edw. 1 c.6) that seems to correct or supplement the law in an important degree. Hobbes lets the reader understand through this implicit but only implicit rebuke of the Philosopher by the Lawyer, that the Philosopher is extending the doctrine laid down incipiently in the disjunction between the deviser or penman of laws, who need not be the king, and the sovereign, who makes them into law by providing means to punish violators. That Hobbes means to leave room for reason— philosophic, not merely legal—in the construction of law appears further from the curtailment of the passage that the Lawyer twice quotes from Coke.[27] Hobbes shows the passage as coming to a full stop after the words "Grave and Learned Men." In fact the sentence continues, "and by long experience grown to such a perfection, for the government of this Realm, as the old rule may be truly verified of it, Neminem oportet esse sapientiorem legibus: No man (out of his own private reason) ought to be wiser than the Law, which is the perfection of reason."[28] Since the addition of this part of the statement would have strengthened the Lawyer's reply when the Philosopher pressed him to defend Coke against the charge that Coke's doctrine implicitly encouraged

26. P. (15).   27. Pp. (4), (16).
28. *Institutes of the Laws of England*, pt. 1, sect. 138, fol. 97b.

disobedience, a reason is needed for the omission of the passage. That reason appears in the context of the second utterance of Coke's formula: in suppressing it, Hobbes appears to deny that no man ought to be wiser than the law and in fact to imply that the Philosopher can be wiser than the law. Here it is well to recall that at the very outset the Philosopher said that his intention in familiarizing himself with his country's laws was to obey and not to judge of their rationality. Perhaps one may take Hobbes to mean that the philosopher can be trusted to be wiser than the law, that is, to be above it, and yet to obey it—at least during his life-time.[29]

The Philosopher turns the Lawyer's repetition of Coke's formula into an occasion for repeating his own depreciation of judicial initiative in making law, reaffirming the crucial import-ance of the king's reason. But he does so with qualifications. He says of the king's reason that, "be it more, or less," it is the soul of the law, and in the same speech he twice associates with the king's reason the "advice" of Parliament, going so far the second time as to say "that the King's Reason, *when it is publickly upon Advice, and Deliberation declar'd*, is that *Anima Legis. . . .*"[30]

There follows an example of the king's acting as legislator pre-cisely in the subordinate sense of putting in force laws that he has not devised: the canons of the church, the imperial law adopted in the admiralty, and several other bodies of law, all of which are law only because the sovereign has declared them to be so in the realm.

The next theme is the limitation of the king's power to levy taxes on his subjects. If he has granted certain liberties or imposed certain restraints upon himself, he is bound to observe those grants and impositions or in other words to keep faith with his subjects except if it be sinful (contrary to the people's safety) so to keep faith. How could the king have granted away what the people's safety requires him to retain? Through "error," which means of course a defect of the royal reason. This staunch defense of the prerogative which rests upon an allusion to the fallibility of the sovereign is followed by another intimation of the need for the monarch to avail himself of the wisdom of his subjects. The Lawyer begins a speech in support of the king's ultimate right to raise money with the following statement: "if Levying of Money be necessary, it is a Sin in the Parliament to refuse, if unnecessary,

29. See pp. 10–11 above.   30. P. (17).

it is a sin both in King and Parliament to Levy. . . ." He says nothing about the case in which the king would unnecessarily and hence sinfully try to levy but would be checked by Parliament nonsinfully refusing. Instead of that he says that it would be sinful in the sovereign to make war or peace without consulting competent and knowing people. Moreover, it is his "consulting with [men] of Military Condition"[31] that apparently makes his martial proceedings lawful and is the basis for the soldiers' obligation to go wherever he sends them to fight. This great weakening of the prerogative as such is concluded with a non sequitur that refers to the sovereign's right to command and the republican motives of the Long Parliament in denying that right.

Passing all of this without a murmur of dissent, the Philosopher himself adds another cause for restraining the king: legislation (dutifully but not very plausibly) ascribed to the sovereigns themselves, binding them from making war for the glory of conquest, is held up to approbation as full of sense and reason. This is followed by a solid reaffirmation of the king's very wide right to judge of the need to levy and use force "to save his own People and himself from Servitude."

It is to be noticed that this reaffirmation[32] is a general repetition of the material with which the present section, "Of Sovereign Power," began.[33] The reason for the repetition may be found partly in the content of the passage that intervenes between the two affirmations of the sovereign's power to levy money and troops according to his own judgment and partly in a point that the repetition contains but that the first statement lacks. Between the two affirmations is the passage in which the defect of the king's reason is acknowledged. In the second affirmation, the Philosopher, in his two final speeches on the present theme, enlarges on the necessity, as distinguished from the desirability, of the king's exercising the ample power for which the Philosopher is here contending. He utters what Hobbes has elsewhere[34] written in his own name: "To think that our Condition being Humane should be subject to no Incommodity, were Injuriously to Quarrel with God Almighty for our own Faults. . . ." Then he makes the Philosopher say that the king is subject only to the laws of God; "and so was *William the Conqueror*, whose Right it all Descended to our present King." But the right of William the

31. P. (20).   32. Pp. (20)–(26).   33. Pp. (8)–(16).
34. *Leviatham*, chap. 20, end.

Conqueror was the right of conquest: Kings as such rule by right of conquest—another way of saying that they are subject only to the laws of God, being above all human contract. It is of the nature of civil life that it provide an incomplete relief of man's estate, a thought that Hobbes apparently retained intact to the end of his life.

There follows a brief interlude[35] on the subject of the king's being sole legislator. The interlude is introduced by a short statement by the Lawyer in which he passes from the law of God that bound William the Conqueror to the thought that God is sole legislator of that law and therefore also of equity. The Philosopher easily brings the Lawyer to admit that the king's reason takes the place of God's on earth, and the Lawyer, in granting that, repeats the point made earlier to the effect that the canons of the church are law in England only because the king made them so. This, it will be remembered, was part of the argument that showed the sovereign to be legislator in the sense of one who makes the law effectual, a sense distinguished from legislator as deviser or intelligent conceiver of the law. In granting what the Lawyer asserts, the Philosopher, in a speech that is marred by an apparent hiatus in the printed text, reintroduces in the same vein the thought that the king's collaboration with Parliament is essential, although it need be observed only to the point that the king's judgment permits. The Lawyer's speech conceding this strengthens the thought that the king must collaborate with Parliament; and if he does not, "he sinneth against God, though he cannot be Compell'd to any thing by his Subjects by Arms, and Force."[36] This statement must have appeared amazing to those many Englishmen alive in 1681 who remembered that Charles I had been compelled by his subjects to lay his head upon the block. Within the context of the *Dialogue*, however, it is noteworthy that Hobbes has led the discourse quickly yet almost imperceptibly from the thought that kingly power is the power of the conqueror to the violence of subjects against the king that is a consequence or potential concomitant of the hostile relation between sovereign and subjects. The taciturnity with which this thought is developed leaves it deprived of those expressions of revulsion in which Hobbes invariably denounces the Revolution and the regicide when they are his manifest theme.

---

35. Pp. (26)–(28).   36. P. (28).

There is at this point an explicit indication in the form of a sub-heading in the text that the interlocutors are turning to a new theme: the king is supreme judge as well as sole legislator. The thought is simply that if the maker of the laws were not also the judge in causes arising under those laws, "there would be no Congruity of Judgments with the Laws."[37] Here as elsewhere Hobbes rejects any formalization of the method of checks and balances. This point is made expeditiously, and the remainder of the section, somewhat less than half of the whole, fails to elaborate the theme of the king's supremacy as judge, from which it can be gathered that the words "The King is the Supreme Judge" are not intended to introduce a formal subsection of the *Dialogue*. What does follow is a demand by the Philosopher that they go no further in speaking of laws without defining them. The definition that emerges incorporates the familiar conception of Hobbes's that law is anterior to justice, which is in turn defined to mean lawabidingness directed to the statutes.

In developing the definition of law as the promulgated command of the sovereign, the Lawyer questions that part of the definition that makes it "of the Essence of a Law to be Publickly and plainly declar'd to the People."[38] This gives the Philosopher an opportunity to urge that everyone be given direct access to printed copies of the statutes. He says to the Lawyer, ". . . what Reason can you give me why there should not be as many Copies abroad of the Statutes, as there be of the Bible?" This evocation of a great issue of the Reformation appears to serve the purpose of suggesting the need for a political reformation through which the mediation of lawyers between subjects and the law will be much mitigated: a private body of men, claiming to possess a "mystery,"[39] interpose themselves between subjects and the power that supervenes over them, to the derogation of the civil authority. The concrete matter as to which that interposition takes place is the raising of money, for the sake of arming the sovereign. In the latter portion of the section "Of Sovereign Power," Hobbes presents forcefully the thought that property is utterly dependent upon sovereignty, for there is no law without sovereign command, nor is there justice without law; and justice is what distinguishes *meum* and *tuum*. He thus lets the taxpayer understand that he is ill-advised to resist as unjust the sovereign's

---

37. Ibid.   38. P. (31).   39. Cf. p. (57).

confiscations, for his own property right rests on the thin crust of justice that is coeval with the foundation of sovereignty itself and cannot have a fate better than what befalls that very sovereignty.

Hobbes places what I have suggested is an evocation of the Reformation between the definition of law and the definition of justice, the three elements followed at some length by the general doctrine of property and sovereignty for which Hobbes is well known. Their conjunction gives a firmer ground to that replacement of the clergy by the legists as the agitators of disobedience which is noticeable in this writing. In general, subjects become disaffected to the sovereign for two kinds of reasons: irrational, having to do with opinion of things beyond reason; and rational, having to do with interest in life and property. The divines have stirred men's minds with respect to the former; the legists have done the same with respect to the latter. Much of Hobbes's life-work dealt with the need for the resumption of supreme clerical power into the civil sovereignty. This small work deals with the resumption of the supreme judicial power into the civil sovereignty, a task made difficult precisely by the fact that in the course of performing it, the claim of natural reason to recognize justice must be weakened, of course without hope or desire of assistance from revelation. The private priests of (legal) reason must be checked as the private priests of revelation needed to be checked.

This construction of the passage following the unique subheading "The King is the Supream Judge" is consistent with the presence and place of that subheading and also with the fact that the next section is "Of Courts," and begins with the characterization of the judicial system as merely administrative of the monarch's function. Before that section opens, Hobbes brings the second section to a conclusion by introducing the theme of the late Revolution in a remarkable way: through a reference to the royal pardon of certain offenders, the interlocutors move to define an "Act of Oblivion" such as that by which the offenders were pardoned. The discussion brings to light the fact that the rebels committed two kinds of offense, one against the king and the other against the multitude of subjects. On the principle that no one can pardon an offense committed against someone else, the interlocutors agree that the king could not have been sole legislator of the Act of Oblivion which is, as they conclude, a general pardon. The "assent" of the injured people was indispensable, and therefore the assent of Parliament was "absolutely necessary." In the important case of injury to life or limb or property, the king cannot rightly be sole legislator as to pardon, that is, remission of obligation to make fair as distinguished from vengeful restitution. The Philosopher then makes it very clear that the term Act of Oblivion is a misnomer, for it provides that certain acts shall be forgiven but not that they be forgotten.

℥ Of Courts

Without explicitly drawing attention to this fact, Hobbes links the section "Of Courts" with the section "Of Sovereign Power" by opening the former with a continuation of the theme with which he brought the latter to a close: the distinction between offenses against the crown and offenses against subjects. The first speech in the new section is by the Philosopher and consists of a request that the Lawyer in effect describe the judicial system in relation to the kinds of controversies that arise. The Lawyer complies, whereupon, in his first noninterrogative speech in this section, the Philosopher declares that "dammages awarded to the party injur'd, has nothing common with the nature of a penalty, but is meerly a Restitution, or satisfaction due to the party griev'd by the Law of Reason, and consequently is no more a punishment than is the paying of a Debt."[40] According to the doctrine laid down in the discussion of the Act of Oblivion, the king cannot in reason pardon an offense against, and thus cannot remit the restitution reasonably owing to, the injured party. Cases between subjects must, however, come before the king as supreme judge, withal before him through his appointed justices. The reader is led to understand that the sovereign is supreme judge in controversies between subjects in such a sense that he is not free, by the dictate of natural reason, to grant pardons in matters of *meum* and *tuum*. Although Hobbes would surely oppugn such an expression as that the sovereign would offend against justice if he remitted the damages due one subject from another, he would not hesitate to say that equity would be violated by one man's remitting the restitution to which another is reasonably entitled. We are thus quickly introduced to the two principal themes of this section: the king himself is supreme judge; and the court of equity, which is the Chancery Court, is the supreme court of the realm.

40. P. (46).

The first concrete subject that the interlocutors discuss is the jurisdiction of the several courts in the English judiciary, or more exactly, what is the scope of each court's power. For the most part, the discussion concerns the two great courts of King's Bench and Common Pleas. The Philosopher learns from the Lawyer that the distribution of causes between the courts is apparently a matter of custom or common law. He therefore asks the Lawyer to cite the Letters Patent by which the King appoints the chief justice of the King's Bench and of the Common Pleas, for the sake of showing that there is no need to resort to mere custom in order to know what each court, that is, each chief justice, is empowered to do. The assignment of functions to the courts is an act of regality.

After a digression on the shortcomings of attorneys, the Philosopher brings the discussion back to jurisdiction, but now more specifically with respect to correction and amendment of the errors of other judges: which judges or courts can overrule which others? The common-law view, which is that of Coke, generally favors the Court of King's Bench, as being what would now be called a "supreme court of appeal." Hobbes makes the Philosopher show that, both historically and according to reason, the claim of Chancery to be that ultimate court for the revision of all others is the best claim. To do this the Philosopher must show that the statutes which are thought to oppose this claim are either misinterpreted by Coke or are in a state of confusion; and he must also show that the king does not alienate his supremacy in the judiciary by appointing judges to assist him and therefore has a prerogative in empowering these judges that the merely customary privileges of certain courts assuredly cannot displace. Now the Philosopher proceeds more positively to press the claims of the chancellor to review the judgments given in both King's Bench and Common Pleas. He argues eventually to the proposition that "there was a necessity of a Higher Court of Equity, than the Courts of Common-Law, to remedy the Errors in Judgment given by the Justices of the Inferior Courts. . . ."[41] He next disposes of the argument (prejudicial to the removal of some causes into Chancery) that it is unlawful to remove a cause from one court to another if that removal would transfer the trial from one procedure to another; for example, from trial before a jury

---

41. Pp. (76)–(77).

to trial before judges alone. His argument is simply common sense, or equity: only the witnesses can say what the facts are; and judges are fully as able to hear and measure witnesses as any jury might be. The customs moreover are not to be pleaded on behalf of any court, its powers, or its scope. "I deny that any Custome of its owne Nature, can amount to the Authority of a Law: For if the Custom be unreasonable, . . . it is no Law, but ought to be abolished; and if the Custom be reasonable, it is not the Custom, but the Equity that makes it Law."[42] He ends the bulk of his argument by making the very language of statutes subject to equitable review in order to prevent the literal (he says "grammatical") adherence to the letter from hindering the consummation of the lawmaker's intention.

As the section draws to a close, the Philosopher makes an uncharacteristic suggestion: that bishops ought to be appointed chancellors. Apparently gratuitously, the clergy and the legists, now on a rather high level, are again juxtaposed. The Philosopher describes the bishops as being commonly the most able and rational men. The Lawyer recoils from the suggestion, and (in a speech of his that is evidently assigned to the Philosopher only by a typographical error[43]) says that "to be able enough is not enough; when, not the difficulty of the Case only, but also the Passion of the Judge is to be Conquer'd." After this remarkable exchange the section is brought to a close by the Philosopher who once more praises and elevates equity.

Upon reviewing the course of the dialogue in the section "Of Courts," it is fair to say that what begins as an assertion of the royal judicial prerogative becomes an argument for Chancery as the supreme court and equity as the supreme law—through the supremacy of the king as judge. The Philosopher has argued for the rule of reason or equity as against custom and as against the letter of the statute itself. The section as a whole maintains the royal sovereignty as the ground for the rule of natural reason as opposed to legal reason, whatever that latter might mean if it means anything different from error and disorder. But to raise a claim for reason is to raise an empty claim until some sign is given of what is concretely reasonable. This is precisely what Hobbes will do in the next section, in which he takes up capital crimes. The first of those is high treason, in the elaboration of which

---

42. P. (80).   43. P. (85).

Hobbes will let it appear that the *salus populi* is that good to which the existence of the king is subordinate. In this way the *Dialogue* approaches a more specific conception of the dictate of sovereign reason.

Of Crimes Capital

The section begins with a long quotation from the statute of 25 Edw. 3 in which the various acts that shall constitute treason are specified. The Philosopher is dissatisfied with the mere enumeration of acts that are treasonous, for he wishes to understand what is the very nature of treason as a crime in or of itself, such an offense as "Reason without a Statute makes it a Crime."[44] This may be said because treason is the crime against civil society as such and therefore against the basis or possibility of law. It cannot therefore be a crime by virtue of law. So at least we may conjecture about the Philosopher's reason for speaking of *malum in se*; he himself does not take the matter up, uncharacteristic of Hobbes's doctrine as it is.

The Lawyer declining this difficult assignment, the Philosopher himself undertakes it. He takes as the first premise of his argument that *salus populi* is *suprema lex*: the safety of the people is the highest law. He then infers that seven acts or kinds of acts[45] are treacherous according to the light of "mere natural reason." Two things may be noticed with respect to the seven treasons.

First, the Philosopher explains why each of the seven is treason even before the statute, and in most cases he derives the particular treason for the premise of *salus populi suprema lex*. That is, of five of the treasons he says that the acts in question would lead to the destruction of the people. In the case of one of the treasons, numbered the third, he shows the act as harmful to the king but fails even to use the word "people" in the explanatory sentence. The statement reads, "That to Levy war against the King within the Realm, and Aiding the Kings Enemies, either within, or without the Realm, are tending to the Kings Destruction, or Disherison, and was High Treason, before this Statute by the Common-Law." The destruction or disherison of the king tends to commotion and thus to endangering the people, and one cannot rationally infer from Hobbes's silence on that fact in this case that he meant to deny that aiding the king's enemies was treason. But that there is some special problem connected with

---

44. P. (89).   45. Pp. (90)–(91).

the understanding of this treason is indicated partly by the silence just referred to and more conspicuously by the Philosopher's polemic against Coke a few pages later on the related subject of whether the king may treat a traitor as an enemy (summarily) or whether he must proceed against him through indictment, using the forms of law. More specifically, the question concerns a subject who is under arms, in the field against the king in open hostility, in a state of deliberate rebellion against him. Hobbes makes the Philosopher ridicule Coke for insisting that there is a difference between the treatment to be accorded an enemy and a traitor. Coke says that an enemy may be killed or ransomed, but a traitor must be tried. The Philosopher tries to make it appear that Coke could not understand that a traitor, as hostile to the king, was thus an "enemy." There is no evidence that Coke failed to understand this. He appears rather to mean that the penalty for treason (as the Philosopher himself must know) was not merely death but in the first place a particularly elaborate death, and in the second place the attainder and the disherison of the traitor; and these ought not to be inflicted summarily. In any case, Hobbes has made the Philosopher move from a statement about aiding the king's enemies (as well as making war on him) that failed to mention the sovereign premise for treason, namely, endangering the people, to another statement in which he asserts the king's right to punish arbitrarily those of his subjects who are his overt enemies in the field or in rebellion. The key to the understanding of this development is given by the difference between "aiding the king's enemies"—which is not connected explicitly with endangering the people—and engaging in acts of war, which does endanger the people. To clarify this, a single example will suffice. Oliver Cromwell was surely the king's enemy, whether by "the king" is meant Charles the First or the Second. Once Oliver became in effect the king regnant, was a resident subject in England who "aided" him a traitor? There is one other treason, namely the one numbered seven, which includes denying "the King Regnant to be their Lawful King," that exposes men to the ultimate penalties. This is the only other passage among those explanatory of the treasons that makes no explicit mention of the people or their destruction, but makes the judgment "for the Reasons aforesaid."

That the third and seventh treasons stand out and are linked to each other and to the subsequent blundering polemic against

Coke is made more probable by a remark in Hobbes's "Considerations upon the Reputation, Loyalty, Manners, and Religion of Thomas Hobbes, etc."[46] "If a man be taken by the Turk, and brought by terror to fight against his former master, I see how he may be killed for it as an enemy, but not as a criminal; nor can I see how he that hath liberty to submit, can at the same time be bound not to submit." Hobbes speaking in his own name presents quite clearly the objection to Coke and to the law—which, as we know, he studied only to obey it and never to reason critically about it: a subject taken in arms against the king is visibly an enemy, but is, so to speak, merely or no more than an enemy. Whereas the Philosopher is made to argue that a subject in arms does not deserve indictment and the due process of law but may be despatched summarily as any other enemy, Hobbes in his own name shows that a subject taken in hostility might deserve no more than to be executed summarily—not tortured, disgraced, and impoverished in his survivors. The decisive point is that the subject might have been intimidated out of one loyalty and into another. To deprive him of the right to respond "naturally" to his fears is impossible and to attempt to do so is therefore irrational and inequitable, the statute to the contrary notwithstanding. Moreover, as the conjunction of the third and seventh treasons indicates, not everything that the law understandably enough considers treason is necessarily destructive of the people's safety (as distinguished from the safety of an individual as such.) On the contrary, a certain loyalty or fealty to an ousted sovereign might itself have something of the fanatic about it and might prove perpetually threatening to the people's safety. Perhaps it is to bring this theme to the reader's mind that Hobbes injects the old oath of homage into the Philosopher's speech,[47] for that oath, quoted again when the subject is property near the end of the *Dialogue*,[48] was an archaism in an age when the crucial point was how the king might obtain money to pay his soldiers precisely because military service was not a condition of land tenure.

The second point to be noticed in the definition of the seven natural treasons is the fact that the last three are not contained in "the Statute" (25 Edw. 3). Here, therefore, are three acts that the natural reason recognizes but the statute fails to recognize as being treason. There follows on the other hand a reference to the

---

46. Molesworth, *English Works*, 4:422.   47. P. (93).   48. P. (201).

killing of a justice or other officer, which is "not otherwise High Treason, but by the Statute." The Philosopher has become increasingly willing to consider the disjunction between reason and the law, although surely without any visible trace of an encouragement to disobedience.

The interlocutors take up next the question as to what constitutes evidence of an intention to commit treason. The law demands that there be proof of an "overt act." The Philosopher shows that the truest "overt act" is speech: to utter the words that convey an intention is infinitely more incriminating than to be in possession of the weapons or poisons with which a treasonous murder might be committed. From this illustration of equity or reason the interlocutors pass to another: if counterfeiting the Great Seal is treason, then lifting the Seal from one document and affixing it to another should also be punished as treason although the statute does not say so: "I think it reason to understand it as within the Statute."[49] As for misprision of treason, or concealment of any knowledge or suspicion one has of a treason, the point at issue is how to regard a man who utters what proves to be an unfounded suspicion. The Philosopher's judgment is pure Hobbes: if the suspicion prove incorrect yet reasonable, the informer had better not be punished as a false accuser lest all people with such suspicions, rationally preferring their own good to the public's, conceal them rather than run the risk.

The interlocutors' next task is to investigate the meaning of felony, especially with a view to the question whether it is "in its own Nature a Crime, or that only which is made a Crime by some Statute."[50] The Philosopher rejects a certain speculation of Coke's on the meaning of felony and replaces it with one of his own, drawn from the thought that a felon is a "Man that maketh it his Trade to maintain himself by the breaking and contemning of all Laws generally."[51] For this reason felonies are "Crimes in their own Nature without the help of Statute."[52] The kinship of treason and the class of felony is apparent: both are hostility to civil society and are therefore criminal by virtue of the meaning of law rather than by the prescription of any specific law.

The interlocutors now begin to consider particular felonies, and first murder. Coke is shown as interpreting 52 Hen. 3 c.25 to mean that accidental homicide was considered to be murder

---

49. P. (101).   50. P. (102).   51. P. (104).   52. P. (105).

before that statute. The Philosopher denies this, arguing rather that, from Saxon times, murder had been the name given to the cause of any violent death while the actual circumstances of the death were still unknown. Thus, before the statute, nonfelonious and felonious homicides were alike called murder—but apparently only provisionally and by reference to the mysteriousness of the circumstances only. This argument repels what appears as the unreasonable notion of Coke's that the law could consider nonfelonious homicide to be murder, murder itself being innately felonious. It almost appears as if the Philosopher were arguing that, because the law is reasonable, the law cannot mean anything that our extra-legal reason determines to be irrational. This form of argument bears a close resemblance to Hobbes's theological cogitations.

There is, however, a complication. As he goes on to controvert Coke, the Philosopher draws in the legislation of King Canute on fining the neighborhood in which a corpse is found and the killer unknown. The Philosopher shows that Canute relieved his subjects of this burdensome charge, *except if the victim were English*. If the victim were French (i.e., foreign, especially Norman) the neighborhood was not to be fined. How different things would be in detail, though not in principle, after the Norman Conquest need not be labored. Thus one may understand why the Philosopher concludes his major speech on this theme by saying that "Murder is distinguished from Homicide by the Statute-Laws, and not by any Common-Law without the Statute; and that it is comprehended under the general name of Felony."[53] His point is twofold: murder is necessarily felonious, and it is misleading to describe a nonfelonious homicide as a felony; but there is so much latitude in the statutory treatment of manslaying that under one regime the mysterious killing of an Englishman must be assessed upon the hundred and the like killing of a Norman not, and under another regime the reverse. The Philosopher remarks that it was "unreasonable to deny the Justice to a stranger,"[54] which is as much as saying that the statute of Canute was unreasonable and unjust. The Philosopher's thought appears to be that there is such a thing as a naturally felonious act and the statute law is capable of ignoring or misunderstanding it, as the common law manifestly is.

---

53. P. (107).   54. Ibid.

Much of the remainder of the section "Of Crimes Capital" takes up points of the common law which appear to be quibbling follies, one of the more outrageous being that it is not a great crime to cut someone else's wheat if the offender throw the booty straight into a cart, but it is death to put it into the cart if it has been first laid on the ground. Another is that the unsuccessful attempt to commit an act that is felonious not expose the perpetrator to indictment of felony. It is on this account that the Philosopher says, "Surely the King has power to Punish him (on this side of Life or Member) as he please,"[55] a notion that is consistent with Bacon's conception of the court of equity as the court of the king's perfect prerogative—for justice untrammeled by law.

In the last few lines of the present section, the interlocutors prepare for the transition to the next subject in a way that deserves notice. The Philosopher says, "Let us now come to crimes not capital"—the same thought and virtually the same words with which he is going to terminate the section now about to begin. The Lawyer's response implies that if they now leave behind the subject of capital crime, they must leave heresy undiscussed. He adds another thought: Coke ranked heresy before murder. Evidently, the Philosopher considers heresy to be either a crime but not capital, or conceivably not a crime at all. By following up the Lawyer's reference to Coke's ranking of heresy before murder, we can gain some intimation of the Philosopher's thought. We must go back to the transition in the present section from treason to murder—which would have been the transition from treason to heresy if Coke's order had been followed—to see the reason for the actual sequence. In fact, the transition from treason to murder was via felony, which was seen as a class of acts innately harmful to law and mankind, consisting of offenses that are crime in their own nature without the help of statute. Passing over heresy tacitly at that point and then seeking to pass over it again here prepares the question where heresy is a felony or even a crime. The section on heresy will show that heresy does not exist as a crime before enactment and after repeal of the statute forbidding it. It is not one of those offenses harmful of their own nature to law and mankind.

---

55. P. (123).

Of Heresy

The broad direction of this section is shown in the first two speeches. The Lawyer opens with Coke's enumeration of the five chief points concerning heresy, of which one is, What shall be judged heresy. The Philosopher immediately replies that "the principal thing to be considered, which is the Heresie it self, he leaveth out; viz. What it is. . . ." The Philosopher begins to investigate the question "What is an act of heresy?" by ascending to the Greek origins of the word. He shows it to be anyone's "taking" or "grasping" a doctrine upon trust in the originator of it, adhering to the literal meaning of the word and presenting it as meaning the act of a mere sectarian as such. The Philosopher's discussion consists of one very long speech followed by numerous speeches of moderate length. The first contains the etymology of *heresy* and the application of the literal meaning of the word to the formation of Greek philosophical sects. That speech sketching the history of the sects ends with the remark that "there were always, though not New Sects of Philosophy, yet New Opinions continuously arising." The Lawyer briefly interrupts. The Philosopher seems to override or brush aside the interruption, and launches into the part of his discourse that brings the word into its Christian context. He begins this part by referring to the communication of the Gospel to Asia Minor, Greece, and Italy—the places of those congregations to which the Pauline Epistles are addressed. Of the converted heathen, some must have been exposed to the philosophic teachings while of course many had not. The Philosopher wants to know what kind of Christian would be most apt at propagating the faith (which, according to the recently accomplished etymology, would mean, at making heretics.) The Lawyer surprisingly answers that those would who could make the best use of Aristotle's rhetoric and logic. This notion is similar to that expressed by Locke in the reflections on the Pauline Epistles contained in his *Paraphrase and Notes* on five of those letters. The Philosopher next asks, "Who were the most prone to Innovation?" In the same vein, these are said by the Lawyer to be the ones "most confident of Aristotle's and Plato's (their former Masters) Natural Philosophy." Those innovators drew men to versions of Christianity that were based upon classical natural philosophy. When these sectarian doctrines conflicted with those held in repute, they could be denounced by provincial councils and their adherents reproached as refusing to give up the philosophy of their sect. It is obvious that heresy means, according to this account, the doctrine that failed to prevail.

What follows is to the effect that heresy or what is not to be believed is in the concrete very much a matter of legislation, indeed entirely a matter of legislation, coming into being, having a certain content, and passing away according to the dictate of those with the power to make and enforce laws. This is complementary to Hobbes's doctrine that what is to be believed as religion is within the sovereign's legislative scope. Hobbes however seems to go further: he describes the repeal of all heresy laws in England in Elizabeth's time as changing the nature of heresy to what originally it was, namely, a private opinion,[56] although a commission for taking cognizance of it continued to exist. If heresy were by its unalterable nature what it was originally, namely, a private opinion, then making it a public matter and culpable would be unreasonable and inequitable. But if heresy had one nature originally, when it was a private opinion, and another nature when it was made criminal, there can be no complaint on the ground of justice when the authorities lawfully oppress the dissident. The interlocutors do not take this question up explicitly: Hobbes keeps them for the most part on the question whether there is any law under which a man could be punished or punished with death for heresy in England after Elizabeth's repeal. Since one man was so punished, the question with which the Philosopher presses the Lawyer is, "By what law was he burned?" The answer is the common law. In the course of attacking this answer, the Philosopher makes a remark of some general interest. If the common law is to be understood as the law of reason, "and if you will say he was burn't by the Law of Reason, you must tell me how there can be Proportion between Doctrine and Burning; there can be no Equality, nor Majority, nor Minority Assigned between them."[57] The Philosopher is using "Reason" in its literal sense as carried in the word *ratio* to mean relation or proportion. Reasoning is then ascertaining the proportion or ratio between things, their equality in the case of reasoning to a definition, their just, equitable, or right relation in the case, for example, of adjusting a punishment or reward to a given act. The Philosopher in denying that there can be any proportion between a teaching and burning (one may wonder

---

56. P. (135).   57. P. (140).

whether he means only terrestrial burning) denies that any teaching is in its own nature bad. Doctrines are bad only in their effects, especially their public effects. It must therefore at all times be irrational to punish the holding of a doctrine as such, for the doctrine and the punishment are essentially incommensurable. On the other hand, the law can rationally order punishment for charitable almsgiving if the public effects of that charity be harmful.[58] The power of the lawmaker to make the just and the unjust seems to have a limit in respect of doctrine and belief: there are essentially private things, and there must be an irrationality, hence an inequity, when the law tries to reach them. It goes without saying that they forfeit immunity as soon as, or to the extent that, they leave the sanctuary of the mind.

Having proved that heresy is no crime or that it is no capital crime in England, the Philosopher brings this section to a close, as he did the previous one, by proposing that they pass on to crimes not capital. The section as a whole is thus given the appearance of a digression.

Of Premunire

This section is in some respects a continuation of the section "Of Courts," for in that section Hobbes maintains the supremacy of the Chancery court as the locus for supervision of the common-law courts of Common Pleas and King's Bench; and in this present section he maintains that the powerful writ of premunire does not lawfully run against those who bring or try causes in Chancery by transfer out of a common-law court, especially on appeal (as it would now be called). This section therefore fortifies the position of Chancery as a leading and independent jurisdiction and correspondingly restricts the common law, which is the law applied in Common Pleas and King's Bench, to the advantage of equity.

In the twenty-fifth year of Edward the Third (1350-51), the Statute of Provisors was enacted in order to make punishable those derogations from the royal dignity implied in a subject's respecting the papal jurisdiction above the king's. Coke interpreted the statute as a defense of the common-law courts against encroachments by the other courts and especially Chancery. Hobbes sets forth the matter and the ground of Coke's notion of

58. P. (47).

it, but says nothing of an important case involving Coke as chief justice of the King's Bench and Bacon as attorney-general, in which this very point was at issue. Coke had given a decision in King's Bench. One of the litigants, thinking himself injured, sought relief in Chancery. The appellee refused to appear there, apparently supported by Coke who threatened the chancellor with a writ of premunire. Bacon was active in resisting Coke's appropriation of premunire to the defense of certain of the king's courts against some others. King James ordered Coke examined by the Privy Council, which rejected Coke's interpretation of the law and rebuked him to the point of disgrace. He was dismissed from the King's Bench shortly thereafter, in 1616.

With this defense of equity and the court in which it is the rule, Hobbes brings to a close the discussion of crimes not capital. Offense against the Statute of Provisors proves to be the only such crime that is taken up as a crime, presumably because it is the one that is of greatest interest to Hobbes in view of his intention in writing. The other offenses not capital are taken up in the course of the discussion of punishments, which occurs in the next section.

Of punishments

The first weighty notion to emerge in this section is that there is no natural rational criterion for punishments such that a punishment can be found for each crime that perfectly fits that crime. This thought of the Philosopher's is supported by the argument that if punishments were assigned out of natural reason, crimes would be similarly punished everywhere and always. Reverting to the thought mentioned above, there seems to be no natural ratio joining the offense and the punishment—a thought that is expressed in the present context more emphatically than before.[59] The Philosopher's conclusion is that, since the assignment of punishments cannot be strictly rational, the condition of reasonableness is fulfilled by promulgation of the assigned punishment as it has been established by whoever has power to enforce it, namely, the sovereign man or men: "it is manifest Reason, that for breaking the known Laws, [one] should suffer the known Punishments."[60] One might say that clear and distinct knowledge of the laws determining the relation of crime and punishment is

59. Cf. p. (140).   60. P. (158).

the just replacement of the natural or rationally just relation of crime and punishment.

At this point in the Philosopher's speech there is a conspicuously abrupt break, or apparent break, in his thought: he is suddenly describing the confrontation of King David by Nathan in the matter of Uriah the Hittite. David is aroused to anger by Nathan's story of the rich man's slaying the poor one's lamb, and in heat exclaims that the offender shall die. This overstates the Scriptural version of David's exclamation, but the point is not material. The Philosopher now asks, curiously, whether this was a royal or tyrannical judgment. The Lawyer replies that the kings of England may do as much in their realm as the good kings of Israel could do in theirs, and that punishing with death in the absence of a precedent law would be permissible in English kings if there were any certainty that all of them would be as good as David. Considering why Nathan found it necessary to tell David the story of the stolen lamb, the Lawyer's remark may be regarded as an unconcealed irony. The intention of it is not hard to see. The concupiscent and irate heats of sovereigns are kept from perverting the relation of crimes and punishments in the direction of brutality by "promulgation," that is, by prior assignment in the absence of heat. Almost any assignment of punishments to offenses will be acceptable as rational if it is done in freedom from passion.

Much earlier in the *Dialogue*,[61] there is a reference to the same confrontation of David by Nathan, and it happens to be also in the context of promulgation as being indispensable to legality, the concrete point there being that the statutes ought to be as widely distributed as the Bible. If we put together what we learned through that passage and its context with what we have seen in the interim and what we can collect from this passage and its context, the thought seems to be this: there have been two great classes of indoctrinators, both private but both usurping a public function of indoctrination, not to say legislation. The clerical indoctrinators or legislators have introduced a great punitiveness into the legal system particularly in connection with the crime or noncrime of heresy. The legistic indoctrinators or legislators have also contributed very much to making the punishments in English practice irrationally vengeful, as the rest of the present

---

61. P. (35), where the *legal* penalty for sheep stealing is given.

section will show.[62] The monarch of course is not to be trusted, tempted as he is into tyrannical ways by the heats of his passions. An intimation of Hobbes's solution is given on page (140) of the *Dialogue* in the passage on proportion between crime and punishment: "the Punishing of Offences can be determined by none but by the King, and that, if it extend to life or member, with the Assent of Parliament." Hobbes is in the position of a Parliamentarist modifying the punitive prerogatives of the monarch by appearing to reassert the sole sovereignty of the monarch against the encroachments of that Parliamentary activist, Sir Edward Coke. Why he should have undertaken a polemic against Coke thus becomes clearer: Coke's doctrine, and therewith the common law, was menacing to the civil order in England in visibly depreciating the prerogative while weakening the crown additionally through making the legal system unreasonably vengeful, and to that extent odious and unendurable. In the last pages of this book, where Parliament is the theme, the Philosopher will go so far as to say that if a king is sane, he will consult with his discreet subjects to the end that the laws may be endurable.

The Philosopher pursues his argument against the excessive harshness of the common-law punishments throughout the first portion of the present section down to the transition from punishments to pardons. Before he leaves the subject, he shows that, for example, in the case of the judgment upon an innocent man who flees the law in despair of proving his innocence, the common-law rule that he is guilty of flight itself is an irrational controversion of every man's natural right to preserve his life. The common law is repeatedly shown to be excessively punitive because it is, far from being the law of reason, unreflective and removed from reason. The Philosopher had a right to reply as he did to the speech with which the Lawyer opens the *Dialogue*.

The next subject is pardoning. The Philosopher's thought here is the continuation of what developed in the first part of this section. Coke and the common law, still in their punitive state, would restrict the king's power of pardoning at every point possible. The Philosopher is able to unite therefore the argument

---

62. Cf. the doctrine of *Leviathan*, chap. 28, to the effect that punishment should be prospective rather than retrospective—deterrent rather than vengeful—and that it is an essentially public act, to be done for public reasons and by its executor acting in a public or politic capacity.

in favor of the royal prerogative with the argument for increased discretion in pardoning. In a curious remark[63] repeated from the earlier discussion of the true limit on the king's power to pardon,[64] the Philosopher reserves to the king only so much vengefulness as belongs to him in his capacity as executor of God's revenges.

There is at last a speech by the Philosopher[65] denoting a radical change of subject, from crimes and punishments to the laws of property. Since no manuscript of this work is extant, a question arises in the reader's mind concerning the last pages of the *Dialogue*, namely, whether the material contained therein fails through a typographical error to appear as a separate section. This question affects the question whether the *Dialogue* as a whole is a complete work. We must see what light is cast on these questions by the closing pages of the book as we have it.

As the subject changes to the laws of property, the Lawyer suggests that they examine the statutes, to which the Philosopher agrees but with the familiar proviso that they do so not to dispute of the justice of the laws, for men are bound to observe the laws that they have consented to. That remark is worth bearing in mind, for in what follows the point will be made that with respect to the basic distribution of landed property by the king, Parliamentary consent was not sought or obtained. At any rate, in a sentence that appears to be incorrectly incorporated in a speech of the Philosopher's, the suggestion is made that they turn to Coke on Magna Charta and other laws. The Philosopher replaces this suggestion with the thought that to understand Magna Charta they will have to remount to the ancient customs, the law of nature, and various general subjects; and in fact they never do return to Coke on Magna Charta or indeed to Magna Charta itself in the existing remainder of the book.

The Philosopher has given himself an opportunity to describe the evidently prehistoric origin of "all Dominion among Men" as being "in Families," and to elaborate the subject at some length. In recounting the natural autocracy of fathers and the environing condition in which it was exercised, Hobbes never uses the expression "state of nature," although that is what he has called it in his other writings. The discussion passes on to the explicit subject of this section or subsection, namely, property. Property is the consequence of appropriation, peaceful or armed,

---

63. Pp. (184)–(185).   64. P. (43).   65. P. (190).

by the sovereign heads of families acting solely—if the appropriation is to be "lawful"—out of an intention to benefit themselves, not to harm others. In the discussion of the pre-civil state as well as in the treatment of punishment and pardon just preceding, Hobbes does not rule out the inflicting of pain as such nor does he condemn the passions that lead men to inflict pain; he condemns the merely selfish or merely private indulgence of those passions as distinguished from their public or useful exercise. It is appropriate, in this portion on property, to take notice of that characteristic of Hobbes's thought which has so much in common with the subsequent development of the economic state.

Having shown how the first landed property belonged to the heads of families as such, the Philosopher has shown that there was landed property in those individuals who were to become the subjects of kings before there could have been landed property in the kings themselves. Whereas in the *Leviathan*[66] Hobbes makes clear that the new subjects must be understood tacitly at least to give up their property to the new sovereign and then to receive it back, there is no mention of such a proceeding in the *Dialogue*. On the contrary, the Lawyer makes a speech alluding to the difficulty implicit in the *Leviathan* account: "Whereas you say, that the Lands so won by the Sovereign Lord of a Family, are his in propriety, you deny (methinks) all property to the Subjects. . ."; and the sequel turns on the point of bare conquest. The broader question to which I am referring is how Hobbes can make the argument that the civil sovereign is the source of all landed property, by assignment, when it is obvious that landed property existed in the domestic sovereigns at the earlier stage. The answer must of course be that the civil sovereign's "assignment" follows either a voluntary or a coerced sequestration of the domestic properties. This is provisionally cleared up in the Philosopher's rhetorical question, "And was not all the Land in *England* once in the hands of *William* the Conqueror?" The subsequent discussion presupposes the case of conquest, and the question therefore is how the property of subjects as such came into being.

The interlocutors proceed to this theme by way of the Lawyer's distinction between the sovereign's "natural Capacity, as he is a Man, and [his] politick Capacity, as a King": if William ever owned all the land in England, it must have been in his politic

---

66. Chap. 24.

or public capacity. To this the Philosopher rejoins in a complicated speech, with the following tendency: (1) if William were sole landowner in his politic capacity, then he must dispose of the land only for the benefit of the people. (2) The people's benefit is to be known either through his own or through the people's discretion, "that is, by Act of Parliament." (3) Parliament (i.e., the existing Parliament of the conquered English) was not consulted. (4) William retained lands for his own recreation or magnificence. (5) The landed possessions of the kings of England are not a grant to them by the people for discharging public burdens. (6) The lands that William disposed of "were properly, and really his own." A very crude version of this argument would be: if William were proprietor in his public capacity, his acts as proprietor would have to have been solely in the interest of the *salus populi*; but they were not, therefore all the land was properly and really his own. This is a defense of regality that kings might wish to dispense with.

The Lawyer agrees with all that is said and now desires to pass from the origin to the growth of monarchies (the "origin" having come to an unpromising conclusion in the exposure of the monarch as being in significant degree a merely private or selfish being). The Philosopher again responds with a speech that, although quite short, appears greatly confused. He tries to make an enumeration of only two major items, but succeeds in creating the impression that there are three or perhaps more, for he says "first" twice and "secondly" only once, and after saying "secondly" he again says "first" with no "secondly" uniquely following it but with various sequels all equally possible in any order. His speech unfolds in this manner: (1) great monarchies have proceeded from small families, "first" by war. (He does not show a second way in which great monarchies have proceeded from small families.) (2) "Other forms of Commonwealths" have grown in other ways, "first" by the voluntary confederation of heads of families to make an aristocracy. (3) "Secondly, by Rebellion proceeded first, *Anarchy* . . ." and from anarchy either monarchy, aristocracy, or democracy. This "secondly" apparently belongs to the second "first" and not to the first because it gives an account of other forms of commonwealth besides monarchy. He now goes over the ground again with illustrations which will help to clarify the thought. (1) The greatest kingdoms in the world are seven in number, four ancient and three modern;

perhaps the greatest monarchy is more characteristic of antiquity than of modernity. All grew up after the first manner, which is by war. The fourth of the seven is the Macedonian monarchy, that of Alexander the Great. The reader must recall that on pages (13) and (20) of this *Dialogue*, Hobbes tacitly allows that it would be very reasonable to restrain kings from levying taxes and troops in pursuit of wars of mere conquest, particularly naming Alexander. Having behind us the recent distinction between the natural and the politic character of a monarch, we might use that distinction to characterise wars of monarchical aggrandisement as to some extent inspired by the private good of the conqueror. In general, the greatness of monarchies is inseparable from war. (2) The second of the three illustrations is wholly contained in this remark: "The second manner was the original of the *Venetian Aristocracy.*" The second manner was peaceful or at least voluntary confederation. (3) The third way is rebellion, which according to the single example of Rome is the means of producing monarchy through and in chaos. The two originals of monarchy, namely, war and rebellion, surround the inconspicuous example of aristocracy formed by voluntary association.

The immediately subsequent speech is the apparently inconsequent question of the Lawyer's, "Do you think the distinction between natural and politic Capacity is insignificant?" The Philosopher replies with no and explains that in monarchy alone the natural and politic capacity are in the same person, which opens up a great field of possible confusion, obviated by the Philosopher's declaring that what a king does or commands by consent of the people is done in his politic or public capacity and all the rest apparently is in his natural or private capacity. This of course means that what William the Conqueror did in assigning the confiscated lands of the English he did in his private capacity, by private right and not by public right.[67]

---

67. William held the whole land of England as his private property, we are told. He made his dispositions without reference to any Parliament; he stood between the Saxon Parliament and the Norman-English Parliament, apparently uniting successfully the natural and politic capacities in his own person. More directly, he had no need of the assent of any Parliament for he had troops that were "his own," as Machiavelli might say. They were his own because they were foreign conquerors in a subjugated country. His successors, who would have to reign or who would perhaps weakly submit to reign as native kings rather than as foreign conquerors, would be compelled to draw on their

(continued on next page)

As can now be seen, the foregoing portion of the *Dialogue* has this structure: a passage on the natural versus the politic capacity of the sovereign; a somewhat invidious passage on the violent root of monarchy; and a recurrence to the theme of the natural versus the politic capacity of the king, making as it were one uninterrupted whole.

The Lawyer once again proposes a new question: "what were the Laws and Customs of our Ancestors?" The new question proves to be a means to the continuation of a familiar theme, now explicit in the Lawyer's question, "How came a Subject to have a propriety in their [*sic*] Lands?" understanding that the land was to begin with totally engrossed by some monarch ruling on a level, either domestic or politic—which level is not made perfectly clear. Next, the kings "part with" some or much of their land in exchange for military service to be rendered by the recipients, who bind themselves by oaths of fealty to do their duty. Then an important development occurs, with respect to those duties of military service and of husbandry that are the conditions for land-tenure of the king: they "were quickly after turned into Rents." About a century after the composition of this *Dialogue*, Adam Smith was to say in the *Wealth of Nations* that the short-sighted selfishness of the feudal barony and clergy, in commuting dues in kind to money rents which they could apply to luxurious consumption, deprived them at last of their political power, for it deprived them of their military retinue. Hobbes does not speak of commutation of feudal service exclusively into money rents except in England; in Scotland and France the commutation was into food. But in any case the direct control of an always available militia was lost to the monarch. Hobbes does not explain this in language like Adam Smith's; he does not explain it at all—except by putting it in the context of the distinction between the monarch's natural or private capacity and his politic or public capacity. In principle, therefore, nothing but reticence stands between Hobbes's thought and Smith's explanation.

(67 continued)

subjects for troops. Perhaps the monarch must be a foreign conqueror in order effectually to unite the politic and natural capacities in his own person. Perhaps, in other words, pure monarchy is the state of deepest hostility between ruler and subjects, or the naturally polemic regime. We have sufficient reason for thinking that this was a notion available to Hobbes, who denied in the name of the king's prerogative that there was any compact between king and subjects.

There is one more apparent turning of the subject, brought on this time by a question of the Philosopher's: "In what manner proceeded those Ancient Saxons, and other Nations of Germany, especially the Northern parts, to the making of their Laws?" Pursuit of the answer to this question leads the interlocutors to the closing theme of Parliament. It appears immediately that the Saxon kings consulted the wisest and discreetest of their subjects when legislating.[68] The Philosopher responds that to legislate any other way would be incompatible with sanity. In other words, for the good of the people and also of the king it is necessary that legislation be with the advice and consent of the people or, in this case, Parliament. It is to be remembered that a few pages earlier[69] Hobbes made it appear that what the king does with consent he does in his public or politic capacity. We are now entitled to draw the conclusion that he is not rational if he tries to govern in his private or natural capacity—as would have been said earlier, tyrannically.

The interlocutors must now establish whether Parliament truly voices the people's consent. It is shown to do so through an exchange in the course of which the Lawyer reveals that from the remotest times on, the local people judged of the discretion and wisdom of the men who were to advise the king and express the people's consent, and those same local people were the electors of the members of Parliament: but the king called his discreet and wise advisers not by naming them but by directing his voting subjects to elect them. Hobbes says nothing of royal management of Parliamentary elections; but it is clear enough that that practice must destroy the essential principle of Parliament that enables it to be the support of kingly action as performed in the king's politic capacity.

The interlocutors have spoken of Parliament; it now appears that they meant the House of Commons. The Lawyer says "it is commonly receiv'd, that for the making of a Law, there ought to be had the assent of the Lords Spiritual and Temporal. . . ." The Philosopher characteristically has rejected mere custom as a rule for practice; but he is now silent on this point. In the last speech

---

68. The formula used might be of interest: "the Kings called together the Bishops, and a great part of the wisest and discreetest Men of the Realm, . . ." as if a Bishop were called ex officio and the laity for reasons of merit.
69. P. (197).

of the *Dialogue*, he shows that nobles were always called to Parliament, constituting a House of Lords, while after the introduction of Christianity, the Bishops were called as well. Thus Parliament is shown to have been complete from remote times, to express the people's assent, and the *Dialogue* abruptly terminates.

The promise to examine the laws of *meum* and *tuum* is not kept. Instead Hobbes has carried further his examination of the damage to the common good that is caused when the boundary between what is essentially private and what is essentially politic is disregarded. In other writings, Hobbes has drawn attention to the clergy as one class of offenders in this regard. In the present *Dialogue*, the legists are considered and criticized with a view to this matter, and so, perhaps surprisingly, is the royal sovereign himself, particularly in the latter part. There is an implicit praise of aristocracy that is almost imperceptible, and surely is not developed as an alternative to monarchy. Through the discussion of the assent of Parliament, a dim view appears of a collaborative regime—king, Lords, and Commons—in which, without overt checks and balances or any suggestion that sovereignty is divisible, there would yet be a rational, equitable unity in a nation purged so far as possible of endemic punitiveness. Hobbes cannot be said to have aimed at restoring the *polis*; he appears however to have aimed at restoring the politic as distinguished from the merely private in its clerical, legalistic, and tyrannical manifestations. That the fruit of his labors has been largely inherited by regimes that seek to sanctify a private sphere of life is not necessarily a sign that his larger purposes have been defeated. And if this testamentary book of his has the meaning that my interpretation indicates, then the *Dialogue* is in an important sense, and thus perhaps even literally, complete.

EDITOR'S NOTE

Two kinds of brackets are used to indicate emendations of the text: square brackets [ ] enclose material added to the text by me, and broken brackets ⟨ ⟩ enclose material printed in the first edition but removed by me. Where I have replaced words or punctuation with other words or punctuation, my material stands [thus] in the text with an index to the removed material which stands ⟨thus⟩ in the footnote. I have recorded even petty changes in order to place in the reader's hands what amounts to a copy of the first edition. I have changed as little as possible, leaving spelling and usage untouched ("then" for "than" and "through" for "thorough") except where there has simply been a mistake. Punctuation is unaltered except where the meaning appears seriously affected. Periods have been retained after numerals, and should not, of course, be read as full stops. I have not inserted quotation marks, partly for the reason that many of Hobbes's quotations are to some extent paraphrases. He never, to my knowledge, corrupts the sense of what he renders, but he does quite often improve the expression or the translation even of the Statutes, and certainly in presenting Coke. There are no footnotes in the first edition; all such are my own. Arabic numerals in parentheses, appearing in the left margin of the text and in footnotes, correspond to the pagination of the first edition. The text of the *Dialogue* begins on page (1), which is a facsimile.

THE
ART
OF
Rhetoric,
WITH A
DISCOURSE
OF
The Laws of *England*.

By *Thomas* Hobbes of *Malmesbury*.

Dent Umbræ tenuem Divi & sine pondere terram,
Spirantesque crocos & in urnâ perpetuum ver.

LONDON,
Printed for *William Crooke* at the Green
Dragon without *Temple-Bar*, 1681.

A DIALOGUE

Between

A *PHYLOSOPHER*

AND

A *STUDENT*,

OF

The Common-Laws of *England*.

Of the Law of Reason.

Law. **W**Hat makes you say, that the Study of the Law is less Rational, than the study of the Mathematicks?

Phylosoph. I say not that, for all study is Rational, or nothing worth ; but I say that the great Masters of the *Mathematicks* do not so often err as the great Professors of the Law.

B *Law.*

Law. If you had applyed your reason to the Law, perhaps you would
(2) have been of another mind.

Ph. In whatsoever Study, I examine whether my Inference be rational,
and have look't over the Titles of the Statutes from *Magna Charta*
downward to this present time. I left not one unread, which I
thought might concern my self, which was enough for me that
meant not to plead for any but my self. But I did not much examine
which of them was more, or less rational; because I read them not
to dispute, but to obey them, and saw in all of them sufficient
reason for my obedience, and that the same reason, though the
Statutes themselves were chang'd, remained constant. I have also
diligently read over *Littleton*'s Book of *Tenures*, with the Commentaries thereupon of the Renowned Lawyer Sir *Ed. Coke*,[1] in
which I confess I found great subtility, not of the Law, but of
Inference from Law, and especially from the Law of Humane
Nature, which is the Law of reason: and I confess that it is truth
which he[2] sayes in the Epilogue to his Book; that by Arguments
and Reason in the Law, a Man shall sooner come to the certainty
and knowledge of the Law: and I agree with Sir *Edw. Coke*, who
[comments] upon that Text, farther[3] that Reason is the Soul of the
(3) Law, and | upon sect. 138. [Coke comments,] *Nihil quod est Rationi
contrarium est licitum*; that is to say, nothing is Law that is against
Reason: and that Reason is the life of the Law, nay the Common
Law it self is nothing else but Reason. And upon Sect. 21. [Coke
comments,] *Æquitas est perfecta quædam Ratio, quæ Jus scriptum inter-
pretatur & emendat, nulla scriptura comprehensa, sed solus in vera
Ratione consistens. i. e.* Equity is a certain perfect Reason that interpreteth and amendeth the Law written, it self being unwritten,
and consisting in nothing else but right Reason.[4] When I consider this, and find it to be true, and so evident as not to be denied
by any Man of right sense,[5] I find my own reason at a stand; for
it frustrates all the Laws in the World: for upon this ground any
Man, of any Law whatsoever may say it is against Reason, and

---

1. Littleton's treatise *On Tenures* is the fifteenth-century legal work reproduced
in and commented upon by Coke in the first of the four parts of his *Institutes
of the Law of England*.   2. Littleton.   3. ⟨;⟩
4. In the foregoing passage, Hobbes's version of quoted material includes
minor emendation: for example, his "Rationi contrarium" replaces "contra
rationem." Such deviations will be allowed to stand, here and throughout,
without future indication to the reader, except if the intelligibility of the passage
is affected.   5. However, cf. p. (87) below.

thereupon make a pretence for his disobedience. I pray you clear this passage, that we may proceed.

La. I clear it thus out of Sir *Edw. Coke. 1 Inst. Sect.* 138. that this is to be understood of an artificial perfection of Reason gotten by long Study, Observation and Experience,[6] and not of every Mans natural Reason; for *Nemo nascitur Artifex.* This Legal Reason is *summa Ratio*; and therefore if all the Reason that is dispersed into

(4) so many several heads were united into one, yet could he | not make such a Law as the Law of *England* is, because by so many successions of Ages it hath been fined and refined by an infinite number of Grave and Learned Men.[7]

Ph. This does not clear the place, as being partly obscure, and partly untrue[;][8] that the Reason which is the Life of the Law, should be not Natural, but Artificial I cannot conceive.[9] I understand well enough, that the knowledge of the Law is gotten by much study, as all other Sciences are, which when they are studyed and obtained, it is still done by Natural, and not by Artificial Reason. I grant you that the knowledge of the Law is an Art, but not that any Art of one Man, or of many how wise soever they be, or the work of one and more Artificers, how perfect soever it be, is Law. It is not Wisdom, but Authority that makes a Law. Obscure also are the words Legal Reason; there is no Reason in Earthly Creatures, but Humane Reason; but I suppose that he means, that the Reason of a Judge, or of all the Judges together (without the King) is that *Summa Ratio*, and the very Law, which I deny, because none can make a Law but he that hath the Legislative Power. That the Law hath been fined by Grave and Learned Men, meaning the Professors of the Law is manifestly untrue, for all

(5) the Laws | of *England* have been made by the Kings of *England*, consulting with the Nobility and Commons in *Parliament*, of which not one of twenty was a Learned Lawyer.

La. You speak of the Statu[t]e Law, and I speak of the Common Law.

Ph. I speak generally of Law.

La. Thus far I agree with you, that Statute Law taken away, there would not be left, either here, or any where, any Law at all that would conduce to the Peace of a Nation; yet Equity, and Reason

---

6. This much of the passage from Coke is quoted, and the matter discussed, in chapter 26 of *Leviathan*.

7. This speech, from "is to be understood" to the end, is a virtual quotation from Coke.   8. ⟨,⟩

9. Cf. *Leviathan*, chap. 15, where Hobbes makes equity the law of nature.

which Laws Divine and Eternal, which oblige all Men at all times, and in all places, would still remain, but be Obeyed by few: and though the breach of them be not punished in this World, yet they will be punished sufficiently in the World to come. Sir *Edw. Coke* for drawing to the Men of his own Profession as much Authority as lawfully he might, is not to be reprehended; but to the gravity and Learning of the Judges they[10] ought to have added in the making of Laws, the Authority of the King, which hath the Soveraignty: for of these Laws of Reason, every Subject that is in his Wits, is bound to take notice at his Peril, because Reason is part of his Nature, which he continually carryes about with him, and may read it, if he will.[11] |

Ph. 'Tis very true; and upon this ground, if I pretend within a Month,
(6) or two to make my self able to perform the Office of a Judge, you are not to think it Arrogance; for you are to allow to me, as well as to other Men, my pretence to Reason, which is the Common Law (remember this that I may not need again to put you in mind, that Reason is the Common Law) and for Statute Law, seeing it is Printed, and that there be Indexes to point me to every matter contained in them, I think a Man may profit in them very much in two Months.

La. But you will be but an ill Pleader.

Ph. A Pleader commonly thinks he ought to say all he can for the Benefit of his Client, and therefore has need of a faculty to wrest the sense of words from their true meaning; and the faculty of *Rhetorick* to seduce the Jury, and sometimes the Judge also, and many other Arts, which I neither have, nor intend to study.[12]

La. But let the Judge how good soever he thinks his Reasoning, take heed that he depart not too much from the Letter of the Statute: for it is not without danger.

Ph. He may without danger recede from the Letter, if he do not from the meaning and sense of the Law,[13] which may be by a Learned
(7) Man, (such as Judges commonly | are) easily found out by the Preamble, the time when it was made, and the Incommodities for

---

10. "They" should perhaps read "he" to refer to Coke.
11. The clause "for of these Laws . . . if he will" is more closely connected with the first part of the speech than with the part to which it is immediately subjoined; but its coherence with the next speech should dispose of speculation about chance disarrangement of the speech as a whole.
12. The present *Dialogue* was first published, withal posthumously, together with Hobbes's *The Art of Rhetoric*.   13. Cf. below, p. (81).

which it was made: but I pray tell me, to what end were Statute-Laws ordained, seeing the Law of Reason ought to be applyed to every Controversie that can arise.

La. You are not ignorant of the force of an irregular Appetite to Riches, to Power, and to sensual Pleasures, how it Masters the strongest Reason, and is the root of Disobedience, Slaughter, Fraud, Hypocrisie, and all manner of evil habits; and that the Laws of Man, though they can punish the fruits of them, which are evil Actions, yet they cannot pluck up the roots that are in the Heart. How can a Man be Indicted of Avarice, Envy, Hypocrisie, or other vitious Habit, till it be declared by some Action, which a Witness may take notice of; the root remaining, new fruit will come forth till you be weary of punishing, and at last destroy all Power that shall oppose it.

Ph. What hope then is there of a constant Peace in any Nation, or between one Nation, and another?

La. You are not to expect such a Peace between two Nations, because there is no Common Power in this World to punish their Injustice: mutual fear may keep them quiet for a time, but upon every
(8) visible | advantage they will invade one another, and the most visible advantage is then, when the one Nation is obedient to their King, and the other not; but Peace at home may then be expected durable, when the common people shall be made to see the benefit they shall receive by their Obedience and Adhæsion to their own Soveraign, and the harm they must suffer by taking part with them, who by promises of Reformation, or change of Government deceive them. And this is properly to be done by Divines, and from Arguments not only from Reason, but also from the Holy Scripture.

Ph. This that you say is true, but not very much to that I aim at by your Conversation, which is to inform my self concerning the Laws of *England*: therefore I ask you again, what is the end of Statute-Laws?

Of Soveraign Power.

La. I SAY THEN THAT THE SCOPE OF ALL HUMANE LAW IS Peace, and Justice in every Nation amongst themselves, and defence against Forraign Enemies.

Ph. But what is Justice?

La. Justice is giving to every Man his own. |

Ph. The Definition is good, and yet 'tis *Aristotles*; what is the Defi-
(9) nition agreed upon as a Principle in the Science of the Common
Law?

La. The same with that of *Aristotle.*

Ph. See you Lawyers how much you are beholding to a Philosopher,
and 'tis but reason, for the more General and Noble Science, and
Law of all the World is true Philosophy, of which the Common
Law of *England* is a very little part.

La. 'Tis so, if you mean by Philosophy nothing but the Study of
Reason, as I think you do.

Ph. When you say that Justice gives to every Man his own, what mean
you by his own? How can that be given me which is my own
already? or, if it be not my own, how can Justice make it mine?

La. Without Law every thing is in such sort every Mans, as he may
take, possess, and enjoy without wrong to any Man, every thing,
Lands, Beasts, Fruits, and even the bodies of other Men, if his
Reason tell him he cannot otherwise live securely: for the dictates
of Reason are little worth, if they tended not to the preservation
and improvement of Mens Lives[. S]¹eeing then without Humane
Law all things would be Common, and this Community a cause
(10) of Incroachment, Envy, Slaughter, and continual War | of one
upon another, the same Law of Reason Dictates to Mankind (for
their own preservation) a distribution of Lands, and Goods, that
each Man may know what is proper to him, so as none other might
pretend a right thereunto, or disturb him in the use of the same.
This distribution is Justice, and this properly is the same which
we say is [one's own]²: by which you may see the great Necessity
there was of Statute Laws, for preservation of all Mankind. It is
also a Dictate of the Law of Reason, that Statute Laws are a
necessary means of the safety and well being of Man in the present
World, and are to be Obeyed by all Subjects, as the Law of
Reason ought to be Obeyed, both by King and Subjects, because
it is the Law of God.

Ph. All this is very Rational; but how can any Laws secure one Man
from another [w]³hen the greatest part of Men are so unreasonable, and so partial to themselves as they are, and the Laws of
themselves are but a dead Letter, which of it self is not able to

---

1. ⟨, s⟩   2. ⟨one owns⟩   3. ⟨? W⟩

compel a Man to do otherwise than himself pleaseth, nor punish, or hurt him when he hath done a mischief[?]⁴

La. By the Laws, I mean, Laws living and Armed: for you must suppose, that a Nation that is subdued by War to an absolute
(11) submission of a Conqueror, it may by | the same Arm that compelled it to Submission, be compelled to Obey his Laws. Also if a Nation choose a Man, or an Assembly of Men to Govern them by Laws, it must furnish him also with Armed Men and Money, and all things necessary to his Office, or else his Laws will be of no force, and the Nation remains, as before it was, in Confusion. 'Tis not therefore the word of the Law, but the Power of a Man that has the strength of a Nation, that makes the Laws effectual. It was not *Solon* that made *Athenian* Laws (though he devised them) but the Supream Court of the People; nor, the Lawyers of *Rome* that made the Imperial Law in *Justinian*'s time, but *Justinian* himself.

Ph. We agree then in this, that in *England* it is the King that makes the Laws, whosoever Pens them, and in this, that the King cannot make his Laws effectual, nor defend his People against their Enemies, without a Power to Leavy Souldiers, and consequently, that he may Lawfully, as oft as he shall really think it necessary to raise an Army (which in some occasions be very great) I say, raise it, and Money to Maintain it. I doubt not but you will allow this to be according to the Law (at least) of Reason.

La. For my part I allow it. But you have heard how, in, and before the
(12) late Trou- | bles the People were of another mind. Shall the King, said they, take from us what he please, upon pretence of a necessity whereof he makes himself the Judg[e]? What worse Condition can we be in from an Enemy! What can they take from us more than what they list?

Ph. The People Reason ill; they do not know in what Condition we were in the time of the Conqueror, when it was a shame to be an *English-Man*, who if he grumbled at the base Offices he was put to by his *Norman* Masters, received no other Answer but this, Thou art but an *English-Man*[;]⁵ nor can the People, nor any Man that humors them in their Disobedience, produce any Example of a King that ever rais'd any excessive Summ's, either by himself, or by the Consent of his Parliament, but when they had great need thereof; nor can shew any reason that might move any of them

---

4. ⟨.⟩   5. ⟨,⟩

so to do. The greatest Complaint by them made against the un-thriftiness of their Kings was for the inriching now and then a Favourite, which to the Wealth of the Kingdom was inconsiderable, and the Complaint but Envy. But in this point of raising Souldiers, what is I pray you the Statute Law?

La. The last Statute concerning it, is 13 *Car.2.c.*6. By which the
(13) Supream Government Command, and disposing of the | Militia of *England* is delivered to be, and always to have been the Antient Right of the Kings of *England*: But there is also in the same Act a Proviso, that this shall not be Construed for a Declaration, that the King may Transport his Subjects, or compel them to march out of the Kingdom, nor is it, on the contrary declared to be unlawful.

Ph. Why is not that also determined?

La. I can imagine cause enough for it, though I may be deceiv'd. We love to have our King amongst us, and not be Govern'd by Deputies, either of our own, or another Nation: But this I verily believe, that if a Forraign Enemy should either invade us, or put himself int[o] a readiness to invade either *England, Ireland,* or *Scotland* (no Parliament then sitting) and the King send *English* Souldiers thither, the Parliament would give him thanks for it. The subjects of those Kings who affect the Glory, and imitate the Actions of *Alexander* the Great, have not always the most comfortable lives, nor do such Kings usually very long enjoy their Conquests. They March to and fro perpetually, as upon a Plank sustained only in the midst, and when one end rises, down goes the other.

Ph. 'Tis well. But where Souldiers (in the Judgment of the Kings
(14) Conscience) are indeed necessary, as in an insurrection, or | Rebellion at home; how shall the Kingdom be preserved without a considerable Army ready, and in pay? How shall Money be rais'd for this Army, especially when the want of publick Treasure inviteth Neighbour Kings to incroach, and unruly Subjects to Rebel?

La. I cannot tell. It is matter of Polity, not of Law; but I know, that there be Statutes express, whereby the King hath obliged himself never to Levy Money upon his Subjects without the consent of his Parliament. One of which Statutes is 25 *Ed.* 1.*c.*6. in these words, *We have granted for us, and our Heirs, as well to Arch-Bishops, Bishops, Abbots, and other Folk of the Holy Church, as also Earls, Barons, and to all the Commonalty of the Land, that for no Business from* *henceforth, we shall take such Aids, Taxes, or Prizes, but by the common Consent of the Realm.* There is also another Statute of *Ed.* 1. in these words, *No Taxes, or Aid shall be taken or Levyed by us, or our Heirs in our Realm, without the good will, and assent of the Arch-Bishops, Bishops, Earls, Barons, Knights, Burgesses, and other Freemen of the Land;* which Statutes have been since that time Confirmed by divers other Kings, and lastly by the King that now Reigneth.[6]

Ph. All this I know, and am not satisfied. I am one of the Common
(15) People, and | one of that almost infinite number of Men, for whose welfare Kings, and other Soveraigns were by God Ordain'd: For God made Kings for the People, and not People for Kings.[7] How shall I be defended from the domineering of Proud and Insolent Strangers that speak another Language, that scorn us, that seek to make us Slaves? Or how shall I avoid the Destruction that may arise from the cruelty of Factions in a Civil War, unless the King, to whom alone, you say, belongeth the right of Levying, and disposing of the Militia[,][8] by which only it can be prevented, have ready Money,. upon all Occasions, to Arm and pay as many Souldiers, as for the present defence, or the Peace of the People shall be necessary? Shall not I, and you, and every Man be undone? Tell me not of a Parliament when there is no Parliament sitting, or perhaps none in being, which may often happen; and when there is a Parliament if the speaking, and leading Men should have a design to put down Monarchy, as they had in the Parliament which began to sit *Nov.* 3. 1640. Shall the King, who is to answer to God Almighty for the safety of the People, and to that end is intrusted with the Power to Levy and dispose of the Souldiery, be disabled to perform his Office by virtue of these
(16) Acts of Parliament which you have | cited? If this be reason, 'tis reason also that the People be Abandoned, or left at liberty to kill one another, even to the last Man; if it be not Reason, then you have granted it is not Law.

La. 'Tis true, if you mean *Recta Ratio,* but *Recta Ratio* which I grant to be Law, as Sir *Edw. Coke* says, 1 *Inst. Sect.* 138. Is an Artificial perfection of Reason gotten by long Study, Observation, and Experience, and not every Mans natural Reason; for *Nemo nascitur Artifex.* This Legal Reason is *summa Ratio;* and therefore, if all

---

6. Charles II.
7. The argument of this speech should be compared with the comments on Hobbes expressed by Rousseau in chapter 2 of *The Social Contract.*   8. ⟨;⟩

the Reason that is dispersed into so many several Heads were united into one, yet could he not make such a Law as the Law of *England* is, because by many Successions of Ages it hath been fined and refined, by an infinite number of Grave and Learned Men. And this is it he calls the Common-Law.

Ph. Do you think this to be good Doctrine? [T][9]hough it be true, that no Man is born with the use of Reason, yet all Men may grow up to it as well as Lawyers; and when they have applyed their Reason to the Laws (which were Laws before they Studyed them, or else it was not Law they Studied) may be as fit for, and capable of Judicature as Sir *Edw. Coke* himself, who whether he had more,

(17) or less use of Reason, was not thereby a Judge, but because | the King made him so: And whereas he says, that a Man who should have as much Reason as is dispersed in so many several Heads, could not make such a Law as this Law of *England* is; if one should ask him who made the Law of *England*? Would he say a Succession of *English* Lawyers, or Judges made it, or rather a Succession of Kings; and that upon their own Reason, either solely, or with the Advice of the Lords and Commons in Parliament, without the Judges, or other Professors of the Law? You see therefore that the Kings Reason, be it more, or less, is that *Anima Legis*, that *Summa Lex*, whereof *Sir Edw. Coke* speaketh, and not the Reason, Learning, or Wisdom of the Judges; but you may see, that quite through his Institutes of Law, he often takes occasion to Magnifie the Learning of the Lawyers, whom he perpetually termeth the Sages of the Parliament, or of the Kings Council: therefore unless you say otherwise, I say, that the Kings Reason, when it is publickly upon Advice, and Deliberation declar'd, is that *Anima Legis*, and that *Summa Ratio*, and that Equity which all agree to be the Law of Reason, is all that is, or ever was Law in *England*, since it became Christian, besides the Bible. |

La. Are not the Canons of the Church part of the Law of *England*, as
(18) also the Imperial Law used in the Admiralty, and the Customs of particular places, and the by-Laws of Corporations, and Courts of Judicature.

Ph. Why not? for they were all Constituted by the Kings of *England*; and though the Civil Law used in the Admiralty were at first the Statutes of the *Roman* Empire, yet because they are in force by

---

9. ⟨t⟩

no other Authority than that of the King, they are now the Kings Laws, and the Kings Statutes. The same we may say of the Canons; such of them as we have retained, made by the Church of *Rome*, have been no Law, nor of any force in *England*, since the beginning of Queen *Elizabeth*'s Raign, but by Virtue of the Great Seal of *England*.

La. In the said Statutes that restrain the Levying of Money without consent of Parliament, Is there any thing you can take exceptions to?

Ph. No, I am satisfied that the Kings that grant such Liberties are bound to make them good, so far as it may be done without sin: But if a King find that by such a Grant he be disabled to protect his Subjects if he maintain his Grant, he sins; and therefore may,

(19) and ought to take no Notice | of the said Grant: For such Grants as by Error, or false Suggestion are gotten from him, are as the Lawyers do Confess, Void and of no Effect, and ought to be recalled. Also the King (as is on all hands Confessed) hath the Charge lying upon him to Protect his People against Forraign Enemies, and to keep the Peace betwixt them within the Kingdom; if he do not his utmost endeavour to discharge himself thereof, he Committeth a Sin, which neither King, nor Parliament can Lawfully commit.

La. No Man I think will deny this: For if Levying of Money be necessary, it is a Sin in the Parliament to refuse, if unnecessary, it is a sin both in King and Parliament to Levy: But for all that it may be, and I think it is a Sin in any one that hath the Soveraign Power, be he one Man, or one Assembly, being intrusted with the safety of a whole Nation, if rashly, and relying upon his own Natural sufficiency, he make War, or Peace without Consulting with such, as by their Experience and Employment abroad, and Intelligence by Letters, or other means have gotten the Knowledge in some measure of the strength, Advantages and Designs of the Enemy, and the Manner and Degree of the Danger that

(20) may from thence arise. In like man-|ner, in case of Rebellion at Home, if he Consult not with [men] of Military Condition, which if he do, then I think he may Lawfully proceed to Subdue all such Enemies and Rebels; and that the Souldiers ought to go on without Inquiring whether they be within the Country, or without: For who shall suppress Rebellion, but he that hath Right to Levy, Command, and Dispose of the Militia? The last long Parliament denied this. But why? Because by the Major part of their Votes

the Rebellion was raised with design to put down Monarchy, and to that end Maintained.

Ph. Nor do I hereby lay any Aspersion upon such Grants of the King and his Ancestors. Those Statutes are in themselves very good for the King and People, as creating some kind of Difficulty, [f]or such Kings as for the Glory of Conquest might spend one part of their Subjects Lives and Estates, in Molesting other Nations, and leave the rest to Destroy themselves at Home by Factions. That which I here find fault with, is the wresting of those, and other such Statutes to a binding of our Kings from the use of their Armies in the necessary defence of themselves and their People. The late long Parliament that in 1648, Murdered their King (a King that sought no greater Glory upon Earth,
(21) but | to be indulgent to his People, and a Pious defender of the Church of *England*) no sooner took upon them the Soveraign Power, then they Levyed Money upon the People at their own Discretion. Did any of their Subjects Dispute their Power? Did they not send Souldiers over the Sea to Subdue *Ireland*, and others to Fight against the Dutch at Sea, or made they any doubt but to be obeyed in all that they Commanded, as a Right absolutely due to the Soveraign Power in whomsoever it resides? I say[10] not this as allowing their Actions, but as a Testimony from the Mouths of those very Men that denyed the same Power to him, whom they acknowledged to have been their Soveraign immediately before, which is a sufficient Proof, that the People of *England* never doubted of the Kings Right to Levy Money for the Maintenance of his Armies, till they were abused in it by Seditious Teachers, and other prating Men, on purpose to turn the State and Church into Popular Government, where the most ignorant and boldest Talkers do commonly obtain the best preferments; again, when their New Republick returned into Monarchy by *Oliver*, who durst deny him Money upon any pretence of *Magna Charta*, or of these other Acts of Parliament which you
(22) have Cited? You may therefore think it good Law, for | all your Books; that the King of *England* may at all times, that he thinks in his Conscience it will be necessary for the defence of his People, Levy as many Souldiers, and as much Money as he please, and that himself is Judge of the Necessity.

La. Is there no body harkning at the door?

10. ⟨,⟩

Ph. What are you afraid of?

La. I mean to say the same that you say: but there be very many yet, that hold their former Principles, whom, neither the Calamities of the Civil Wars, nor their former Pardon have throughly cur'd of their Madness.

Ph. The Common People never take notice of what they hear of this Nature, but when they are set on by such as they think Wise; that is, by some sorts of Preachers, or some that seem to be Learned in the Laws, and withal speak evil of the Governors. But what if the King upon the sight, or apprehension of any great danger to his People; as when their Neighbours are born down with the Current of a Conquering Enemy, should think his own People might be involved in the same Misery, may he not Levy, Pay, and Transport Souldiers to help those weak Neighbours by way of prevention, to save his own People and himself from Servitude? Is that a sin? |

La. First, If the War upon our Neighbour be Just, it may be ques-
(23) tion'd whether it be Equity or no to Assist them against the Right.

Ph. For my part I make no Question of that at all, unless the Invader will, and can put me in security, that neither he, nor his Successors shall make any Advantage of the Conquest of my Neighbour, to do the same to me in time to come; but there is no Common Power to bind them to the Peace.

La. Secondly; when such a thing shall happen, the Parliament will not refuse to Contribute freely to the safety of themselves, and the whole Nation.

Ph. It may be so, and it may be not: For if a Parliament then sit not, it must be called; that requires 6 Weeks time; Debating and Collecting what is given requires as much, and in this time the Opportunity perhaps is lost. Besides, how many wretched Souls have we heard to say in the late Troubles; What matter is it who gets the Victory? We can pay but what they please to Demand, and so much we pay now: and this they will Murmur, as they have ever done whosoever shall Raign over them, as long as their Coveteousness and Ignorance hold together, which will be till Dooms-
(24) day, if better order be not taken for their | [In]struction in their Duty, both from Reason and Religion.

La. For all this I find it somewhat hard, that a King should have Right to take from his Subjects, upon the pretence of Necessity what he pleaseth.

Ph. I know what it is that troubles your Conscience in this Point. All

Men are troubled at the Crossing of their Wishes; but it is our own fault. First, we wish Impossibilities; we would have our Security against all the World, upon Right of Property, without Paying for it: This is Impossible. We may as well Expect that Fish, and Fowl should Boil, Rost, and Dish themselves, and come to the Table; and that Grapes should squeeze themselves into our Mouths, and have all other the Contentments and ease which some pleasant Men have Related of the Land of *Cocquany*. Secondly, There is no Nation in the World where he, or they that have the Soveraignty do not take what Money they please, for Defence of those respective Nations, when they think it necessary for their safety. The late long Parliament denyed this; but why? Because there was a Design amongst them to Depose the King. Thirdly, There is no Example of any King of *England* that I have Read of, that ever pretended any such Necessity for

(25) Levying of Money, against | his Conscience. The greatest [sums][11] that ever were Levyed (Comparing the value of Money, as it was at that time, with what now it is) were Levied by King *Edw*. 3d. and King *Henry* the 5th. Kings of whom we Glory now, and think their Actions great Ornaments to the *English* History. Lastly, As to the enriching of now and then a Favourite, it is neither sensible to the Kingdom, nor is any Treasure thereby Conveyed out of the Realm, but so spent as it falls down again upon the Common People. To think that our Condition being Humane should be subject to no Incommodity, were Injuriously to Quarrel with God Almighty for our own Faults; for he hath done his part in annexing our own Industry and Obedience.

La. I know not what to say.

Ph. If you allow this that I have said; then, say that the People never were, shall be, or ought to be free from being Taxed at the will of one or other; being hindred, that if Civil War come, they must Levy all they have, and that Dearly, from the one, or from the other, or from both sides.[12] Say, that adhering to the King, their Victory is an end of their Trouble; that adhering to his Enemies

---

11. ⟨founds⟩

12. The passage "being hindred . . . both sides" is obscure. Without reference to an authoritative MS, it is hard to say whether "being hindred" is a typesetter's misreading or perhaps belongs elsewhere. Also doubtful is the antecedent, or antecedents, of the two "theys," and therefore the sense in which "Levy" is being used. The following conjecture is offered as being generally compatible with the gist of the speech: "lest, if civil war come, the people must redeem all their property, and at a high price too, from either or both sides."

there is no end; for the War will continue by a perpetual Sub-
(26) division, and when it ends, they will be in the same | Estate they
were before. That they are often Abused by Men who to them
seem wise, when then their Wisdom is nothing else but Envy to
those that are in Grace, and in profitable Employments, and that
those Men do but abuse the Common People to their own ends,
that set up a private Mans Propriety against the publick Safety.
But say withal, that the King is Subject to the Laws of God, both
Written, and Unwritten, and to no other; and so was *William the
Conqueror*, whose Right it all Descended to our present King.

La. As to the Law of Reason, which is Equity, 'tis sure enough there
is but one Legislator, which is God.

Ph. It followeth then that which you call the Common-Law, Distinct
from Statute-Law, is nothing else but the Law of God.

La. In some sense it is, but it is not Gospel, but Natural Reason, and
Natural Equity.

Ph. Would you have every Man to every other Man alledge for Law
his own particular Reason? There is not amongst Men an
Universal Reason agreed upon in any Nation, besides the Reason
of him that hath the Soveraign Power; yet though his Reason be
but the Reason of one Man, yet it is set up to supply the place of
(27) that | Universal Reason, which is expounded to us by our Saviour
in the Gospel, and consequently our King is to us the Legislator
both of Statute-Law, and of Common-Law.

La. Yes, I know that the Laws Spiritual, which have been Law in this
Kingdom since the Abolishing of Popery, are the Kings Laws,
and those also that were made before; for the Canons of the
Church of *Rome* were no Laws, neither here, nor any where else
without the Popes Temporal Dominions, farther than Kings, and
States in their several Dominions respectively did make them so.

Ph. I grant that. But you must grant also, that those Spiritual Laws
[were enacted in England by consent of the Lords and Commons
assenting in the Kings' actions as sole][13] Legislators of the

---

13. It is evident that the passage, as originally printed, is defective between the
words "Laws" and "Legislators." The editor of the 1750 *Works* and Molesworth emended the passage by inserting the words "were made by" at this
place, which appears unsatisfactory. The insertion proposed above has been
constructed to cohere with the argument of the preceding and succeeding
speeches, and to take account of the apparent tone of the exchange. For
example, the defective speech begins with the Philosopher saying that he grants
something, but the Lawyer must in turn also concede a certain point—something, presumably, that goes beyond what the Lawyer has allowed in the
(*continued on next page*)

Spiritual Law; and yet not all Kings, and States make Laws by Consent of the Lords and Commons; but our King here is so far bound to their Assents, as he shall Judge Conducing to the Good, and safety of his People; for Example, if the Lords and Commons should Advise him to restore those Laws Spiritual, which in Queen *Maries* time were in Force, I think the King were by the Law of Reason obliged, without the help of any other Law of God, to neglect such Advice.

La. I Grant you that the King is sole Legislator, but with this Restric-
(28) tion, that if | he will not Consult with the Lords of Parliament and hear the Complaints, and Informations of the Commons, that are best acquainted with their own wants, he sinneth against God, though he cannot be Compell'd to any thing by his Subjects by Arms, and Force.

Ph. We are Agreed upon that already[. S][14]ince therefore the King is sole Legislator, I think it also Reason he should be sole Supream Judge.

La. There is no doubt of that; for otherwise there would be no Congruity of Judgments with the Laws. I Grant also that he is the

The King is the   Supream Judge over all Persons, and in all
Supream Judge.   Causes Civil, and Ecclesiastical within his

own Dominions, not only by Act of Parliament at this time, but that he has ever been so by the Common-Law: For the Judges of both the Benches have their Offices by the Kings Letters Patents, and so (as to Judicature) have the Bishops. Also the Lord Chancellour hath his Office by receiving from the King the Great Seal of *England*; and to say all at once, there is no Magistrate, or Commissioner for Publick Business, neither of Judicature, nor Execution in State, or Church, in Peace, or War, but he is made so by Authority from the King.

Ph. 'Tis true; But perhaps you may think otherwise, when you Read
(29) such Acts of Parliament, as say, that the King shall have Power and Authority to do this, or that by Virtue of that Act, as *Eliz.* *c.* 1. That your Highness, your Heirs, and Successors, Kings, or Queens of this Realm shall have full Power and Authority, by Virtue of this Act, by Letters Patents under the Great Seal of

---

(13 continued)

preceding speech. What ensues is on the theme of the collaboration of king and advisers with a view to the difference between English and alien practice. The missing words appear to introduce or contribute to that distinction.

14. ⟨, s⟩

England to Assign, *&c.* Was it not this Parliament that gave this Authority to the Queen?

La. No; For the Statute in this Clause is no more than (as Sir *Edw. Coke* useth to speak) an Affirmance of the Common-Law;[15] for she being Head of the Church of *England* might make Commissioners for the deciding of Matters Ecclesiastical, as freely as if she had been Pope, who did you know pretend his Right from the Law of God.

Ph. We have hitherto spoken of Laws without considering any thing of the Nature and Essence of a Law; and now unless we define the word Law, we can go no farther without Ambiguity, and Fallacy, which will be but loss of time; whereas, on the contrary, the Agreement upon our words will enlighten all we have to say hereafter.

La. I do not remember the Definition of Law in any Statute. |

Ph. I think so: For the Statutes were made by Authority, and not (30) drawn from any other Principles than the care of the safety of the People. Statutes are not Philosophy as is the Common-Law, and other disputable Arts, but are Commands, or Prohibitions which ought to be obeyed, because Assented to by Submission made to the Conqueror here in *England*, and to whosoever had the Soveraign Power in other Common wealths; so that the Positive Laws of all Places are Statutes. The Definition of Law was therefore unnecessary for the makers of Statutes, though very necessary to them, whose work it is to Teach the sence of the Law.

La. There is an Accurate Definition of a Law in *Bracton*, Cited by Sir *Edw. Coke* ([2 *Inst.* p. 588, n. 14]) *Lex est sanctio justa, jubens honesta, & prohibens contraria.*[16]

Ph. That is to say, Law is a just Statute, Commanding those things which are honest, and Forbidding the contrary. From whence it followeth, that in all Cases it must be the Honesty, or Dishonesty that makes the Command a Law, whereas you know that but for the Law we could not (as saith St. *Paul*) have known what is sin; therefore this Definition is no Ground at all for any farther Dis- (31) course of Law. Besides, you know the Rule of Honest, and | Dishonest refers to Honour, and that it is Justice only, and Injustice that the Law respecteth. But that which I most except against in this Definition, is, that it supposes that a Statute made by the

---

15. 1 *Inst.* fol. 70a.
16. First edition is blank within the parentheses. The definition appears in Bracton, fol. 2a.

Soveraign Power of a Nation may be unjust. There may indeed in a Statute Law, made by Men be found Iniquity, but not Injustice.

La. This is somewhat subtil; I pray deal plainly, what is the difference between Injustice and Iniquity?

Ph. I pray you tell me first, what is the difference between a Court of Justice, and a Court of Equity?

La. A Court of Justice is that which hath Cognizance of such Causes as are to be ended by the Positive Laws of the Land; and a Court of Equity [is][17] that, to which belong such Causes as are to be determined by Equity; that is to say, by the Law of Reason.

Ph. You see then that the difference between Injustice, and Iniquity is this; that Injustice is the Transgression of a Statute-Law, and Iniquity the Transgression of the Law of Reason, [but that the dictate of obedience to the statute law][18] was nothing else but the Law of Reason, and that the Judges of that Law are Courts of Justice, because the breach of the Statute-Law is Iniquity, and Injustice also.[19] But perhaps you mean by Common-Law, not the

(32) Law it self, | but the manner of proceeding in the Law (as to matter of Fact) by 12 Men, Freeholders, though those 12 Men are no Court of Equity, nor of Justice, because they determine not what is Just, or Unjust, but only whether it be done, or not done; and their Judgment is nothing else but a Confirmation of that which is properly the Judgment of the Witnesses; for to speak exactly there cannot possibly be any Judge of Fact besides the Witnesses.

La. Seeing all Judges in all Courts ought to Judge according to Equity, which is the Law of Reason, a distinct Court of Equity seemeth to me to be unnecessary, and but a Burthen to the People, since Common-Law, and Equity are the same Law.

Ph. It were so indeed[, i][20]f Judges could not err, but since they may err, and that the King is not Bound to any other Law but that of Equity, it belongs to him alone to give Remedy to them that by the Ignorance, or Corruption of a Judge shall suffer dammage.

---

17. ⟨in⟩

18. Down to "Transgression of the Law of Reason," the passage is intelligible; as originally printed, the remainder rendered the whole sentence defective. The editor of the 1750 *Works* met the problem by deleting "was nothing else but the Law of Reason"; Molesworth deletes "was nothing else . . . and Injustice also." It appears, though, that the emendation of the passage calls for filling a hiatus rather than excision of introduced material.

19. Cf. *Leviathan,* chap. 15.   20. ⟨; I⟩

La.[21] How would you have a Law defin'd?

Ph. Thus; A Law is the Command of him, or them that have the Soveraign Power, given to those that be his or their Subjects, declaring Publickly, and plainly what every of them may do, and what they must forbear to do. |

La. By your Definition of a Law, the Kings Proclamation under the
(33) Great Seal of *England* is a Law; for it is a Command, and Publick, and of the Soveraign to his Subjects.

Ph. Why not? If he think it necessary for the good of his Subjects: For this is a Maxim at the Common-Law Alledged by Sir *Edward Coke* himself. [2 *Inst.* p. 306][22] *Quando Lex aliquid concedit, concedere videtur & id per quod devenitur ad illud.* And you know out of the same Author, that divers Kings of *England* have often, to the Petitions in Parliament which they granted, annexed such exceptions as these, unless there be necessity, saving our Regality; which I think should be always understood, though they be not expressed; and are understood so by Common Lawyers, who agree that the King may recall any Grant wherein he was deceiv'd.

La. Again, whereas you make it of the Essence of a Law to be Publickly and plainly declar'd to the People, I see no necessity for that. Are not all Subjects Bound to take notice of all Acts of Parliament, when no Act can pass without their Consent?

Ph. If you had said that no Act could pass without their knowledge, then indeed they had been bound to take notice of them; but none
(34) can have knowledge of them but | the Members of the Houses of Parliament, therefore the rest of the People are excus'd; or else the Knights of the [Shires][23] should be bound to furnish People with a sufficient Number of Copies (at the Peoples Charge) of the Acts of Parliament at their return into the Country; that every man may resort to them, and by themselves, or Friends take notice of what they are obliged to; for otherwise it were Impossible they should be obeyed: And that no Man is bound to do a thing Impossible is one of Sir *Edw. Cokes* Maxims at the Common-Law.[24] I know that most of the Statutes are Printed,

---

21. This speech and the following one by the Philosopher were printed originally above the Lawyer's speech that begins "Seeing all Judges in all Courts. . . ." In that place the two-speech passage so obviously interrupts one line of argument, and loses its contiguity with another which it clearly introduces, that I venture to change its position.

22. ⟨1 *Inst. Sect.* 306⟩ Also at 1 *Inst.* Sect. 68 fol. 56a; Sect. 232, fol. 153a. Cf. *Leviathan*, chap 14. (When the law grants something, it evidently grants also the means thereto.)   23. ⟨Sheirs⟩   24. E.g., 1 *Inst.* fol. 92a.

but it does not appear that every Man is bound to Buy the Book of Statutes, nor to search for them at *Westminster* or at the *Tower*, nor to understand the Language wherein they are for the most part Written.

La. I grant it proceeds from their own Faults; but no Man can be excused by the Ignorance of the Law of Reason; that is to say, by Ignorance of the Common-Law, except Children, Mad-men, and Idiots: But you exact such a notice of the Statute-Law, as is almost Impossible. Is it not enough that they in all Places have a sufficient Number of the Pœnal Statutes?

Ph. Yes; If they have those Pœnal Statutes near them, but what
(35) Reason can you give me why there should not be as many | Copies abroad of the Statutes, as there be of the Bible?

La. I think it were well that every Man that can Read had a Statute-Book; for certainly no knowledge of those Laws, by which Mens Lives and Fortunes can be brought into danger, can be too much. I find a great Fault in your Definition of Law; which is, that every Law either forbiddeth or Commandeth something. 'Tis true that the Moral-Law is always a Command or a Prohibition, or at least Implieth it; but in the Levitical-Law, where it is said; that he that Stealeth a Sheep shall Restore four Fold;[25] what Command, or Prohibition lyeth in these words?

Ph. Such Sentences as that are not in themselves General, but Judgments[;][26] nevertheless, there is in those words Implied a Commandment to the Judge, to cause to be made a Four-fold Restitution.

La. That's Right.

Ph. Now Define what Justice is, and what Actions, and Men are to be called Just.

La. Justice is the constant will of giving to every Man his own; that is to say, of giving to every Man that which is his Right, in such manner as to Exclude the Right of all Men else to the same thing.
(36) A Just Action is that which is not against the Law. | A Just Man is he that hath a constant Will to live Justly; if you require more, I doubt there will no Man living be Comprehended within the Definition.

Ph. Seeing then that a Just Action (according to your Definition) is that which is not against the Law; it is Manifest that before there was a Law, there could be no Injustice, and therefore Laws are in

---

25. Exod. 21:37. Cf. 2 Sam. 12:6. See below, p. (159). 26. ⟨,⟩

their Nature Antecedent to Justice and Injustice, and you cannot deny but there must be Law-makers, before there [were][27] any Laws, and Consequently before there was any Justice, I speak of Humane Justice; and that Law-makers were before that which you call Own, or property of Goods, or Lands distinguished by *Meum, Tuum, Alienum.*

La. That must be Granted; for without Statute-Laws, all Men have Right to all things; and we have had Experience when our Laws were silenced by Civil War, there was not a Man, that of any Goods could say assuredly they were his own.

Ph. You see then that no private Man can claim a Propriety in any Lands, or other Goods from any Title, from any Man, but the King, or them that have the Soveraign Power; because it is in
(37)　virtue of the Soveraignty, that every Man may not enter | into, and Possess what he pleaseth; and consequently to deny the Soveraign any thing necessary to the sustaining of his Soveraign power, is to destroy the Propriety he pretends to. The next thing I will ask you is, how you distinguish between Law and Right, or *Lex* and *Jus.*

La. Sir *Ed. Coke* in divers places makes *Lex* and *Jus* to be the same,[28] and so *Lex Communis*, and *Jus Communis* to be all one; nor do I find that he does in any places distinguish them.

Ph. Then will I distinguish them, and make you judge whether my distinction be not necessary to be known by every Author of the Common Law: for Law obligeth me to do, or forbear the doing of something; and therefore it lies upon me an Obligation; but my Right is a Liberty left me by the Law to do any thing which the Law forbids me not, and to leave undone any thing which the Law commands me not. Did Sir *Ed. Coke* see no difference between being bound and being free?

La. I know not what he [saw][29], but he has not mention'd it, though a man may dispense with his own Liberty, that cannot do so with the Law.

Ph. But what are you better for your Right, if a rebellious Company
(38)　at home, or an Enemy from abroad take away the Goods, | or dispossess you of the Lands you have a right to? Can you be defended, or repair'd, but by the strength and authority of the King? What reason therefore can be given by a man that

---

27. ⟨was⟩
28. E.g., 1 *Inst.* fol. 142a. Cf. Bracton, fol. 2a; *Leviathan*, chap. 26.
29. ⟨was⟩

endeavours to preserve his Propriety, why he should deny, or malignly contribute to the Strength that should defend him, or repair him? Let us see now what your Books say to this point, and other points of the Right of Soveraignty. *Bracton*, the most authentick Author of the Common Law, *fol. 55.* saith thus: *Ipse Dominus Rex habet omnia Jura in manu suâ, est Dei Vicarius; habet ea quæ sunt Pacis, habet etiam coercionem ut Delinquentes puniat; habet in potestate suâ Leges; nihil enim prodest Jura condere, nisi sit qui Jura tueatur.* That is to say, our Lord the King hath all Right in his own Hands; is Gods Vicar; he has all that concerns the Peace; he has the power to punish Delinquents; all the Laws are in his power; To make Laws is to no purpose, unless there be some-body to make them obeyed.[30] If *Bracton's* Law be Reason, as I, and you think it is; what temporal power is there which the King hath not? Seeing that at this day all the power Spiritual which *Bracton* allows the *Pope*, is restored to the Crown; what is there that the King cannot do, excepting sin against the Law of God? The same

(39) *Bracton Lib.* [1][31] | *c.* 8. saith thus; *Si autem a Rege petitur (cum Breve non curret contra ipsum) locus erit supplicationi, quod factum suum corrigat, & emendet; quod quidem si non fecerit, satis sufficit ad pœnam, quod Dominum expectet Ultorem; nemo quidem de factis ejus præsumat disputare, multo fortius contra factum ejus venire:* That is to say, if any thing be demanded of the King (seeing a Writ lyeth not against him) he is put to his Petition, praying him to Correct and Amend his own Fact; which if he will not do, it is a sufficient Penalty for him, that he is to expect a punishment from the Lord: No Man may presume to dispute of what he does, much less to resist him. You see by this, that this Doctrine concerning the Rights of Soveraignty so much Cryed down by the long Parliament, is the Antient Common-Law, and that the only Bridle of the Kings of *England*, ought to be the fear of God. And again *Bracton, c.* 24. of the second Book says, That the Rights of the Crown cannot be granted away; *Ea vero quæ Jurisdictionis [sunt] & Pacis, & ea quæ sunt Justitiæ & Paci annexa, ad nullum pertinent, nisi ad Coronam & Dignitatem Regiam, nec a Corona separari possunt, nec a privata persona possideri.*[32] That is to say, those things which belong to Juris-

---

30. This is a collection of expressions from Bracton, not a consecutive passage.
31. ⟨21⟩ The Latin differs slightly from Bracton, fols. 5b–6.
32. Bracton reads, ". . . *nec a corona separari poterunt, cum faciant ipsam coronam*": "since they constitute the crown itself." The expression "*nec a privata persona possideri*" is brought up by Hobbes from Bracton's next paragraph. Fol. 55b.

diction and Peace, and those things that are annexed to Justice,

(40) and | Peace, appertain to none, but to the Crown and Dignity of the King, nor can be separated from the Crown, nor be possest by a private Person. Again you'l find in *Fleta* (a Law-Book written in the time of *Edw.* 2.) That Liberties though granted by the King, if they tend to the hinderance of Justice, or subversion of the Regal Power, were not to be used, nor allowed: For in that Book *c.* 20. concerning Articles of the Crown, which the Justices Itinerant are to enquire of, the 54th Article is this, you shall inquire *De Libertatibus concessis quæ impediunt Communem Justitiam, & Regiam Potestatem subvertunt.* Now what is a greater hindrance to Common Justice, or a greater subversion of the Regal Power, than a Liberty in Subjects to hinder the King from raising Money necessary to suppress, or prevent Rebellions, which doth destroy Justice, and subvert the power of the Soveraignty? Moreover when a Charter is granted by a King in these words, *Dedita & coram   pro me & Hæredibus meis*[, t][33]he grantor by the Common-Law (as Sir *Edw. Coke* sayes in his Commentaries on *Littleton*)[34] is to warrant his Gift; and I think it Reason, especially if the Gift be upon Consideration of a price Paid. Suppose a Forraign State should [lay][35] claim to this Kingdom ('tis

(41) no Matter as to the Que-|stion I am putting, whether the Claim be unjust) how would you have the King to warrant to every Free-holder in *England* the Lands they hold of him by such a Charter? If he cannot Levy Money, their Estates are lost, and so is the Kings Estate, and if the Kings Estate be gone, how can he repair the Value due upon the Warranty? I know that the Kings Charters are not so meerly Grants, as that they are not also Laws;[36] but they are such Laws as speak not to all the Kings Subjects in general, but only to his Officers; implicitly forbidding them to Judge, or Execute any thing contrary to the said Grants. There be many Men that are able Judges of what is right Reason, and what not; when any of these shall know that a Man has no Superiour, nor Peer in the Kingdom, he will hardly be perswaded he can be bound by any Law of the Kingdom, or that he who is Subject to none but God, can make a Law upon himself,

---

33. ⟨. T⟩
34. I find in Coke neither such a form of words for a charter nor the formula that a grantor is to warrant his gift. Cf. 2 *Inst.* Stat. de Bigamis (4 Edw. 1), esp. c. 6; and 1 *Inst.* bk. 3 chap. 13, esp. sect. 733.   35. ⟨say⟩
36. Cf. *Leviathan,* chap. 26, end.

which he cannot also as easily abrogate, as he made it. The main Argument, and that which so much taketh with the throng of People, proceedeth from a needless fear put into their minds by such Men as mean to make use of their Hands to their own ends; for if (say they) the King may (notwithstanding the Law) do what

(42) he please, and nothing to restrain him but the | fear of punishment in the World to come, then (in case there come a King that fears no such punishment) he may take away from us, not only our Lands, Goods, and Liberties, but our Lives also if he will: And they say true; but they have no reason to think he will, unless it be for his own profit, which cannot be; for he loves his own Power; and what becomes of his power when his Subjects are destroyed, or weaked, by whose multitude, and strength he enjoyes his power, and every one of his Subjects his Fortune? And lastly, whereas they sometimes say the King is bound, not only to cause his Laws to be observ'd, but also to observe them himself; I think the King causing them to be observ'd is the same thing as observing them himself: For I never heard it taken for good Law, that the King may be Indicted, or Appealed, or served with a Writ, till the long Parliament practised the contrary upon the good King *Charles*, for which divers of them were Executed, and the rest by this our present King pardoned.

La. Pardoned by the King and Parliament.

Ph. By the King in Parliament if you will, but not by the King, and Parliament; you cannot deny, but that the pardoning of Injury,

(43) [belongs] to the Person that is Injur'd[.][37] Trea-|son, and other Offences against the Peace, and against the Right of the Soveraign are Injuries done to the King; and therefore whosoever is pardoned any such Offence, ought to acknowledge he ow[e]s his Pardon to the King alone: But as to such Murders, Felonies, and other Injuries as are done to any Subject how mean soever, I think it great reason that the parties endammaged ought to have satisfaction before such pardon be allow'd. And in the death of a Man, where restitution of Life is Impossible, what can any Friend, Heir, or other party that may appeal, require more than reasonable satisfaction some other way? Perhaps he will be content with nothing but Life for Life; but that is Revenge, and belongs to God, and under God to the King, and none else; therefore if there be reasonable satisfaction tendred, the King, without sin

---

37. ⟨,⟩ Cf. below p. (181).

(I think) may pardon him. I am sure, if the pardoning him be a sin, that neither King, nor Parliament, nor any earthly Power can do it.

La. You see by this your own Argument, that the Act of *Oblivion*,[38] without a Parliament could not have passed; because, not only the King, but also most of the Lords, and abundance of Common People had received Injuries; which not being pardonable, but (44) by their own Assent, it was absolutely ne-|cessary that it should be done in Parliament, and by the assent of the Lords and Commons.

Ph. I grant it; but I pray you tell me now what is the difference between a general Pardon, and an Act of *Oblivion*?

La. The word Act of *Oblivion* was never in our Books before; but I believe it is in yours.

Ph. In the State of *Athens* long ago, for the Abolishing of the Civil War, there was an Act agreed on; that from that time forward, no Man should be molested for any thing (before that Act done) whatsoever without exception, which Act the makers of it called an Act of *Oblivion*; not that all Injuries should be forgotten (for then we could never have had the story) but that they should not rise up in Judgment against any Man. And in imitation of this Act the like was propounded (though it took no effect) upon the death of *Julius Cæsar*, in the Senate of *Rome*. By such an Act you may easily conceive that all Accusations for offences past were absolutely dead, and buried, and yet we have no great reason to think, that the objecting one to another of the Injuries pardoned, was any violation of those Acts, except the same were so expressed in the Act it self. |

La. It seems then that the Act of *Oblivion* was here no more, nor of (45) other nature than a General Pardon.

Of Courts.

Ph. SINCE YOU ACKNOWLEDGE THAT IN ALL CONTROVERsies, the Judicature originally belongeth to the King, and seeing that no Man is able in his own person to execute an Office of so much business; what order is taken for deciding of so many, and so various Controversies?

---

38. Cf. below, pp. (187)-(190).

La. There be divers sorts of Controversies, some of which are concerning Mens Titles to Lands and Goods; and some Goods are
Corporeal, [as]¹ Lands, Money, Cattel, Corn, and the like, which
may be handled, or seen; and some Incorporeal, as Priviledges,
Liberties, Dignities, Offices, and many other good things, meer
Creatures of the Law, and cannot be handled or seen: And both
of these kinds are concerning *Meum*, and *Tuum*. Others there are
concerning Crimes punishable divers wayes; and amongst some
of these, part of the punishment is some Fine, or Forfeiture to the
King, and then it is called a Plea of the Crown, in case the King
sue the party, otherwise it is but a private Plea, which they call an
(46) Appeal: And though upon Judg-|ment in an Appeal the King
shall have his Forfeiture; yet it cannot be called a Plea of the
Crown, but when the Crown pleadeth for it. There be also other
Controversies concerning the Government of the Church, in
order to Religion, and virtuous Life. The offences both against
the Crown, and against the Laws of the Church are Crimes; but
the offences of one Subject against another, if they be not against
the Crown, the King pretendeth nothing in those Pleas, but the
Reparation of his Subjects injur'd.

Ph. A Crime is an offence of any kind whatsoever, for which a penalty
is Ordain'd by the Law of the Land: But you must understand
that dammages awarded to the party injur'd, has nothing common with the nature of a penalty, but is meerly a Restitution, or
satisfaction due to the party griev'd by the Law of Reason, and
consequently is no more a punishment than is the paying of a
Debt.

La. It seems by this Definition of a Crime you make no difference
between a Crime, and a sin.

Ph. All Crimes are indeed Sins, but not all Sins Crimes. A Sin may be
in the thought or secret purpose of a Man, of which neither a
Judge, nor a Witness, nor any Man take notice; but a Crime is
(47) such a Sin as consists in an Action against the Law, of | which
Action he can be accused, and Tryed by a Judge, and be Con-
vinced, or Cleared by Witnesses. Farther; that which is no Sin in
it self, but indifferent, may be made Sin by a positive Law. As
when the Statute was in force; that no Man should wear Silk in
his Hat, after the Statute, such wearing of Silk was a Sin, which
was not so before: Nay sometimes an Action that's good in it

---

1. ⟨and⟩

self, by the Statute Law may be made a Sin; as if a Statute should be made to forbid the giving of Alms to a strong and sturdy Beggar; such Alms after that Law would be a Sin, but not before: For then it was Charity, the Object whereof is not the strength, or other Quality of the poor Man, but his Poverty. Again, he that should have said in Queen *Maries* time, that the *Pope* had no Authority in *England*, should have been Burnt at a Stake; but for saying the same in the time of Queen *Elizabeth*, should have been Commended. You see by this, that many things are made Crimes, and no Crimes, which are not so in their own Nature, but by Diversity of Law, made upon Diversity of Opinion, or of Interest by them which have Authority: And yet those things, whether good, or evil, will pass so with the Vulgar (if they hear them often with odious terms recited) for hainous Crimes in themselves, as

(48) many | of those Opinions, which are in themselves Pious, and Lawful, were heretofore by the Popes Interest therein called Detestable Heresie. Again; some Controversies are of things done upon the Sea, others of things done upon the Land. There need be many Courts to the deciding of so many kinds of Controversies. What order is there taken for their Distribution?

La. There be an extraordinary great number of Courts in *England*; First; there be the Kings Courts both for Law, and Equity in matters Temporal, which are the Chancery, the Kings-Bench, the Court of Common-Pleas, and for the Kings Revenue the Court of the Exchequer, and there be Subjects Courts by Priviledge, as the Courts in *London*, and other priviledg'd places. And there be other Courts of Subjects, as the Court of Landlords, called the Court of Barons, and the Courts of Sherifs. Also the Spiritual Courts are the Kings Courts at this day, though heretofore they were the *Popes* Courts. And in the Kings Courts, some have their Judicature by Office, and some by Commission, and some Authority to Hear, and Determine, and some only to Inquire, and to Certifie into other Courts. Now for the Distribution of what Pleas every Court may hold; it is commonly held, that all

(49) the Pleas of the Crown, and of all | Offences contrary to the Peace are to be holden in the Kings-Bench, or by Commissioners, for *Bracton* saith;[2] *Sciendum est, quod si Actiones sunt Criminales, in Curia Domini Regis debent determinari; cum sit ibi pœna Corporalis infligenda, & hoc coram ipso Rege, si tangat personam suam, sicut Crimen Læsæ*

---

2. (Virtually), at fol. 104b.

Majestatis, vel coram Justitiariis ad hoc specialiter assignatis. That is to say; That if the Plea be Criminal, it ought to be determin'd in the Court of our Lord the King, because there they have power to inflict Corporeal punishment, and if the Crime be against his person, as the Crime of Treason, it ought to be determin'd before the King himself, or if it be against a private person, it ought to be determin'd by Justices Assigned; that is to say, before Commissioners. It seems by this, that heretofore Kings did hear and determine Pleas of Treason against themselves, by their own Persons; but it has been otherwise a long time, and is now: For it is now the Office of the Lord Steward of *England* in the Tryal of a Peer, to hold that Plea by a Commission especially for the same. In Causes concerning *Meum*, and *Tuum*, the King may sue, either in the Kings-Bench, or in the Court of Common Pleas, as it appears by *Fitzherbert* in his *Natura Brevium*,[3] at the Writ of Escheat. |

Ph. A King perhaps will not sit to determine of Causes of Treason
(50) against his Person, lest he should seem to make himself Judge in his own Cause; but that it shall be Judged by Judges of his own making, can never be avoided, which is also one as if he were Judge himself.

La. To the Kings-Bench also (I think) belongeth the Hearing, and Determining of all manner of Breaches of the Peace whatsoever, saving alwayes to the King that he may do the same, when he pleaseth, by Commissioners. In the time of *Henry* the 3d, and *Edward* the 1st, (when *Bracton* wrote) the King did usually send down every seven years into the Country Commissioners called Justices Itinerant, to Hear, and Determine generally all Causes Temporal, both Criminal, and Civil, whose places have been now a long time supplyed by the Justices of Assize, with Commissions of the Peace of *Oyer*, and *Terminer*, and of Goal-delivery.

Ph. But why may the King only Sue in the Kings-Bench, or Court of Common-Pleas, which he will, and no other Person may do the same?

La. There is no Statute to the contrary, but it seemeth to be the Common-Law; for Sir *Edw. Coke*, 4 *Inst.*[4] setteth down the Juris-diction of the Kings-Bench; which (he says) has; First, Juris-
(51) diction in all | Pleas of the Crown. Secondly, The Correcting of all manner of Errors of other Justices, and Judges, both of Judgments and Process (except of the Court of Exchequer) which he

---

3. Sir Anthony Fitzherbert (1470-1538), *On the Nature of Writs.*   4. Chap. 7.

sayes, is to this Court *Proprium quarto modo*.[5] Thirdly; That it has power to Correct all Misdemeanours *extrajudicial* tending to the breach of the Peace, or oppression of the Subjects, or raising of Factions, Controversies, Debates, or any other manner of Misgovernment. Fourthly; It may hold Plea by Writ out of the Chancery of all Trespasses done *Vi & Armis*. Fifthly; It hath power to hold Plea by Bill for Debt, Detinu[e], Covenant, Promise, and all other personal Actions; but of the Jurisdiction of the Kings-Bench in Actions real he says nothing; save, that if a Writ in a Real Action be abated by Judgment in the Court of Common-Pleas, and that the Judgment be by a Writ of Error, reversed in the Kings-Bench, then the Kings-Bench may proceed upon the Writ.

Ph. But how is the Practice?

La. Real Actions are commonly decided, as well in the Kings-Bench, as in the Court of Common-Pleas.

Ph. When the K[i]ng by Authority in Writing maketh a Lord-Chief-Justice of the Kings-Bench; does he not set down what he makes him for? |

La. Sir *Edw. Coke* sets down the Letters Patents, whereby of Antient
(52) time the Lord Chief-Justice was Constituted, wherein is expressed to what end he hath his Office; *viz. Pro Conservatione nostra, & tranquilitatis Regni nostri, & ad Justitiam universis & singulis de Regno nostro exhibendam, Constituimus Dilectum & Fidelem nostrum P. B. Justitiarium Angliæ, quamdiu nobis placuerit Capitalem, &c.*[6] That is to say, for the preservation of our self, and of the Peace of our Realm, and for the doing of Justice to all and singular our Subjects, we have Constituted our Beloved and Faithful *P. B.* during our pleasure, Chief Justice of *England*, &c.

Ph. Methinks 'tis very plain by these Letters Patents, that all Causes Temporal within the Kingdom (except the Pleas that belong to the Exchequer) should be decidable by this Lord-Chief-Justice. For as for Causes Criminal, and that concern the Peace, it is granted him in these words, for the Conservation of our self, and peace of the Kingdom, wherein are contained all Pleas Criminal; and, in the doing of Justice to all and singular the Kings Subjects are comprehended all Pleas Civil. And as to the Court of Common-Pleas, it is manifest it may hold all manner of Civil-Pleas (except
(53) those of the Exchequer) by *Magna Charta, Cap.* 11. | So that all

---

5. Hobbes will of course deny that it belongs singularly to the King's Bench to correct errors, below, pp. (70)-(87).   6. 4 *Inst.* chap. 7.

original Writs concerning Civil-Pleas are returnable into either of the said Courts; but how is the Lord-Chief-Justice made now?

La. By these words in their Letters Patents; *Constituimus vos Justitiarium nostrum Capitalem ad Placita coram nobis tenenda, durante beneplacito nostro.*[7] That is to say, we have made you our Chief-Justice to hold Pleas before our self, during our pleasure. But this Writ, though it be shorter, does not at all abridge the power they had by the former. And for the Letters Patents for the Chief-Justice of the Common-Pleas, they go thus, *Constituimus dilectum & Fidelem, &c. Capitalem Justitiarium de Communi Banco. Habendum, &c. quamdiu nobis placuerit, cum vadiis & foedis ab antiquo debitis & consuetis.*[8] *Id est*, We have Constituted our Beloved and Faithful, *&c.* Chief-Justice of the Common-Bench, To have, *&c.* during our pleasure, with the ways, and Fees thereunto heretofore due, and usual.

Ph. I find in History, that there have been in *England* always, a Chancellour and a Chief-Justice of *England*, but of a Court of Common-Pleas there is no mention before *Magna Charta*. Common-Pleas there were ever both here, and I think, in all Nations; for Common-Pleas and Civil-Pleas I take to be the same. |

La. Before the Statute of *Magna Charta* Common-Pleas (as Sir *Edw.*
(54) *Coke* granteth, 2 *Inst.* p. 21.) might have been holden in the Kings-Bench; and that Court being removeable at the Kings will, the Returns of Writs were *Coram Nobis ubicunque fuerimus in Anglia*; whereby great trouble of Jurors ensued, and great charges of the parties, and delay of Justice; and that for these causes it was Ordain'd, that the Common-Pleas should not follow the King, but be held in a place certain.

Ph. Here Sir *Edw. Coke* declares his Opinion, that no Common-Plea can be holden in the Kings-Bench, in that he says they might have been holden then. And yet this doth not amount to any probable proof, that there was any Court of Common-Pleas in *England* before *Magna Charta*: For this Statute being to ease the Jurors, and lessen the Charges of Parties, and for the Expedition of Justice had been in Vain, if there had been a Court of Common-Pleas then standing; for such a Court was not necessarily to follow the King, as was the Chancery, and the Kings-Bench. Besides,

---

7. The Lawyer refers to these words as taken from letters patent, but Coke shows (4 *Inst.* p. 75) that the Chief Justice had not been made by letters patent since Edward I. Following the translation, the Lawyer will speak of "this Writ," which accords with Coke. 8. 4 *Inst.* p. 99.

unless the Kings-Bench, wheresoever it was, held Plea of civil Causes, the Subject had not at all been eased by this Statute: For supposing the King at *York*, had not the Kings Subjects about (55) *London*, Jurors, and parties as much | trouble, and charge to go to *York*, as the People about *York* had before to go to *London*? Therefore I can by no means believe otherwise, then that the Erection of the Court of Common-Pleas was the effect of that Statute of *Magna Charta, Cap.* 11. And before that time not existent, though I think that for the multiplicity of Suits in a great Kingdom there was need of it.

La. Perhaps there was not so much need of it as you think: For in those times the Laws, for the most part, were in setling, rather than setled; and the old Saxon Laws concerning Inheritances were then practised, by which Laws speedy Justice was Executed by the Kings Writs, in the Courts of Barons, which were Land-lords to the rest of the Freeholders, and Suits of Barons in County-Courts, and but few Suits in the Kings Courts, but when Justice could not be had in those Inferior Courts; but at this day there be more Suits in the Kings Courts, than any one Court can dispatch.

Ph. Why should there be more Suits now, than formerly? For I believe this Kingdom was as well Peopled then as now.

La. Sir *Edw. Coke*, 4 *Inst.* p. 76, assigneth for it six Causes, 1. Peace, 2. Plenty, 3. The Dissolution of Religious Houses, and dispersing of their Lands among so many several persons, 4. The multitude (56) of Infor-|mers, 5. The number of Concealers, 6. The multitude of Attorneys.

Ph. I see Sir *Edw. Coke* has no mind to lay any fault upon the Men of his own Profession; and that he Assigns for Causes of the Mischiefs, such things as would be Mischief, and Wickedness to amend; for if Peace, and Plenty, be the cause of this Evil, it cannot be removed but by War and Beggery; and the Quarrels arising about the Lands of Religious Persons cannot arise from the Lands, but from the doubtfulness of the Laws. And for Informers they were Authorised by Statutes, to the Execution of which Statutes they are so necessary, as that their number cannot be too great, and if it be too great the fault is in the Law it self. The number of Concealers, are indeed a number of Couseners, which the Law may easily Correct. And lastly for the multitude of Attorneys, it is the fault of them that have the power to admit, or refuse them. For my part I believe that Men at this day have better learn't the Art of Caviling against the words of a Statute, than heretofore

they had, and thereby encourage themselves, and others, to undertake Suits upon little reason. Also the variety and repugnancy of Judgments of Common-Law do oftentimes put Men to hope for
(57) Victory in causes, whereof in reason they had no | ground at all. Also the ignorance of what is Equity in their own causes, which Equity not one Man in a thousand ever Studied, and the Lawyers themselves seek not for their Judgments in their own Breasts, but in the precedents of former Judges, as the Antient Judges sought the same, not in their own Reason, but in the Laws of the Empire. Another, and perhaps the greatest cause of multitude of Suits is this, that for want of Registring of conveyances of Land, which might easily be done in the Townships where the Lands ly, a Purchase cannot easily be had, which will not be litigious. Lastly, I believe the Coveteousness of Lawyers was not so great in Antient time, which was full of trouble, as [it has]⁹ been since in time of Peace, wherein Men have leisure to study fraud, and get employment from such Men as can encourage to Contention. And how ample a Field they have to exercise this Mystery in is manifest from this, that they have a power to Scan and Construe every word in a Statute, Charter, Feofment, Lease, or other Deed, Evidence, or Testimony. But to return to the Jurisdiction of this Court of the Kings-Bench, where, as you say, it hath power to correct and amend the Errors of all other Judges, both in Process,
(58) and in Judgments; cannot the Judges of the Com-|mon-Pleas correct Error in Process in their own Courts, without a Writ of Error from another Court?

La. Yes; and there be many Statutes which Command them so to do.

Ph. When a Writ of Error is brought out of the Kings-Bench, be it either Error in Process, or in Law, at whose Charge is it to be done?

La. At the Charge of the Clyent.

Ph. I see no reason for that; for the Clyent is not in fault, who never begins a Suit but by the advice of his Council Learned in the Law, whom he pays for his Council given. Is not this the fault of his Councellor? Nor when a Judge in the Common-Pleas hath given an Erroneous Sentence, it is always likely that the Judge of the Kings-Bench will reverse the Judgment (though there be no Question, but as you may find in *Bracton*, and other Learned Men, he has power to do it) because being Professors of the same

---

9. ⟨they have⟩

Common-Law, they are perswaded, for the most part, to give the same Judgments: For Example; if Sir *Edw. Coke* in the last Terme that he sate Lord-Chief-Justice in the Court of Common-Pleas, had given an Erroneous Judgment, that when he was removed, and made Lord-Chief-Justice of the Kings-Bench, (59) would therefore have reversed the said Judgment, it is possi-|[ble] he might, but not very likely. And therefore I do believe there is some other power, by the King constituted, to reverse Erroneous Judgments, both in the Kings-Bench, and in the Court of Common-Pleas.

La. I think not; for there is a Statute to the contrary, made 4°, *Hen.* 4. *cap.* 23. in these words; Whereas, as well in Plea Real, as in Plea Personal, after Judgment [given] in the Court[s] of our Lord the King, the Parties be made to come upon grievous pain, sometimes before the King himself, sometimes before the Kings Council, and sometimes to the Parliament to answer thereof anew, to the great Impoverishing of the Parties aforesaid, and to the subversion of the Common-Law of the Land, it is ordained and established, that after Judgment given in the Court[s] of our Lord the King, the Parties, and their Heirs shall be there[of] in Peace, until the Judgment be undone by Attaint, or by Error, if there be Error, as hath been used by the Laws in the times of the Kings Progenitors.

Ph. This Statute is so far from being repugnant to that, I say, as it seemeth to me to have been made expressly to confirm the same: For the substance of the Statute is, that there shall be no Suit made by either of the Parties for any thing adjudged, either in the (60) Kings-Bench, or Court of Common-|Pleas, before the Judgment be undone by Error, or Corruption prov'd; and that this was the Common-Law before the making of this Statute, which could not be, except there were (before this Statute) some Courts authorised to examine, and correct such Errors as by the Plaintiff should be assign'd. The inconvenience which by this Statute was to be remedied was this, that often Judgment given in the Kings Courts, by which are meant in this place the Kings-Bench, and Court of Common-Pleas, the Party against whom the Judgment was given, did begin a new Suit, and cause his Adversary to come before the King himself; here by the King himself must be understood the King in Person; for though in a Writ by the words *Coram nobis* is understood the Kings-Bench, yet in a Statute it is never so; nor is it strange, seeing in those days the King did usually sit in Court with his Council, to hear (as sometimes King *James*) and sometimes the same Parties commenced their Suit before the Privy-Council, though the King were absent; and sometimes before the Parliament the former Judgment yet standing. For remedy whereof, it was ordained by this Statute, that no Man should renew his Suit, till the former Judgment was undone by Attaint, or Error; which Reversing of a Judgment had been

(61) impossi-|ble, if there had been no Court (besides the aforesaid two Courts) wherein the Errors might be Assigned, Examin'd, and Judg'd; for no Court can be esteemed in Law, or Reason, a Competent Judge of its own Errors. There was therefore before this Statute some other Court existent for the hearing of Errors, and Reversing of Erroneous Judgments. What Court this was I enquire not yet, but I am sure it could not be either the Parliament or the Privy-Council, or the Court wherein the Erroneous Judgment was given.

La. The Doctor and Student[10] discourses of this Statute, *cap.* 18. much otherwise than you do: For the Author of that Book saith, that against an Erroneous Judgment all Remedy is by this Statute taken away. And though neither Reason, nor the Office of a King, nor any Law positive can prohibit the remedying of any Injury, much less of an unjust Sentence, yet he shows many Statutes, wherein a Mans Conscience ought to prevail above the Law.

Ph. Upon what ground can he pretend, that all Remedy in this case is by this Statute prohibited?

La. He says it is thereby enacted, that Judgment given by the Kings Courts shall not be examin'd in the Chancery, Parliament, nor elsewhere. |

Ph. Is there any mention of Chancery in this Act? It cannot be
(62) examin'd before the King and his Council, nor before the Parliament, but you see that before the Statute it was examin'd somewhere, and that this Statute will have it examin'd there again.

And seeing the Chancery was altogether the highest Office of Judicature in the Kingdom for matter of Equity, and that the Chancery is not here forbidden to examine the Judgments of all other Courts, at least it is not taken from it by this Statute. But what Cases are there in this Chapter of the Doctor and Student,

10. *Doctor and Student* is the familiar title of the work attributed to Christopher Saint German (1460?-1540) called *A Dialogue in English betwixt a Doctor of Divinity and a Student in the Laws of England. . . .* The parallel and difference between that title and the title of the present work are conspicuous.

by which it can be made probable, that when Law, and Conscience, or Law and Equity seem to oppugne one another, the written Law should be preferr'd?

La. If the Defendant wage his Law in an Action of Debt brought upon a true Debt, the Plaintiff hath no means to come to his Debt by way of Compulsion, neither by *Subpœna*, nor otherwise, and yet the Defendant is bound in Conscience to pay him.[11]

Ph. Here is no preferring that, I see, of the Law above Conscience, or Equity; for the Plaintiff in this case loseth not his Debt for want either of Law, or Equity, but for want of Proof; for neither Law, nor Equity can give a Man his Right, unless he prove it. |

La. Also if the Grand-Jury in Attaint affirm a false Verdict given by
(63) the Petty-Jury, there is no farther Remedy, but the Conscience of the party.

Ph. Here again the want of Proof is the want of Remedy; for if he can prove that the Verdict given was false, the King can give him remedy such way as himself shall think best, and ought to do it, in case the Party shall find surety, if the same Verdict be again affirmed, to satisfie his Adversary for the Dammage, and Vexation he puts him to.

La. But there is a Statute made since; *viz.* 27 *Eliz.* *c.* 8. by which that Statute of [4] *Hen.* 4. 23. is in part taken away; for by that Statute[12] Erroneous Judgments given in the Kings-Bench, are by a Writ of Error to be examin'd in the Exchequer-Chamber, before the Justices of the Common-Bench, and the Barons of the Exchequer, and by the preamble of this Act[13] it appears, that Erroneous Judgments are only to be reform'd by the High Court of Parliament.

Ph. But here is no mention, that the Judgments given in the Court of Common-Pleas should be brought in to be examin'd in the Exchequer-Chamber[;][14] why therefore may not the Court of Chancery examine a Judgment given in the Court of Common-Pleas? |

La. You deny not but, by the Antient Law of *England*, the Kings-
(64) Bench may examine the Judgment given in the Court of Common-Pleas.

Ph. 'Tis true; but why may not also the Court of Chancery do the same, especially if the fault of the Judgment be against Equity, and not against the Letter of the Law?

---

11. This speech and the next one by the Lawyer are quotations from *Doctor and Student*, chap. 18.   12. 4 Hen. 4 c. 23.   13. 27 Eliz. c. 8.   14. ⟨,⟩

La. There is no necessity of that; for the same Court may examine both the Letter and the Equity of the Statute.

Ph. You see by this, that the Jurisdiction of Courts cannot easily be distinguished, but by the King himself in his Parliament. The Lawyers themselves cannot do it; for you see what Contention there is between Courts, as well as between particular Men. And whereas you say, that Law of 4 *Hen.* 4. 23. is by that of 27 *Eliz.* *cap.* 8. taken away, I do not find it so. I find indeed a Diversity of opinion between the makers of the former and the latter Statute, in the preamble of the latter and Conclusion of the former. The Preamble of the latter is; forasmuch as Erroneous Judgments given in the Court called the Kings-Bench, are only to be reformed in the High Court of Parliament, and the Conclusion of the former is, that the contrary was Law in the times of the Kings Progenitors. These are no parts of those Laws, but Opinions only
(65) con-|cerning the Antient Custom in that Case, arising from the different Opinions of the Lawyers in those different times, neither Commanding, nor Forbidding any thing; though of the Statutes themselves, the one forbids that such Pleas be brought before the Parliament, the other forbids it not: But yet if after the Act of *Hen.* 4. such a Plea had been brought before the Parliament, the Parliament might have Heard, and Determin'd it: For the Statute forbids not that! nor can any Law have the force to hinder the [lawmakers][15] of any Jurisdiction whatsoever they please to take upon them, seeing it is a Court of the King and of all the People together, both Lords, and Commons.

La. Though it be, yet seeing the King (as Sir *Edw. Coke* affirms, 4 *Inst.* p. 71) hath committed all his power Judicial, some to one Court, and some to another, so as if any Man would render himself to the Judgment of the King, in such case where the King hath committed all his power Judicial to others, such a render should be to no effect. And p. 73. he saith farther; That in this Court the Kings of this Realm have sitten on the High Bench, and the Judges of that Court on the Lower Bench, at his feet; but Judicature belongeth only to the Judges of that Court, and in his presence they answer all Motions. |

Ph. I cannot believe that Sir *Edw. Coke*, how much soever he desir'd
(66) to advance the authority of himself, and other Justices of the Common-Law, could mean that the King in the Kings-Bench sate

---

15. ⟨Law⟩

as a Spectator only, and might not have answered all motions, which his Judges answer'd, if he had seen cause for it: For he knew that the King was Supream Judge then in all causes Temporal, and is now in all Causes both Temporal, and Ecclesiastical; and that there is an exceeding great penalty ordained by the Laws for them that shall deny it. But Sir *Edw. Coke* as he had (you see) in many places before, hath put a Fallacy upon himself, by not distinguishing between Committing, and Transferring. He that Transferreth his power, hath deprived himself of it, but he that Committeth it to another to be Exercised in his name, and under him, is still in the Possession of the same power. And therefore if a Man render himself; that is to say, Appealeth to the King from any Judge whatsoever, the King may receive his Appeal; and it shall be effectual.

La. Besides these 2 Courts, the Kings-Bench for Pleas of the Crown, and the Court of Common-Pleas for Causes Civil, according to the Common-Law of *England*, there is another Court of Justice,

(67) that hath Jurisdiction in Causes both Civil, and Cri-|minal, and is as Antient a Court, at least as the Court of Common Pleas, and this is the Court of the Lord Admiral, but the proceedings therein are according to the Laws of the *Roman* Empire, and the Causes to be determin'd there are such as arise upon the Marine Sea: For so it is ordain'd by divers Statutes, and confirm'd by many Precedents.

Ph. As for the Statutes they are always Law, and Reason also; for they are made by the Assent of all the Kingdom, but Precedents are Judgments one contrary to another; I mean divers Men, in divers Ages, upon the same case give divers Judgments. Therefore I will ask your Opinion once more concerning any Judgments besides those of the King, as to their validity in Law. But what is the difference between the proceedings of the Court of Admiralty, and the Court of Common-Law?

La. One is, that the Court of Admiralty proceedeth by two Witnesses, without any either Grand-Jury, to Indict, or Petty to Convict, and the Judge giveth Sentence according to the Laws Imperial, which of old time were in force in all this part of Europe, and now are Laws, not by the Will of any other Emperor or Forraign Power, but by the Will of the Kings of *England*

(68) that have given them force in their own Domi-|nions; the reason whereof seems to be, that the causes that arise at Sea are very often between us, and People of other Nations, such as

are Governed for the most part by the self same Laws Imperial.

Ph. How can it precisely enough be determin'd at Sea, especially near the Mouth of a very great River, whether it be upon the Sea, or within the Land? For the Rivers also are, as well as their Banks, within, or a part of one Country or other.

La. Truly the Question is difficult, and there have been many Suits about it, wherein the Question has been, whose Jurisdiction it is in.

Ph. Nor do I see how it can be decided, but by the King himself, in case it be not declar'd in the Lord Admirals Letters Patents.

La. But though there be in the Letters Patents a power given to hold Plea in some certain cases[,]¹⁶ to any of the Statutes concerning the Admiralty[;] the Justices of the Common-Law may send a Prohibition to that Court, to proceed in the Plea, though it be with a *non-obstante* of any Statute.¹⁷

Ph. Methinks that That should be against the Right of the Crown, which cannot be taken from it by any Subject: For that Argument of Sir *Edw. Coke*'s, that the King has given away all his Judicial (69) Power, is worth | nothing; because (as I have said before) he cannot give away the Essential Rights of his Crown, and because by a *non-obstante* he declares he is not deceived in his Grant.

La. But you may see by the Precedents alledged by Sir *Edw. Coke*, the contrary has been perpetually practised.

Ph. I see not that perpetually; for who can tell, but there may have been given other Judgments in such cases, which have either been not preserv'd in the Records, or else by Sir *Edw. Coke* (because they were against his opinion) not alledged: For this is possible, though you will not grant it to be very likely; therefore I insist only upon this, that no Record of a Judgment is a Law, save only to the party Pleading, until he can by Law reverse the former Judgment. And as to the proceeding without Juries by two sufficient Witnesses, I do not see what harm can proceed from it to the Common-wealth, nor consequently any just Quarrel that

---

16. ⟨ ; ⟩
17. In the letters patent of Henry IV appointing Sir Thomas Beaufort to be Lord High Admiral, for example, after the instruction to conduct certain legal proceedings the following expression is used: ". . . aliquibus statutis sive ordinacionibus incontrarium factis non obstantibus . . ." (*The Black Book of the Admiralty*, ed. Sir Travers Twiss, 1871, in Rolls Series, vol. 1, p. 374). This royal mandate to the Admiral to act "any statute to the contrary notwithstanding" is what is referred to here by "a *non-obstante.*" The context thus indicates the need for the changes in punctuation.

the Justice of the Common-Law can have against their proceedings in the Admiralty: For the Proof of a Fact in both Courts lyeth meerly on the Witnesses, and the difference is no more, but that in the Imperial-Law, the Judge of the Court Judgeth of the Testimony of the Witnesses, and the Jury doth in a Court of Common-Law. Besides, if a Court of Common-Law should

(70) chance to | Incroach upon the Jurisdiction of the Admiral, may not he send a Prohibition to the Court of Common-Law to forbid their proceeding? I pray you tell me what Reason there is for the one, more than for the other?

La. I know none but long Custom; for I think it was never done.

Ph. The Highest ordinary Court in *England* is the Court of Chancery, wherein the Lord Chancellour, or otherwise Keeper of the Great Seal is the only Judge. This Court is very Antient, as appears by Sir *Edw. Coke*, 4 *Inst.* p. [78][18]. where he nameth the Chancellors of King *Edgar*, King *Etheldred*, King *Edmund*, and King *Edward* the Confessor. His Office is given to him without Letters Patents by the Kings delivery to him of the Great Seal of *England*; and whosoever hath the keeping of the Great Seal of *England* hath the same, and the whole Jurisdiction that the Lord Chancellour ever had by the Statute of 5 *Eliz. cap.* 18. wherein it is declar'd, that such is, and always has been the Common-Law.

[*La.*][19] And Sir *Edw. Coke* says, he has his name of Chancellour from the highest point of his Jurisdiction; *viz.* a *Cancellando*; that is, from Cancelling the Kings Letters Patents, by drawing strokes through it like a Lattice.[20]

Ph. Very pretty. It is well enough known that *Cancellarius* was a great
(71) Officer under | the *Roman Empire*, whereof this Island was once a Member, and that the Office came into this Kingdom, either with, or in Imitation of the *Roman* Government. Also it was long after the time of the 12 *Cæsars*, that this Officer was created in the State of *Rome*. For till after *Septimius Severus* his time, the Emperors did diligently enough take cognizance of Causes and Complaints for Judgments given in the Courts of the Prætors, which

---

18. ⟨87⟩
19. In the first edition, two consecutive speeches are attributed to the Philosopher, viz., "The Highest ordinary Court . . ." and "Very pretty. . . ." Molesworth adopts an attribution that joins "The Highest ordinary Court . . ." to the previous speech of the Lawyer, thus restoring the alternation. I believe that the present arrangement, for which I am indebted to Mr. William Galston, is more harmonious with the context.   20. 4 *Inst.* p. 88.

were in *Rome* the same that the Judges of the Common-Law are here; but by the continual Civil Wars in after-times for the choosing of Emperors, that diligence by little and little ceased; and afterwards (as I have Read in a very good Author of the *Roman* Civil Law) the number of complaints being much increased, and being more than the Emperor could dispatch, he appointed an Officer as his Clerk, to receive all such Petitions; and that this Clerk caused a partition to be made in a Room convenient, in which partition-Wall, at the heighth of a Mans reach, he placed at convenient distances certain Bars; so that when a Suitor came to deliver his Petition to the Clerk, who was sometimes absent, he had no more to do, but to throw in his Petition between those Bars, which in *Latin* are called properly *Cancelli*; not that any

(72) certain Form of those Bars, or any Bars at all were ne-|cessary; for they might have been thrown over, though the whole space had been left open; but because they were *Cancelli*, the Clerk Attendant, and keeping his Office there, was called *Cancellarius*: And any Court Bar may properly enough be called *Cancelli*, which does not signifie a Lattice; for that is but a meer Conjecture grounded upon no History nor Grammar, but taken up at first (as is likely) by some Boy that could find no other word in the Dictionary for a Lattice but *Cancelli*. The Office of this Chancellour was at first but to Breviate the matter of the Petitions, for the easing of the Emperor, but Complaints encreasing daily, they were too many, considering other Businesses more necessary for the Emperor to determine, and this caused the Emperor to commit the Determination of them to the Chancellor again; what Reason doth Sir *Edw. Coke* alledge to prove, that the highest point of the Chancellors Jurisdiction is to Cancel his Masters Letters Patents, after they were Sealed with his Masters Seal; unless he hold Plea concerning the validity of them, or of his Masters meaning in them, or of the surreptitious getting of them, or of the abusing of them, which are all causes of Equity? Also, seeing the Chancellor hath his Office only by the delivery of the Great Seal, without any

(73) Instruction, or Limitati-|on of the Process in his Court to be used; it is manifest, that in all Causes whereof he has the hearing, he may proceed by such manner of hearing, and examining of Witnesses (with Jury, or without Jury) as he shall think fittest for the Exactness, Expedition and Equity of the Decrees. And therefore, if he think the Custome of proceeding by Jury, according to the Custome of *England* in Courts of Common-Law, tend

more to Equity (which is the scope of all the Judges in the World, or ought to be) he ought to use that method, or if he think better of another proceeding, he may use it, if it be not forbidden by a Statute.

La. As for this Reasoning of yours I think it well enough; but there ought to be had also a reverend respect to Customs not unreasonable; and therefore, I think, Sir *Edw. Coke* says not amiss; that in such Cases, where the Chancellor will proceed by the Rule of the Common-Law, he ought to deliver the Record in the Kings-Bench; and also it is necessary for the Lord Chancellor to take care of not exceeding [his jurisdiction] as it is limited by Statutes.

Ph. What are the Statutes by which his Jurisdiction is limited? I know that by the 27 *Eliz. cap.* 8. He cannot Reverse a Judgment given in the Kings-Bench for Debt, Detinue, &c. Nor before the Statute
(74) could | he ever by virtue of his Office, Reverse a Judgment in Pleas of the Crown, given by the Kings-Bench that hath the Cognizance of such Pleas, nor need he; for the Judges themselves, when they think there is need to relieve a Man opprest by ill Witnesses, or power of great Men prevailing on the Jury, or by Error of the Jury, though it be in case of Felony, may stay the Execution, and Inform the King, who will in Equity relieve him. As to the regard we ought to have to Custome, we will Consider of it afterward.

La. First in a Parliament holden the 13th of *Rich.* 2. the Commons Petitioned the King, that neither the Chancellor, nor other Chancellor[21] do make any order against the Common-Law, nor that any Judgment be given without due Process of Law.

Ph. This is no unreasonable Petition; for the Common-Law is nothing else but Equity: And by this Statute it appears, that the Chancellors, before that Statute, made bolder with the Courts of Common Law, than they did afterward; but it does not appear that Common-Law in this Statute signifies any thing else, but generally the Law Temporal of the Realm, nor was this Statute ever Printed, that such as I might take notice of it; but whether it
(75) be a Statute or not, I know not, till you tell me what the | [King][22] Answer'd to this Petition.

La. The Kings Answer was, the [usages][23] heretofore shall stand, so as the Kings Royalty be saved.

---

21. That is, neither the present chancellor nor any other.
22. ⟨Parliament⟩   23. ⟨Wages⟩ See 4 *Inst.* p. 82.

Ph. This is flatly against Sir *Edw. Coke*, concerning the Chancery.

La. In another Parliament, 17 *Rich.* 2. It is Enacted, at the Petition of the Commons; That forasmuch as People were Compelled to come before the Kings Council, or in Chancery, by Writs grounded upon untrue Suggestions, that the Chancellor for the time being, presently after such Suggestions, be duly found, and proved untrue, shall have power to Ordain, and Award Dammages, according to his discretion, to him which is so [troubled][24] unduly, as is aforesaid.

Ph. By this Statute it appears, that when a Complaint is made in Chancery upon [untrue][25] Suggestions, the Chancellor shall have the Examination of the said Suggestions, and as he may avoid Dammages when the Suggestions are untrue, so he may also proceed by Process to the determining of the Cause, whether it be Real, or Personal, so it be not Criminal.

La. Also the Commons Petitioned in a Parliament of 2 *Hen.* 4. not Printed; That no Writs, nor Privy-Seals be sued out of Chancery,

(76) Exchequer, or other places to | any Man to appear at a day, upon a pain, either before the King and his Council, or in any other place, contrary to the ordinary Course of Common-Law.

Ph. What Answer was given to this Petition by the King?

La. That such Writs should not be granted without necessity.

Ph. Here again you see the King may deny, or Grant any Petitions in Parliament, either as he thinks it necessary, as in this place, or as he thinks it prejudicial, or not prejudicial to his Royalty, as in the Answer of the former Petition, which is a sufficient proof, that no part of his Legislative Power, or any other Essential part of Royalty can be taken from him by a Statute. Now seeing it is granted, that Equity is the same thing with the Law of Reason, and seeing Sir *Edw. Coke*, 1 *Inst. Sect.* 21. Defines Equity to be a certain Reason comprehended in no Writing, but consisting only in right Reason, which interpreteth and amendeth the Written-Law; I would fain know to what end there should be any other Court of Equity at all, either before the Chancellor or any other Person, besides the Judges of the Civil, or Common-Pleas? Nay I am sure you can alledge none but this, that there was a necessity of a Higher Court of Equity, than the Courts of

(77) Common-Law, to | remedy the Errors in Judgment given by the

---

24. ⟨Travelled⟩ This word translates "travaillez" of the statute. Coke writes "travelled," 4 *Inst.* p. 83.   25. ⟨undue⟩

Justices of Inferior Courts, and the Errors in Chancery were irrevocable, except by Parliament, or by special Commission appointed thereunto by the King.

La. But Sir *Edw. Coke* says, that seeing matters of Fact by the Common Law are Tryable by a Jury of 12 Men, this Court should not draw the matter *ad aliud Examen, i. e.* to another kind of Examination, *viz.* by Deposition of Witnesses, which should be but evidence to a Jury.[26]

Ph. To the Deposition of Witnesses any more or less, then to evidence to the Lord-Chancellor? 'Tis not therefore another kind of Examination; nor is a Jury more capable of duly examining Witnesses than a Lord-Chancellor. Besides, seeing all Courts are bound to Judge according to Equity, and that all Judges in a Case of Equity, may sometimes be deceiv'd, what harm is there to any Man, or to the State, if there be a subordination of Judges in Equity, as well as of Judges in Common-Law? Seeing it is provided by an Act of Parliament[27] to avoid Vexation, that *Subpœnas* shall not be granted, till surety be found to satisfie the Party so grieved and vexed for his Dammages and Expences, if so be the matter may not be made good which is contained in the Bill. |

La. There is another Statute of 31 *Hen.* 6. *cap.* 2. wherein there is a
(78) Proviso cited by Sir *Edw. Coke* in these words; "Provided, that no matter determinable by the Laws of the Realm, shall be by the said Act determined in other Form, then after the course of the same Law in the Kings Courts having the Determination of the same Law."

Ph. This Law was made but for Seven years, and never continued by any other Parliament, and the motive of this Law was the great

---

26. At 4 *Inst.* p. 84, Coke writes, "Whereas matters of fact by the common law are triable by a jury of twelve men, this court [Chancery] should draw the matter *ad aliud examen*, that is, to judge upon deposition of witnesses, which should be but evidence to a jury in actions real, personall, or mixt." The Lawyer's speech reads ". . . should not draw . . ." where Coke reads ". . . should draw. . . ." The difference in readings, surprisingly, has little effect on the meaning of the passage. The Lawyer has Coke mean that a matter should not be removed from the common law courts to Chancery because cases ought not to be tried under other forms of examination than those appointed for their trial; while Coke himself says that were a matter to be removed from the common law courts to Chancery, the effect would be unlawfully to change the mode of examination, etc.

27. 4 *Inst.* p. 83: 15 Hen. 6 c. 4. Cf. 17 Rich. 2 c. 6.

Riots, Extortions, Oppressions, &c. used during the time of the Insurrection of *John Cade*, and the Indictments and Condemnations wrongfully had by this usurped Authority; and thereupon the Parliament Ordained, that for 7 years following no Man should disobey any of the Kings Writs under the Great Seal, or should refuse to appear upon Proclamation before the Kings Council, or in the Chancery, to Answer to Riots, Extortions, &c. For the first time he should lose, &c. Wherein there is nothing at all concerning the Jurisdiction of the Chancery, or any other Court, but an extraordinary power given to the Chancery, and to the Kings Privy-Council, to Determine of those Crimes which were not before that time Tryable, but only by the Kings-Bench, or special Commission: For the Act was made expressly for the

(79) punish-|ment of a great Multitude of Crimes committed by those that had Acted by the said *Cade*'s Authority; to which Act the Proviso was added, which is here mention'd, that the [proceedings][28] in those Courts of Chancery, and of the Kings Council should be such, as should be used in the Courts, to which the said [causes][29], before this Act was made, do belong. That is to say, such causes as were Criminal, should be after the order of the Kings-Bench, and such Causes as were not Criminal, but only against Equity, should be Tryed after the manner of the Chancery, or in some cases according to the Proceedings in the Exchequer. I wonder why Sir *Edw. Coke* should cite a Statute (as this is) above two hundred years before expir'd, and other two Petitions; as if they were Statutes, when they were not passed by the King; unless he did it on purpose to diminish (as he endeavours to do throughout his Institutes) the Kings Authority, or to insinuate his own opinions among the People for the Law of the Land: For that also he endeavours by Inserting *Latin* Sentences, both in his Text, and in the Margin, as if they were Principles of the Law of Reason, without any Authority of Antient Lawyers, or any certainty of Reason in themselves, to make Men believe they are the very

(80) grounds of the Law of *England*. Now | as to the Authority you ascribe to Custome, I deny that any Custome of its own Nature, can amount to the Authority of a Law: For if the Custom be unreasonable, you must with all other Lawyers confess that it is no Law, but ought to be abolished; and if the Custom be reasonable, it is not the Custom, but the Equity that makes it Law. For what

---

28. ⟨Proceeds⟩   29. ⟨Courts⟩

need is there to make Reason Law by any Custom how long soever when the Law of Reason is Eternal? Besides, you cannot find in any Statute (though *Lex & Consuetudo* be often mentioned as things to be followed by the Judges in their Judgments) that *Consuetudines*, that is to say, Customs, or Usages did imply any Long continuance of former time; but that it signified such Use, and Custom of proceeding, as was then immediately in being before the making of such Statute. Nor shall you find in any Statute the word Common-Law, which may not be there well Interpreted for any of the Laws of *England* Temporal; for it is not the singularity of Process used in any Court; that can distinguish it so as to make it a different Law from the Law of the whole Nation.

La. If all Courts were (as you think) Courts of Equity, would it not be incommodious to the Common-wealth? |

Ph. I think not; unless perhaps you may say, that seeing the Judges,
(81) whether they have many, or few causes to be heard before them, have but the same wages from the King, they may be too much inclin'd to put off the Causes they use to hear (for the easing of themselves) to some other Court; to the delay of Justice, and dammage of the Parties suing.

La. You are very much deceiv'd in that; for on contrary the Contention between the Courts for Jurisdiction, is of who shall have most Causes brought before them.

Ph. I cry you Mercy, I smelt not that.

La. Seeing also all Judges ought to give their Sentence according to Equity; if it should chance that a Written Law should be against the Law of Reason, which is Equity, I cannot Imagine in that Case how any Judgment can be Righteous.

Ph. It cannot be that a Written Law should be against Reason: For nothing is more reasonable than that every Man should obey the Law, which he hath himself assented to; but that is not always the Law which is signified by *Grammatical* Construction of the Letter, but that which the Legislator thereby intended should be in Force;[30] which Intention, I Confess, is a very hard matter many times to pick out of the words of the Statute, and requires great
(82) Ability | of understanding, and greater Meditations, and Considerations of such Conjuncture of occasions, and Incommodities as needed a new Law for a Remedy; for there is scarce any thing so

---

30. Cf. above, p. (6).

clearly written, that when the Cause thereof is forgotten, may not be wrested by an ignorant Grammarian, or a Cavilling Logician, to the Injury, Oppression, or perhaps Destruction of an honest Man. And for this Reason, the Judges deserve that Honour and Profit they enjoy[. S][31]ince the Determination of what particular Causes every particular Court should have Cognizance, is a thing not yet sufficiently explained, and is in it self so difficult, as that the Sages of the Law themselves (the Reason Sir *Edw. Coke* will leave to Law it self) are not yet agreed upon it; how is it possible for a Man that is no professed, or no profound Lawyer, to take notice in what Court he may Lawfully begin his Suit, or give Council in it to his Client?

La. I confess that no Man can be bound to take notice of the Jurisdiction of Courts, till all the Courts be agreed upon it amongst themselves; but what Rule to give Judgment by a Judge can have, so as never to contradict the Law written, nor displease his Legislator I understand not.

Ph. I think he may avoid both, if he take care by his Sentence, that he
(83) neither | punish an Innocent, nor deprive him of his dammages due from one that maliciously sueth him without reasonable Cause, which to the most of Rational Men, and unbiassed is not, in my Opinion, very difficult. And though a Judge should (as all Men may do) Erre in his Judgment, yet there is always such power in the Laws of *England*, as may content the Parties, either in the Chancery, or by Commissioners of their own choosing, Authorized by the King; for every Man is bound to acquiesce in the Sentence of the Judges he chooseth.

La. In what Cases can the true Construction of the Letter be contrary to the meaning of the Lawmaker?

Ph. Very many, whereof Sir *Edw. Coke* nameth 3, Fraud, Accident, and Breach of Confidence;[32] but there be many more; for there be a very great many reasonable Exceptions almost to every General Rule, which the makers of the Rule could not foresee; and very many words in every Statute, especially long ones, that are, as to *Grammar*, of Ambiguous signification, and yet to them that know well, to what end the Statute was made, perspicuous

---

31. ⟨ ; s⟩

32. 4 *Inst.* p. 84. Coke enumerates fraud (or "covins, frauds, and deceits"), accident, and breach of confidence as matters "to be judged in court of conscience" but without explicit reference to any need for transcending the letter of the law.

enough; and many Connections of doubtful reference, which by
a *Grammarian* may be Cavill'd at, though the Intention of the Law-
maker be never so perspicuous. And these are the difficulties |
(84)   which the Judges ought to Master, and can do it in respect of their
Ability for which they are chosen, as well as can be hoped for;
and yet there are other Men can do the same, or else the Judges
places could not be from time to time supplyed. The Bishops
commonly are the most able and rational Men, and obliged by
their profession to Study Equity, because it is the Law of God,
and are therefore capable of being Judges in a Court of Equity.
They are the Men that teach the People what is Sin; that is to say,
they are the Doctors in Cases of Conscience. What reason then
can you shew me, why it is unfit, and hurtful to the Common-
wealth, that a Bishop should be a Chancellor, as they were most
often before the time of *Hen*. 8. and since that time once in the
Raign of King *James*?[33]

La. But Sir *Ed*. says,[34] that soon after that a Chancellor was made,
which was no Professor of the Law, he finds in the Rolls of the
Parliament a grievous Complaint by the whole Body of the Realm,
and a Petition that the most wise and able Men within the Realm
might be chosen Chancellors.

Ph. That Petition was Reasonable, but it does not say which are Abler
Men, the Judges of the Common Law, or the Bishops. |

La. That is not the great Question as to the Ability of a Judge; both
(85)   of one, and the other there are Able Men in their own way; but
when a Judge of Equity has need, almost in every Case, to consider as well the Statute-Law, as the Law of Reason, he cannot
perform his Office perfectly, unless he be also ready in the Statutes.

---

33. Hobbes proceeds curiously here. He makes the Philosopher advocate the
appointment of bishops to be chancellor and asks the Lawyer to say what would
be objectionable in that. One would expect that the Lawyer would immediately
refer to the passage in Coke, 4 *Inst.* p. 79, in which it appears that "in the
parliament *anno* 45 E. 3. a grievous complaint was made by the lords and
commons, that the realme had bin of long time governed by men of the church
in disherison of the crown, and desired that lay men only might be principall
officers, &c." Instead, Hobbes has the Lawyer reply out of the subsequent
passage in the *Institutes*, evading the question as to the clergy and taking up the
question of competence in the common law by itself. Cf. Bacon's letter to the
king, 12 February 1615 (*The Works of Francis Bacon . . .* [London, 1740], 4:607):
"If you take my Lord of Canterbury, I will say no more, but the chancellor's
place requires a whole man; and to have both jurisdictions, spiritual and
temporal, in that height is fit but for a King."   34. 4 *Inst.* p. 79.

Ph. I see no great need he has to be ready in the Statutes; in the hearing of a Cause do the Judges of the Common-Law Inform the Council at the Bar what the Statute is, or the Council the Judges?

La. The Council Inform the Judges.

Ph. Why may they not as well Inform the Chancellor? Unless you will say, that a Bishop understands not as well as a Lawyer what is sense, when he hears it Read in *English*.

[*La.*]³⁵ No; no; both the one, and the other are able enough, but to be able enough is not enough; when, not the difficulty of the Case only, but also the Passion of the Judge is to be Conquer'd. I forgot to tell you of the Statute of the 36 *Edw.* 3. *cap.* 9. That if any Person think himself grieved contrary to any of the Articles above Written, or others contained in divers Statutes, will come to the Chancery, or any for him, and thereof make his Complaint, he shall presently there have Remedy by force of the said Articles, (86) and Statutes, without elsewhere | pursuing to have Remedy.

[*Ph.*]³⁶ By the words of this Statute it is very apparent, in my opinion, that the Chancery may hold Plea upon the Complaint of the Party grieved, in any Case Tryable at the Common-Law, because the party shall have present Remedy in that Court, by force of this Act, without pursuing for Remedy elsewhere.

La. Yes; but Sir *Edw. Coke* Answers this Objection, 4 *Inst.* p. 82. in this manner. These words, says he, *He shall have Remedy*, signifie no more but that he shall have presently there a remedial Writ grounded upon those Statutes to give him Remedy at the Common-Law.

Ph. Very like Sir *Edw. Coke* thought as soon as the Party had his Writ, he had his Remedy, though he kept the Writ in his Pocket, without pursuing his Complaint elsewhere; or else he thought, that in the Common-Bench was not elsewhere than in the Chancery.

La. Then there is the Court of————

Ph. Let us stop here; for this which you have said satisfies me, that

---

35. The first edition prints everything from "Why may they not as well . . ." through ". . . without pursuing for Remedy elsewhere." as a single speech by the Philosopher. The present attribution may be defended on the following grounds. First, the interjection of "No; no;" implies the transition of the conversation to the other interlocutor. Second, the argument from the passion of the judge is in the same vein as the Lawyer's speeches on pages (6) and (7) above. Third, there is precedent in the *Dialogue* for the Lawyer's presenting the statute and the Philosopher's then interpreting it. Cf. page (78) above. I am indebted to Mr. William Galston for the suggestion of the emended attribution.   36. See the preceding note.

seek no more than to distinguish between Justice, and Equity; and from it I Conclude, that Justice fulfils the Law, and Equity Interprets the Law; and amends the Judgments given upon the same Law: Wherein I depart not much from the Definition of
(87) Equity, cited | in Sir *Edw. Coke*, 1 *Inst. Sect.* 21. *viz.*: Equity is a certain perfect Reason that Interpreteth, and Amendeth the Law Written; though I Construe it a little otherwise than he would have done; for no one can mend a Law but he that can make it, and therefore I say not it amends the Law, but the Judgments only when they are Erroneous. And now let us Consider of Crimes in particular (the Pleas whereof are commonly called the Pleas of the Crown) and of the punishments belonging to them; and first of the Highest Crime of all which is High Treason. Tell me what is High Treason.

Of Crimes Capital.

La. THE FIRST STATUTE THAT DECLARETH WHAT IS HIGH Treason, is the Statute of the 25 *Edw.* 3. in these words.[1] *Whereas divers Opinions have been before this time, in what Case Treason shall be said, and in what not; the King, at the Request of the Lords, and of the Commons, hath made Declaration in the manner as hereafter follows; That is to say, when a Man doth Compass, or Imagine the Death of our Lord the King, of our Lady the Queen, or of their Eldest Son and Heir; or if a Man doth violate the Kings Companion, or the Kings Eldest Daughter unmarried, or the Wife of the Kings Eldest Son and Heir;* |
(88) *or if a Man do Levy War against our Lord the King in his Realm, or be adherent to the Kings Enemies in his Realm, giving to them Aid, and Comfort in the Realm, or elsewhere, and thereof be provably Attainted by open Deed, by People of their Condition. And if a Man Counterfeit the Kings Great, or Privy-Seal, or his Money. And if a Man bring false Money into this Realm Counterfeit to the Money of* England, *as the Money called Lushburgh,[2] or other like to the said Money of* England, *knowing the Money to be false, to Merchandize, and make payment in deceit of our said Lord the King, and of his People. And if a Man slay the Chancellor, Treasurer, or the Kings Justices of the one Bench, or the*

1. Substantially.
2. Understood as facsimile of English coin produced in Luxemburg.

other, Justices in Eyre, or Justices of Assises, and all other Justices Assigned to Hear, and Determine, being in their Places, and doing their Offices. And is to be understood in the Cases above rehearsed, that That ought to be adjudged Treason, which extends to our Royal Lord the King, and his Royal Majesty, and of such Treason the Forfeiture of the Escheats pertains to our Lord the King, as well the Lands and Tenements holden of others as himself. And moreover there is another manner of Treason; that is to say, when a Servant Slayeth his Master, or a Wife her Husband; or when a Man Secular, or Religious slayeth his Prelate, to whom he

(89) *oweth Faith, and Obedience; and of | such Treason the Escheats ought to pertain to every Lord of his own Fee. And because many other like Cases of Treason may happen in time to come, which a Man cannot think, nor declare at this present time, it is accorded, that if any Case supposed Treason, which is not above specified, doth happen before any Justices, the Justices shall tarry without giving any Judgment of the Treason till the Cause be shewed, and declared before the King and his Parliament, whether it ought to be adjudged Treason, or other Felony.*

Ph. I desir'd to understand what Treason is, wherein no Enumeration of Facts can give me satisfaction. Treason is a Crime of it self, *Malum in se*, and therefore a Crime at the Common-Law, and High Treason the Highest Crime at the Common Law that can be: And therefore not the Statute only, but Reason without a Statute makes it a Crime. And this appears by the Preamble, where it is intimated, that all Men, though of divers Opinions did Condemn it by the name of Treason, though they knew not what Treason meant, but were forced to request the King to determine it. That which I desire to know is, how Treason might have been defined without the Statute, by a Man that has no other faculty to make a Definition of it, than by meer Natural Reason. |

La. When none of the Lawyers have done it, you are not to expect
(90) that I should undertake it on such a sudden.

Ph. You know that *Salus Populi* is *Suprema Lex*; that is to say, the safety of the People, is the highest Law; and that the safety of the People of a Kingdom consisteth in the safety of the King, and of the strength necessary to defend his People, both against Forraign Enemies, and Rebellious Subjects. And from this I infer, that to Compass (that is) to design the Death of the then present King, was High Treason before the making of this Statute, as being a Designing of a Civil War, and the Destruction of the People. 2. That the Design to Kill the Kings Wife, or to violate her Chastity, as also to violate the Chastity of the [wife of the]

Kings Heir apparent, or of his Eldest Daughter unmarryed, as tending to the Destruction of the certainty of the Kings Issue, and by Consequence by raising of Contentions about the Crown, and Destruction of the People in Succeeding time by Civil War, was therefore High Treason before this Statute. 3. That to Levy war against the King within the Realm, and Aiding the Kings Enemies, either within, or without the Realm, are tending to the Kings Destruction, or Disherison, and was High Treason, before (91) this Statute by the Common-Law. 4. That | Counterfeiting the principal Seals of the Kingdom, by which the King Governeth his People, tendeth to the Confusion of Government, and Consequently to the Destruction of the People, and was therefore Treason before the Statute. 5. If a Souldier design the Killing of his General, or other Officer in time of Battel, or a Captain Hover doubtfully with his Troops, with intention to gain the Favour of him that shall chance to get the Victory, it tendeth to the Destruction both of King, and People, whether the King be present, or absent, and was High Treason before the Statute. 6. If any Man had Imprisoned the Kings Person, he had made him incapable of Defending his People, and was therefore High Treason before the Statute. 7. If any Man had, with design to raise Rebellion against the King, Written, or by words advisedly uttered, denied the King Regnant to be their Lawful King, he that wrought, Preached, or spoke such words, living then under the Protection of the Kings Laws, it had been High Treason before the Statute for the Reasons aforesaid. And perhaps there may be some other Cases upon this Statute, which I cannot presently think upon; but the Killing of a Justice, or other Officer as is determin'd by the Statute, is not otherwise High Treason, (92) but by the Statute. And to | distinguish that which is Treason by the Common-Law, from all other Inferior Crimes; we are to Consider, that if such High Treason should take effect, it would destroy all Laws at once; and being done by a Subject, 'tis a return to Hostility[3] by Treachery; and consequently, such as are Traytors may by the Law of Reason be dealt withal, as Ignoble and Treacherous Enemies; but the greatest of other Crimes, for the most part; are breaches of one only, or at least of very few Laws.

La. Whether this you say be true, or false, the Law is now unquestion-

---

3. Cf. below, p. (95).

able by a Statute made in 1 and 2 of Queen *Mary*,[4] whereby there is nothing to be esteemed Treason, besides those few Offences specially mentioned in the Act of 25 *Ed.* 3.

Ph. Amongst these great Crimes the greatest is that which is Committed by one that has been trusted, and loved by him whose Death he so designeth: For a Man cannot well take heed of those, whom he thinks he hath obliged, whereas an open Enemy gives a Man warning before he Acteth. And this it is for which the Statute hath declared, that it is another kind of Treason, when a Servant killeth his Master, or Mistress, or a Wife killeth her Husband, or a Clerk killeth his Prelate; and I should think it petty

(93) Treason also, though it be | not within the words of the Statute; when a Tenant in Fee, that holdeth by Homage, and Fealty, shall kill the Lord of his Fee; for Fealty is an Oath of Allegiance to the Lord of the Fee; saving he may not keep his Oath in any thing Sworn to, if it be against the King. For Homage, as it is expressed in a Statute of 17 *Edw.* 2. is the greatest submission that is possible to be made to one Man by another; for the Tenant shall hold his Hands together between the Hands of his Landlord, and shall say thus; I become your Man from this day forth for Life, for Member and for Worldly Honour, and shall owe [you][5] Faith for the Lands that I[6] hold of you, saving the Faith that I owe unto our[7] Lord the King, and to [mine][8] other Lords: Which Homage, if made to the King, is Equivalent to a promise of simple obedience, and if made to another Lord, there is nothing excepted but the Allegiance to the King;[9] and that which is called Fealty, is but the same Confirmed by an Oath.

La. But Sir *Edw. Coke*, [3][10] *Inst.* p. 11. denies that a Traytor is in

---

4. Mary reigned for about a year before marrying Philip. After the commencement of their joint reign, the years of that reign would be counted both from her sole and from their joint accession. "1 and 2 of Queen *Mary*" should read "1 and 2 Philip and Mary," meaning in the first year of their joint reign but the second from her sole accession. Cf. 3 *Inst.* p. 215.

5. ⟨that my⟩   6. ⟨shall⟩   7. ⟨Sovereign⟩   8. ⟨many⟩

9. It is obvious that there is confusion in Hobbes's account, for he refers to the oath of homage as capable of being made to the king and he quotes it as containing a reservation of the juror's homage to the king. Hobbes's reference is to statute 2 of the seventeenth year of Edward II (A.D. 1324), which distinguishes "when a freeman shall do homage to his lord of whom he holdeth in chief" and "when a freeman shall do homage to another than his chief Lord." The former homage is "*sauve le foi que jeo doi a nostre seignur le Roi*" and the latter is "*sauve le foi que jeo doy a nostre seignur le Roi & a mes autres seignurages.*" Cf. p. ⟨202⟩ below.   10. ⟨4⟩

Legal understanding the Kings Enemy; for Enemies (saith he) be those that be out of the Allegiance of the King; and his Reason is; because, if a Subject joyn with a Forraign Enemy, and come
(94) into *England* with him, and be taken Pri-|soner here, he shall not be Ransomed, or proceeded with as an Enemy shall, but he shall be taken as a Traytor to the King. Whereas an Enemy coming in open Hostility, and taken, shall either be Executed by Martial-Law, or Ransomed; for he cannot be Indicted of Treason, for that he never was in the Protection and Ligeance of the King, and the Indictment of the Treason saith, *Contra Ligeantiam suam debitam*.

Ph. This is not an Argument worthy of the meanest Lawyer. Did Sir *Edw. Coke* think it [im]possible[11] for a King Lawfully to kill a Man, by what Death soever without an Indictment, when it is manifestly proved he was his open Enemy? Indictment is a form of Accusation peculiar to *England*, by the Command of some King of *England*, and retained still, and therefore a Law to this Country of *England*; but if it were not Lawful to put a Man to Death otherwise than by an Indictment no Enemy could be put to Death at all in other Nations, because they proceed not, as we do, by Indictment. Again, when an open Enemy is taken and put to Death by Judgment of Martial-Law; it is not the Law of the General or Council of War, that an Enemy shall be thus proceeded with, but the Law of the King contained in their Commissions; such as from time to time the Kings have thought fit,
(95) in | whose Will it always resteth, whether an open Enemy, when he is taken, shall be put to Death, or no, and by what Death; and whether he shall be Ransomed, or no, and at what price? Then for the Nature of Treason by Rebellion; is it not a return to Hostility?[12] What else does Rebellion signifie? *William* the Conqueror Subdued this Kingdom; some he Killed; some upon promise of future obedience he took to Mercy, and they became his Subjects, and swore Allegiance to him; if therefore they renew the War against him, are they not again open Enemies; or if any of them lurking under his Laws, seek occasion thereby to kill him secretly, and come to be known, may he not be proceeded against as an Enemy, who though he had not Committed what he Design'd, yet had certainly a Hostile Design? Did not the long Parliament declare all those for Enemies to the State that opposed

11. ⟨is possible⟩
12. Cf. above, p. (92); *Leviathan*, chap. 28; Locke, *Second Treatise*, sect. 226.

their Proceedings against the late King? But Sir *Edw. Coke* does seldom well distinguish when there are two divers Names for one and the same thing;[13] though one contain the other, he makes them always different, as if it could not be that one and the same Man should be both an Enemy, and a Traytor. But now let us come to his Comment upon this Statute; The Statute says (as it (96) is printed in *English*) when a Man doth | Compass, or Imagine the Death of our Lord the King, *&c.* What is the meaning of the word Compassing, or Imagining?

La. On this place Sir *Edw. Coke* says,[14] that before the making of this Act, *Voluntas reputabatur pro facto*, the Will was taken for the Deed. And so saith *Bracton*,[15] *Spectatur Voluntas, & non Exitus; & nihil interest utrum quis occidat, aut causam [mortis] præbeat*; That is to say, the Cause of the killing: Now Sir *Edw. Coke* says, this was the Law before the Statute; and that to be a Cause of the killing, is to ["]declare the same by some open Deed tending to the Execution of his Intent, or which might be Cause of Death.["][16]

---

13. See note 37, p. (110) below.
14. 3 *Inst.* p. 5. See also ibid. p. 161.
15. Fol. 136b. Bracton's subject there is not treason but accidental homicide.
16. Bracton's statement means, "The will is to be regarded and not the outcome; and it does not matter whether one kills, or declares the cause of death." So at least Coke understood *praebeat* ("declares") and Hobbes also. Travers Twiss, in his edition of Bracton (*Rerum Brit.* [London, 1878-80]) translates "it does not matter, whether a person slays or supplies the cause of death." Samuel Thorne's Bracton (Harvard: Cambridge, 1968) reads "or furnishes the cause of death", agreeing with Twiss. If "supplies" or "furnishes" were correct in the context, the reference would most plausibly have to be to the weapons or instruments of slaying; but these are the subject not in Coke's discussion of this branch of the Act but of the subsequent one touching proof of an overt act (3 *Inst.* p. 12). The matter deserves some attention partly because the next few speeches of the present work, and especially the Philosopher's long speech, move to the question of what constitutes a reasonable "proof" of intention to commit a crime, viz., treason, i.e., what constitutes a provable declaring of such an intention, the conclusion aimed at being that the uttering of words is a clearer declaration than any providing of weapons or poisons. Curiously, while Hobbes avoided the modern translation of *praebeat* in favor of Coke's, he seems to have adopted an interpretation of the law that accepts the collapsing of the branches of the law which the modern translation implies.

The awkward expression "declares the cause of death" is explained by Coke in the context of the distinction between compassing the death of a subject and compassing the death of the king. He refers to two precedent cases of declaring the cause of death of a subject, namely, beating a man and leaving him for dead

(continued opposite)

Ph. Is there any *English-man* can understand, that to Cause the Death of a Man, and to declare the same is all one thing? And if this were so, and that such was the Common-Law before the Statute, by what words in the Statute is it taken away?

La. It is not taken away, but the manner how it must be prov'd is thus Determin'd, that it must be prov'd by some open Deed, as providing of Weapons, Powder, Poyson, Assaying of Armour, sending of Letters, *&c.*

Ph. But what is the Crime it self which this Statute maketh Treason? For as I understand the words, To Compass, or Imagine the

(97) Kings Death, *&c.* The Compas-|sing (as it is in the *English*) is the only thing which is made High Treason; so that not only the killing, but the Design is made High Treason; or as it is in the *French* Record, *Fait Compasser*; That is to say, the causing of others to Compass, or Design the Kings Death is High Treason; and the words *par overt fait*, are not added as a specification of any Treason, or other Crime, but only of the Proof that is requir'd by the Law. Seeing then the Crime is the Design and Purpose to kill the King, or cause him to be killed, and lyeth hidden in the Breast of him that is Accused; what other Proof can there be had of it than words Spoken or Written. And therefore if there be sufficient Witness, that he by words Declared, that he had such a Design, there can be no Question, but that he is Comprehended within this Statute: Sir *Edw. Coke* doth not deny, but that if he Confess this Design, either by Word, or Writing,[17] he is within the Statute. As for that Common saying, that bare words may make a Heretick, but not a Traytor, which Sir *Edw. Coke* on this occasion maketh use of,[18] they are to little purpose; seeing that this Statute

---

(16 *continued*)

as a declaration of intention to cause his death; and cutting the throat of a man and leaving him for dead, to the same effect. "But in those days [at or before 25 Edw. 3], in the case of the king, if a man had compassed, or imagined the death of the king (who is the head of the commonwealth) and had declared his compassing, or imagination, by words or writing, this had been high treason, and a sufficient overture [manifestation] by the ancient law" (*ibid.*, p. 5). What emerges is (1) that Coke did not suppose and surely did not say that causing the death of a man and declaring the same is all one thing: on the contrary, the two unsuccessful felons "declared" without causing; and (2) with respect to slaying the king, "compassing" was treasonous before 25 Edw. 3 and thus was not "made" treason by the statute, as is represented by the Philosopher in the next long speech.

17. ⟨but that⟩   18. 3 *Inst.* p. 14.

maketh not the words High Treason, but the Intention, whereof the words are but a Testimony: and that Common-saying is false (98) as it is generally Pronounced; for there were | divers Statutes made afterwards, though now expir'd, which made bare words to be Treason, without any other Deed: As, 1 *El. cap.* 6. & 13. *El. cap.* 1. If a Man should Publickly Preach, that the King were an Usurper, or that the Right of the Crown belonged to any other than the King that Reigned, there is no doubt but it were Treason, not only within this Statute of *E.3.* but also within the Statute of 1 *Ed.* 6. c. 12. which are both still in Force.

La. Not only so; but if a Subject should counsel any other Man to kill the King, Queen, or Heir apparent to the Crown, it would at this day be Judged High Treason; and yet it is no more than bare words. In the third year of King *James*, *Henry Garnet*, a Jesuit-Priest, to whom some of the Gun-Powder Traytors had Revealed their design by way of Confession, gave them Absolution, without any Caution taken for their desisting from their purpose, or other provision against the danger, was therefore Condemned, and Executed as a Traytor, though such Absolution were nothing else but bare words. Also I find in the Reports[19] of Sir *John Davis*, Attorney-General for *Ireland*; that in the time of King *Henry* the 6th, a Man was Condemned of Treason, for saying the King was a Natural Fool, and unfit to Govern; but yet this Clause in the (99) Sta-|tute of *Edw.* 3. *viz.* That the Compassing there mentioned ought to be proved by some *Overt Act*, was by the Framers of the Statute, not without great Wisdom, and Providence inserted: For as Sir *Edw. Coke* very well observeth,[20] when Witnesses are Examin'd concerning words only, they never or very rarely agree precisely about the words they Swear to.

Ph. I deny not but that it was wisely enough done. But the Question is not here of the Treason (which is either Fact, or design) but of the Proof, which, when it is doubtful, is to be Judged by a Jury of 12 Lawful Men: Now whether think you is it a better Proof of a Mans Intention to kill, that he declares that same with his own Mouth, so as it may be Witnessed, or that he provide Weapons, Powder, Poyson, or Assay Arms? If he utter his Design by words, the Jury has no more to do than to consider the

---

19. Sir John Davis, *Les Reports des Cases & Matters en Ley* . . . (London, 1674; Dublin, 1615, as *Le Primer Report*, etc.; English translation, Dublin, 1762, Davis spelled "Davies"). The years covered by the reports are 1604–12.
20. 3 *Inst.* p. 14.

Legallity of the Witnesses, the Harmony of their Testimonies, or whether the words were spoken advisedly[.]²¹ For they might have been uttered in a Disputation for Exercise only, or when he that spake them had not the use of Reason, nor perhaps any Design, or wish at all towards the Execution of what he talked of: But how a Jury from providing, or buying of Armour, or (100) buying of Gun-Powder, or from any o-|ther overt Act, not Treason in it self, can infer a Design of Murdering the King, unless there appear some words also, signifying to what end he made such Provision, I cannot easily conceive. Therefore as the Jury on the whole matter[,] Words and Deeds[,] shall ground their Judgment concerning Design, or not Design, so, in Reason, they ought to give Verdict. But to come to the Treason of Counterfeiting the Great, or Privy-Seal, seeing there are so many ways for a Cheating Fellow to make use of these Seals, to the Cousening of the King, and his People; why are not all such abuses High-Treason, as well as the making of a false Seal?

La. So they are: For Sir *Edw. Coke* produceth²² a Record of one that was Drawn, and Hang'd for taking the Great Seal from an expir'd Patent, and fastning it to a Counterfeit Commission to gather Money: But he approveth not the Judgment, because it is the Judgment for Petty Treason; also because the Jury did not find him Guilty of the Offence laid in the Indictment, which was the Counterfeiting of the Great-Seal, but found the special matter, for which the Offender was Drawn, and Hang'd.

Ph. Seeing this Crime of taking the Great Seal from one Writing, and (101) fastning it to another was not found High Treason by the | Jury, nor could be found upon special matter to be the other kind of Treason mentioned in the same Statute; what ground had either the Jury to find it Treason, or the Judge to pronounce Sentence upon it?

La. I cannot tell. Sir *Edw. Coke* seems to think it a false Record; for hereupon he saith by way of Admonition to the Reader, that hereby it appeareth how dangerous it is to Report a Case by the Ear.

Ph. True; but he does not make it apparent, that this Case was untruly Reported, but on the contrary confesseth, that he had perused the same Record; and a Man may (if it may be done without Proof of the Falsity) make the same Objection to any Record whatsoever. For my part, seeing this Crime produced the same mischief

---

21. ⟨?⟩   22. 3 *Inst.* p. 15.

that ariseth from Counterfeiting, I think it reason to understand it as within the Statute: And for the Difference between the Punishments (which are both of them Capital) I thin[k][23] it is not worthy to be stood upon; seeing Death, which is, *Ultimum supplicium*, is a satisfaction to the Law; as Sir *Edw. Coke* himself hath in another place affirm'd.[24] But let us now proceed to other Crimes.

La. Appendent to this is another Crime called Misprision of Treason;
(102) which is the Concealing of it by any Man that knows | it; and it is called Misprision from the *French Mespriser*, which signifies to contemn, or undervalue; for it is no small Crime in any Subject, so little to take to Heart a known danger to the Kings Person, and Consequently, to the whole Kingdom, as not to discover not only what he knows, but also what he suspecteth of the same, that the Truth therefore may be Examin'd. But for such Discovery, tho the thing prove false, the Discoverer shall not, as I think, be taken for a false Accuser; if for what he directly affirms, he produces a reasonable Proof, and some probability for his Suspition; for else the Concealment will seem justifiable by the Interest, which is to every Man allowed in the preservation of himself from pain and dammage.

Ph. This I consent to.

La. All other Crimes meerly Temporal are comprehended under Felony, or Trespass.

Ph. What is the meaning of the word Felony? Does it signifie any thing that is in its own Nature a Crime, or that only which is made a Crime by some Statute? for I remember some Statutes that make it Felony to Transport Horses, and some other things out of the Kingdom; which Transportation before such Statutes made, and after the Repealing of the same, was no greater Crime than any other usual Traffick of a Merchant. |

La. Sir *Edw. Coke* derives the word Felony from the Latin word *Fel*,
(103) the Gall of a living Creature, and accordingly defines Felony to be an Act done *Animo Felleo*;[25] that is to say, a Bitter [or][26] Cruel Act.

Ph. Etymologies are no Definitions, and yet when they are true they give much light towards the finding out of a Definition; but this

---

23. ⟨g⟩
24. 3 *Inst.* p. 212. Bracton, fol. 105, presents the need to adhere strictly to the legal sentence as part of an argument against vindictiveness in executing sentences.   25. 1 *Inst.* fol. 391b. Also 3 *Inst.* p. 149.   26. ⟨a⟩

of Sir *Edw. Coke*'s carries with it very little of Probability; for there be many things made Felony by the Statute-Law, that proceed not from any bitterness of mind at all, and many that proceed from the contrary.

La. This is matter for a Critick, to be pickt out of the knowledge of History and Forraign Languages, and you may perhaps know more of it than I do.

Ph. All that I, or, I think, any other can say in this matter will amount to no more than a reasonable Conjecture, insufficient to sustain any point of Controversie in Law. The word is not to be found in any of the old *Saxon* Laws, set forth by Mr. *Lambert*,[27] nor in any Statute Printed before that of *Magna Charta*; there it is found. Now *Magna Charta* was made in the time of *Hen.* the 3d, Grand-Child to *Hen.* the 2d, Duke of *Anjou*, a *French-man* born, and bred in the Heart of *France*, whose Language might very well retain (104) many words | of his Ancestors the *German-Franks*, as ours doth of the *German-Saxons*; as also many words of the Language of the *Gaules*, as the *Gaules* did retain many words of the *Greek* Colonie planted at *Marseilles*. But certain it is the *French* Lawyers at this day use the word Felon, just as our Lawyers use the same; whereas the Common People of *France* use the word *Filou* in the same sence; but *Filou* signifieth not the Man that hath committed such an Act, as they call Felony; but the Man that maketh it his Trade to maintain himself by the breaking and contemning of all Laws generally; and comprehendeth all those unruly People called Cheaters, Cutpurses, Pick-locks, Catch-Cloaks, Coyners of false Money, Forgers, Thieves, Robbers, Murderers, and who-soever make use of Iniquity on Land, or Sea, as a Trading, or Living. The *Greeks* upon the Coast of *Asia*, where *Homer* liv'd, were they that Planted the Colony of *Marseilles*; they had a word that signified the same with Felon, which was φιλήτης, *Filetes*, and this *Filetes* of *Homer* signifies properly the same that a Felon signifies with us: And therefore *Homer* makes *Apollo* to call *Mercury* φιλήτην *Fileteen*, and ἄρχος φιλήτων;[28] I insist not upon the truth of this Etymologie; but it is certainly more rational than the *Animus Felleus* of Sir *Edw. Coke*. And for the (105) mat-|ter it self it is manifest enough, that which we now call Murder, Robbery, Theft, and other practices of Felons, are the same that we call Felony, and Crimes in their own nature without

27. William Lambarde (1536–1601), *Archaionomia* (1568).
28. The Homeric *Hymn to Hermes*, line 292.

the help of Statute. Nor is it the manner of punishment that distinguisheth the nature of one Crime from another; but the mind
of the Offender and the Mischief he intendeth, considered together with the Circumstances of Person, Time, and Place.

La. Of Felonies, the [most heinous][29] is Murder.

Ph. And what is Murder?

La. Murder is the Killing of a Man upon Malice forethought, as by
a Weapon, or by Poyson, or any way, if it be done, upon Antecedent Meditation, or thus, Murder is the Killing of a Man in
cold Blood.

Ph. I think there is a good definition of Murder set down by Statute,
52 *Hen.* 3. *cap.* 25.[30] in these words: Murder from henceforth shall
not be Judged before our Justices, where it is found misfortune
only, but it shall take place in such as are slain by Felony. And Sir
Edw. Coke Interpreting this Statute, 2 *Inst.* p. 148. saith; That the
mischief before this Statute was, that he that Killed a Man by
misfortune, as by doing any Act that was not against Law, and yet
against his Intent, if the Death of a Man ensued, this was adjudged

(106) Murder. But I | find no Proof that he alledgeth, nor find I any
such Law amongst the Laws of the *Saxons*, set forth by Mr.
Lambert.[31] For the word, it is (as Sir *Edw. Coke* noteth) old *Saxon*,
and amongst them it signified no more than a Man slain in the
Field, or other place, the Author of his death not known. And
according hereunto, *Bracton*, who lived in the time of *Magna
Charta*, defineth it *fol.* 134, thus; Murder is the secret killing of a
Man, when none besides the killer, and his Companions saw, or
knew it; so that it was not known who did it, nor fresh-suit could
be made after the doer;[32] therefore every such killing was called
Murder before it could be known whether it could be by Felony,
or not: For a Man may be found dead that kills himself, or was
Lawfully kill'd by another. This name of Murder came to be the
more horrid, when it was secretly done, for that it made every
Man to consider of their own danger, and him that saw the dead
Body to boggle at it, as a Horse will do at a dead Horse;[33] and to
prevent the same they had Laws in force to Amerce the Hundred
where it was done, in a sum defined by Law to be the Price of his
Life: For in those dayes the lives of all sorts of Men were valued

---

29. ⟨Crime⟩ See 3 *Inst.* p. 47.   30. Statute of Marlebridge.
31. See above, p. (103), n. 27.   32. The paraphase of Bracton ends here.
33. Cf. the passage in Rousseau, *Second Discourse,* in *Oeuvres complètes de J.-J.
Rousseau* (Paris: Gallimard, 1964). 3:154.

by Money; and the value set down in their Written Laws. And (107) therefore Sir *Edw. Coke* was mistaken in that he | thought that killing a Man by misfortune before the Statute of *Marlebridge* was adjudged Murder, and those secret Murders were abominated by the People, for that they were lyable to so great a Pecuniary Punishment for suffering the Malefactor to escape. But this grievance was by *Canutus*, when he Reign'd, soon eased: For he made a Law, that the Countrey in this Case, should not be Charged, unless he were an *English-man* that was so slain; but if he were a *French-man* (under which name were comprehended all Forraigners, and especially the *Normans*) though the slayer escaped, the County was not to be Amerced. And this Law, though it were very hard, and Chargeable when an *English-man* was so slain, for his Friend to prove he was an *English-man*, and also unreasonable to deny the Justice to a stranger; yet was it not Repealed till the 14th of King *Ed.* the 3d. By this you see that Murder is distinguished from Homicide by the Statute-Laws, and not by any Common-Law without the Statute; and that is comprehended under the general name of Felony.

La. And so also is Petit Treason, and I think so is High Treason also; for in the abovesaid Statute in the 25 *Ed.* 3d. Concerning Treasons there is this Clause. And because that many other like Cases of (108) Trea-|son, may happen in time to come, which a Man cannot think, or declare at the present time; it is accorded, that if any other Case, supposed Treason which is not above specified, doth happen before any the Justices, the Justices shall tarry without any going to Judgment of the Treason, till the Cause be shewed, and declared before the King and his Parliament whether it be Treason, or other Felony;[34] which thereby shews that the King and Parliament thought that Treason was one of the sorts of Felony.

Ph. And so think I.

La. But Sir *Edw. Coke* denies it to be so at this day; for 1 *Inst. Sect.* 745. at the word Felony, he saith; That in Antient time this word Felony was of so large an extent, as that it included High Treason ————But afterwards it was resolved, that in the Kings Pardon, or Charter, this word Felony should extend only to Common Felonies————And at this day, under the word Felony by Law is included Petit Treason, Murder, Homicide, burning of Houses,

---

34. A virtual quotation from 25 Edw. 3 c. 2.

Burglary, Robbery, Rape, &c. Chance-medley, *se defendendo*, and *Petit Larceny.*

Ph. He says it was resolv'd, but by whom?

La. By the Justices of Assize in the time of *Hen.* 4. as it seems in the Margin. |

Ph. Have Justices of Assize any Power by their Commission to alter
(109) the Language of the Land and the received sence of words? Or in the Question in what Case Felony shall be said, [is it][35] referred to the Judges to Determine; as in the Question in what Case Treason shall be said it is referred by the Statute of *Edw.* the 3d. to the Parliament? I think not; and yet perhaps they may be disobliged[36] to disallow a Pardon of Treason, when mentioning all Felonies it nameth not Treason, nor specifies it by any description of the Fact.

La. Another kind of Homicide there is simply called so, or by the name of Manslaughter, and is not Murder, and that is when a Man kills another Man upon suddain Quarrel, during the heat of Blood.

Ph. If two meeting in the Street chance to strive who shall go nearest to the Wall, and thereupon Fighting, one of them kills the other, I believe verily he that first drew his Sword did it of Malice forethought, though not long forethought; but whether it be Felony or no, it may be doubted. It is true, that the harm done is the same as if it had been done by Felony; but the wickedness of the Intention was nothing near so great. And supposing it had been done by Felony, then 'tis manifest by the Statute of *Marlebridge,*
(110) that it was very Murder. And | when a Man for a word, or a trifle

---

35. ⟨it is⟩

36. The word "disobliged" intrudes on the sense of the passage. In *Works* (1750) and Molesworth, it is emended to "obliged." The context makes that revision questionable however. The argument of the text is that although felony originally included high treason, judges on their own authority resolved that the royal pardons of felony in general do not pardon high treason as well. But judges do not have authority to remake the meaning of words; "and yet perhaps they may be disobliged to disallow" the application of the king's general pardon of felony to high treason. Emendation to "obliged" would mean that the precedent of the common law practice evolved in the courts out of a judicial usurpation is now effective in overruling the sovereign's pardon, and judges are "obliged" to continue to rule in that wise. If "disobliged" be understood in the strained sense of "discharged from their (unfounded) obligation," the passage can stand without emendation and without violating the context. It is left standing with a caution to the reader.

shall draw his Sword, and kill another Man, can any Man imagine that there was not some Precedent Malice?

La. 'Tis very likely there was Malice more or less, and therefore the Law hath Ordained for it a punishment equal to that of Murder, saving that the Offender shall have the Benefit of his Clergy.

Ph. The Benefit of Clergy comes in upon another account, and importeth not any extenuation of the Crime; for it is but a Relick of the old usurped Papal priviledge, which is now by many Statutes so pared off, as to spread but to few Offences, and is become a Legal kind of Conveying Mercy, not only to the Clergy, but also to the Laity.

La. The work of a Judge you see is very difficult, and requires a Man that hath a faculty of well distinguishing of Dissimilitudes of such Cases as Common Judgments think to be the same.[37] A small Circumstance may make a great Alteration, which a Man that cannot well discern, ought not to take upon him the Office of a Judge.

Ph. You say very well; for if Judges were to follow one anothers Judgments in Precedent Cases, all the Justice in the World would at length depend upon the Sentence of a few Learned, or Un-
(111) learned, ignorant | Men, and have nothing at all to do with the Study of Reason.

La. A Third kind of Homicide is when a Man kills another, either by misfortune, or in a necessary defence of himself, or of the King, or of his Laws; for such killing is neither Felony, nor Crime, saving (as Sir *Edw. Coke* says, [3][38] *Inst.* p. 56.) that if the Act that a Man is a doing when he kills another Man be Unlawful, then it is Murder. As if *A.* meaneth to steal a Deer in the Park of *B.* Shooteth at the Deer, and by the glance of the Arrow killeth a Boy that is hidden in a Bush; this is Murder, for that the Act was Unlawful; but if the owner of the Park had done the like, shooting at his own Deer, it had been by Misadventure, and no Felony.

Ph. This is not so distinguished by any Statute, but is the *Commonly* only of Sir *Ed. Coke.* I believe not a word of it. If a Boy be Robbing an Apple-tree, and falling thence upon a Man that stands under it, and breaks his Neck, but by the same chance saveth his own Life, Sir *Edw. Coke,* it seems, will have him Hanged for it, as if he had fallen of prepensed Malice. All that can be called Crime in this Business is but a simple Trespass, to the dammage perhaps

---

37. Cf. *Leviathan,* chap. 8; above, p. (95).   38. ⟨4⟩

of sixpence or a shilling. I confess the Trespass was an Offence
(112) against the Law, but the falling was | none, nor was it by the
Trespass, but by the falling that the Man was slain; and as he
ought to be quit of the killing, so he ought to make Restitution
for the Trespass. But I believe the Cause of Sir *Edw. Coke*'s mistake was his not well understanding of *Bracton*, whom he cites in
the Margin: For [fol. 120b][39] he saith thus: *Sed hic erit distinguen-
dum, utrum quis dederit operam rei licitæ, vel illicitæ; si illicitæ, ut si
lapidem projiciebat quis versus locum per quem consueverunt homines
transitum facere, vel dum insequitur equum, vel bovem, & aliquis ab equo,
vel a bove percussus fuerit, & hujusmodi, hoc imputatur ei, i. e.* But here
we are to distinguish whether a Man be upon a Lawful, or Unlawful business; if an unlawful, as he that throws a stone into a
place, where Men use to pass; or if he chase a Horse, or an Ox,
and thereby the Man be stricken by the Horse, or the Ox, this
shall be imputed to him: And it is most reasonable: For the doing
of such an unlawful Act as is here meant, is a sufficient Argument
of a Felonious purpose, or at least a hope to kill some body, or
other, and he cared not whom; which is worse than to design the
death of a certain Adversary, which nevertheless is Murder. Also
on the contrary, though the business a Man is doing be Lawful,
(113) and it chanceth sometimes that a Man be slain | thereby; yet may
such killing be Felony. For if a Car-man drive his Cart through
Cheapside in a throng of People, and thereby he kill a Man; though
he bare him no Malice, yet because he saw there was very great
danger, it may reasonably be inferr'd, that he meant to adventure
the killing of some body, or other, though not of him that was
kill'd.

La. He is a Felon also that killeth himself voluntarily, and is called,
not only by Common Lawyers, but also in divers Statute-Laws,
Felo de se.

Ph. And 'tis well so: For names imposed by Statutes are equivalent
to Definitions; but I conceive not how any Man can bear *Animum
felleum*, or so much Malice towards himself, as to hurt himself
voluntarily, much less to kill himself; for naturally, and necessarily the Intention of every Man aimeth at somewhat, which is
good to himself, and tendeth to his preservation: And therefore,
methinks, if he kill himself, it is to be presumed that he is not
compos mentis, but by some inward Torment or Apprehension of

---

39. ⟨1206⟩

somewhat worse than Death, Distracted.

La. Nay, unless he be *compos mentis* he is not *Felo de se* (as Sir *Edw. Coke* saith, [3]⁴⁰ *Inst.* p. 54.) and therefore he cannot be Judged a *Felo de se*, unless it be first proved he was *compos mentis*. |

Ph. How can that be proved of a Man dead; especially if it cannot be
(114) proved by any Witness, that a little before his death he spake as other Men used to do. This is a hard place; and before you take it for Common-Law it had need to be clear'd.

La. I'le think on't. There's a Statute of 3 *Hen.* 7. *c.* 14. which makes it Felony in any of the Kings Houshold-Servants under the degree of a Lord, to Compass the Death of any of the Kings Privy-Council. The words are these; That from henceforth the Steward, Treasurer, and Controuler of the Kings House for that time being, or one of them, have full Authority and Power, to inquire by 12 sad Men, and discreet Persons of the Chequer-Roll of the King's Honourable Houshold[, i]⁴¹f any Servant, admitted to his Servant Sworn, and his name put into the Chequer-Roll, whatsoever he be serving in any manner, Office, or Room, reputed, had, or taken under the State of a Lord, make any Confederacies, Compassings, Conspiracies, or Imaginations with any Person to Destroy, or Murder the King, or any Lord of this Realm, or any other Person sworn to the Kings Council, Steward, Treasurer, or Controuler of the Kings House[; . . .]⁴² And if such Misdoers shall be found Guilty by Confession, or otherwise, that the said Offence shall be Judged Felony.[. . .] |

Ph. It appears by this Statute, that not only the Compassing the
(115) Death (as you say) of a Privy-Councellor, but also of any Lord of this Realm is Felony; if it be done by Any of the Kings Houshold Servants that is not a Lord.

La. No; Sir *Edw. Coke* upon these words, any Lord of this Realm, or other Person Sworn of the Kings Council infers [3]⁴³ *Inst.* p. 38. that is to be understood of such a Lord only as is a Privy-Councellor.

Ph. For barring of the Lords of Parliament from this Priviledge, he strains this Statute a little farther (in my Opinion) than it reacheth of it self. But how are such Felonies to be Tryed?

La. The Indictment is to be found, before the Steward, Treasurer, and Controuler of the Kings House, or one of them, by 12 of the Kings Houshold Servants. The Petit Jury for the Tryal must be

---

40. ⟨4⟩   41. ⟨. I⟩   42. ⟨.⟩   43. ⟨4⟩

12 other of the Kings Servants, and the Judges are again the Steward, Treasurer, and Controuler of the Kings House, or 2 of them; and yet I see that these Men are not usually great Students of the Law.

Ph. You may hereby be assur'd, that either the King and Parliament were very much overseen in choosing such Officers perpetually for the time being, to be Judges in a Tryal at the Common-Law,

(116) or else | that Sir *Edw. Coke* presumes too much, to appropriate all the Judicature, both in Law, and Equity, to the Common-Lawyers; as if neither Lay-Persons, Men of Honour, nor any of the Lords Spiritual, who are the most versed in the Examination of Equity, and Cases of Conscience, when they hear the Statutes Read, and Pleaded, were unfit to Judge of the intention and meaning of the same. I know, that neither such great Persons, nor Bishops have ordinarily so much spare time from their ordinary Employment as to be so skilful as to Plead Causes at the Bar; but certainly they are, especially the Bishops, the best able to Judge of matters of Reason; that is to say (by Sir *Edw. Coke*'s Confession) of matters (except of Blood) at the Common-Law.

La. Another sort of Felony, though without Man-slaughter, is Robbery; and by Sir *Edw. Coke*, [3][44] *Inst.* p. 68. defined thus, Robbery by the Common-Law is a Felony committed by a violent Assault upon the Person of another, by putting him in fear, and taking away from him his Money, or other Goods of any value whatsoever.

Ph. Robbery is not distinguished from Theft by any Statute. *Latrocinium* comprehendeth them both, and both are Felony, and both Punished with Death. And therefore to distinguish them aright

(117) is the work | of Reason only. And the first difference which is obvious to all Men, is, that Robbery is committed by Force, or Terror, of which neither is in Theft; for Theft is a secret Act, and that which is taken by violence, or Terror, either from his Person, or in his Presence is still Robbery; but if it be taken secretly, whether it be by day, or night from his Person, or from his Fold, or from his Pasture, then it is called Theft. 'Tis Force and Fraud only that distinguisheth between Theft, and Robbery, both which are by the Pravity only of the Intention, Felony, in their Nature. But there be so many Evasions of the Law found out by evil Men, that I know not in this Predicament[45] of Felony how to place

---

44. ⟨4⟩   45. category

them: For suppose I go secretly by day, or night, into another Mans Field of Wheat Ripe, and standing, and Loading my Cart with it I carry it away; Is it Theft, or Robbery?

La. Neither; it is but Trespass: But if you first lay down the Wheat you have cut, and then throw it into your Cart, and carry it away, then it is Felony.

Ph. Why so?

La. Sir *Edw. Coke* tells you the Reason of it, [3]⁴⁶ *Inst.* p. 107. for he defineth Theft to be by the Common-Law a Felonious, and fraudulent taking and carrying away by any Man, or Woman, of the (118) meer Personal Goods | of another, not from the Person, nor by night in the House of the owner. From this Definition he Argues thus, p. 109. Any kind of Corn, or Grain growing upon the ground is a Personal Chattel, and the Executors of the owner shall have them, though they be not severed; but yet no Larceny can be Committed of them, because they are annexed to the Realty: So it is of Grass standing on the Ground, or of Apples, or of any Fruit upon the Trees, *&c.* So it is of a Box, or Chest of Charters, no Larceny can be committed of them, because the Charters concern the Realty, and the Box, or Chest, though it be of great value, yet shall it be of the same nature the Charters are of. *Omne magis dignum trahit ad se minus.*⁴⁷

Ph. Is this Definition drawn out of any Statute, or is it in *Bracton*, or *Littleton*, or any other Writer upon the Science of the Laws?

La. No; it is his own; and you may observe by the Logick-Sentences dispersed through his Works, that he was a Logician sufficient enough to make a Definition.

Ph. But if his Definitions must be the Rule of Law; what is there that he may not make Felony, or not Felony, at his Pleasure? But seeing it is not Statute-Law that he says, it must be very perfect (119) Reason, or | else no Law at all; and to me it seems so far from Reason as I think it ridiculous. But let us Examine it. There can (says he) be no Larceny of Corn, Grass, or Fruits that are growing, that is to say, they cannot be stolen; but why? Because they concern the Realty; that is, because they concern the Land. 'Tis true that the Land cannot be stolen, nor the right of a Mans Tenure; but Corn, and Trees, and Fruit, though growing, may be cut down, and carryed away secretly, and Feloniously, in Contempt, and Despight of the Law. And are they not then stolen?

---

46. ⟨4⟩   47. The more considerable draws to itself the less.

And is there any Act which is Feloniously committed, that is not more than Trespass? Can any Man doubt of it that understands the *English* Tongue? 'Tis true, that if a Man pretend a right to the Land, and on that pretence take the Fruits thereof by way of taking Possession of his own, it is no more than a Trespass, unless he conceal the taking of them; for in that one Case, he but puts the Man that was in Possession before to exhibit his complaint, which purpose is not Felonious, but Lawful; for nothing makes a distinction between Felony, and not Felony, but the purpose. I have heard that if a Man slander another with stealing of a Tree standing, there lies no Action for it, and that upon this ground, (120) To steal a standing Tree is impossi-|ble; and that the Cause of the Impossibility is, that a Man's Free-hold cannot be stolen; which is a very obvious Fallacy; for Free-hold signifieth, not only the Tenement, but also the Tenure; and though it be true that a Tenure cannot be stolen, yet every Man sees the standing Trees, and Corn, may easily be stolen; and so far forth as Trees, *&c.* are part of the Freehold, so far forth also they are Personal Goods; for whatsoever is Freehold is Inheritance, and descendeth to the Heir, and nothing can descend to the Executors, but what is meerly Personal. And though a Box, or Case of Evidences are to descend to the Heir, yet unless you can shew me positive Law to the contrary, they shall be taken into the Executors hands, to be delivered to the Heir. Besides, how unconscionable a thing is it, that he that steals a shillings worth of Wood; which the Wind hath blown down, or which lyeth Rotten on the ground, should be Hang'd for it, and he that takes a Tree worth 20 or 40 shillings, should Answer only for the Dammage?

La. 'Tis somewhat hard, but it has been so practised time out of mind. Then follows Sodomy, and Rape, both of them Felonies.

Ph. I know that, and that of the former he justly says it is detestable, (121) being in a man-|ner an Apostacie from Humane Nature: But in neither of them is there any thing of *Animus Felleus.* The Statutes which make them Felony are exposed to all Mens reading; but because Sir *Edw. Coke*'s Commentaries upon them are more diligent and Accurate than to be free from all uncleanness, let us leap over them both, observing only by the way, that he leaves an Evasion for an impotent Offender, though his design be the same, and pursued to the utmost of his Power.

La. Two other great Felonies are breaking, and Burning of Houses, neither of which are defin'd by any Statute. The former of them is by Sir *Edw. Coke.* [3][48] *Inst.* p. 63. Defined thus: Burglary is by the Common-Law, the Breaking and Entring into the Mansion-house of another, in the night with intent to kill some reasonable Creature, or to commit some other Felony within the same, whether his intent be executed, or not; and defineth Night to be then, when one Man cannot know anothers Face by daylight: And for the parts of a Mansion-house he reckoneth all Houses that belong to Housekeeping, as Barns, Stables, Dary-Houses, Buttery, Kitchin, Chambers, &c. But breaking of a House by day, though Felony, and Punished as Burglary, is not within the Statute. |

Ph. I have nothing to say against his Interpretations here, but I like
(122) not that any private Man should presume to determine, whether such, or such a Fact done be within the words of a Statute, or not, where it belongs only to a Jury of 12 Men to declare in their Verdict, whether the Fact laid open before them be Burglary, Robbery, Theft, or other Felony; for this is to give a leading Judgment to the Jury, who ought not to consider any private Lawyers Institutes, but the Statutes themselves pleaded before them for directions.

La. Burning, as he defines it, p. 66. is a Felony at the Common-Law committed by any that maliciously and voluntarily in the night, or day, burneth the House of another: And hereupon infers, if a Man sets Fire to the House, and it takes not, that then it is not within the Statute.

Ph. If a Man should secretly, and maliciously lay a quantity of Gun-Powder under another Mans House, sufficient to Blow it up, and set a Train of Powder in it, and set Fire to the Train, and some Accident hinder the Effect, is not this Burning? or what is it? What Crime? It is neither Treason, nor Murder, nor Burglary, nor Robbery, nor Theft, nor (no dammage being made) any Trespass, nor contrary to any Statute. And yet (seeing the Common-Law is
(123) the | Law of Reason) it is a sin, and such a sin as a Man may be Accused of, and Convicted, and consequently a Crime committed of Malice prepensed; shall he not then be Punished for the Attempt? I grant you that a Judge has no Warrant from any Statute-Law, Common Law, or Commission to appoint the Punishment; but surely the King has power to Punish him (on this side of Life or Member) as he please; and with the Assent of

---

48. ⟨4⟩

La. Parliament (if not without) to make the Crime for the future Capital.

La. I know not. Besides these Crimes there is Conjuration, Witchcraft, Sorcery and Inchantment, which are Capital by the Statute, 1 of King *James*, *cap.* 12.

Ph. But I desire not to discourse of that Subject; for though without doubt there is some great Wickedness signified by those Crimes; yet I have ever found my self too dull to conceive the nature of them, or how the Devil hath power to do many things which Witches have been Accused of. Let us now come to Crimes not Capital.

La. Shall we pass over the Crime of Heresie, which Sir *Edw. Coke* ranketh before Murder, but the consideration of it will be somewhat long.

Ph. Let us defer it till the Afternoon. |

(124)   *Of Heresie.*

La. CONCERNING HERESIE, SIR EDW. COKE, [3][1] INST. P. 39. says, that 5 things fall into consideration. 1. Who be the Judges of Heresie. 2. What shall be Judged Heresie. 3. What is the Judgment upon a Man Convicted of Heresie. 4. What the Law alloweth him to save his Life. 5. What he shall forfeit by Judgment against him.

Ph. The principal thing to be considered, which is the Heresie it self, he leaveth out; *viz.* What it is, in what Fact, or Words it consisteth, what Law it violateth, Statute-Law, or the Law of Reason. The Cause why he omitteth it, may perhaps be this; that it was not only out of his Profession, but also out of his other Learning. Murder, Robbery, Theft, *&c.* Every Man knoweth to be evil, and are Crimes defined by the Statute-Law, so that any Man may avoid them, if he will. But who can be sure to avoid Heresie, if he but dare to give an Account of his Faith, unless he know beforehand what it is?

La. In the Preamble of the Statute of the 2d, *Hen.* 4. *cap.* 15. Heresie is laid down, as a Preaching or Writing of such Doctrine, as is contrary to the determination of Holy Church. |

---

1. ⟨4⟩

Ph. Then it is Heresie at this day to Preach, or Write against Wor-
(125) shipping of Saints, or the Infallibility of the Church of *Rome*, or
any other determination of the same Church: For Holy-Church,
at that time, was understood to be the Church of *Rome*, and now
with us the Holy-Church I understand to be the Church of
England; and the Opinions in that Statute are now, and were then
the true Christian Faith. Also the same Statute of *Hen.* 4. De-
clareth, by the same Preamble, that the Church of *England* had
never been troubled with Heresie.

La. But that Statute is Repeal'd.

Ph. Then also is the Declaration, or Definition of Heresie repeal'd.

La. What, say you, is Heresie?

Ph. I say Heresie is a singularity of Doctrine, or Opinion contrary to
the Doctrine of another Man, or Men, and the word properly
signifies the Doctrine of a Sect, which Doctrine is taken upon
Trust of some Man of Reputation for Wisdom, that was the first
Author of the same. If you will understand the truth hereof, you
are to Read the Histories and other Writings of the Antient
Greeks, whose word it is, which Writings are extant in these days,
and easie to be had. Wherein you will find, that in, and a little
(126) before the time of *Alexander* the | Great; there lived in *Greece*
many Excellent Wits, that employed their time in search of the
Truth in all manner of Sciences worthy of their Labour, and
which to their great Honour and Applause published their Writings; some concerning Justice, Laws, and Government, some
concerning Good, and Evil Manners, some concerning the
Causes of things Natural, and of Events discernable by sense; and
some of all these Subjects. And of the Authors of these, the
Principal were *Pythagoras*, *Plato*, *Zeno*, *Epicurus* and *Aristotle*, Men
of deep and laborious Meditation, and such as did not get their
Bread by their Philosophy, but were able to live of their own,
and were in Honour with Princes, and other great Personages.
But these Men, though above the rest in Wisdom yet their
Doctrine in many points did disagree; whereby it came to pass,
that such Men as studied their Writings, inclined, some to *Pythagoras*, some to *Plato*, some to *Aristotle*, some to *Zeno*, and some to
Epicurus. But Philosophy it self was then so much in Fashion, as
that every Rich Man endeavour'd to have his Children educated
in the Doctrine of some, or other of these Philosophers, which
were for their Wisdom so much renown'd. Now those that
followed *Pythagoras*, were called *Pythagoreans*; those that followed

(127) *Plato, Academicks*; those that | followed *Zeno, Stoicks*; those that followed *Epicurus, Epicureans*, and those that followed *Aristotle, Peripateticks*, which are the names of Heresie in *Greek*, which signifies no more but taking of an Opinion; and the said *Pythagoreans, Academicks, Stoicks, Peripateticks, &c.* were termed by the names of so many several Heresies. All Men (you know) are subject to Error, and the ways of Error very different; and therefore 'tis no wonder if these Wise, and diligent searchers of the Truth did, notwithstanding their Excellent parts, differ in many points amongst themselves. But this Laudable Custom of Great, Wealthy Persons to have their Children at any price to learn Philosophy, suggested to many idle and needy Fellows, an easie and compendious way of Maintenance; which was to Teach the Philosophy, some of *Plato*, some of *Aristotle, &c.* Whose Books to that end they Read over, but without Capacity, or much Endeavour to examine the Reasons of their Doctrines, taking only the Conclusions, as they lay; and setting up with this, they soon professed themselves Philosophers, and got to be the School-Masters to the Youth of *Greece*; but by Competition for such Employment, they hated and reviled one another with all the bitter Terms

(128) they could invent; and very often, when upon Occa-|sion they were in Civil Company, fell first to Disputation, and then to Blows, to the great trouble of the Company, and their own shame. Yet amongst all their reproachful words the name of Heretick came never in, because they were all equally Hereticks, their Doctrine not being theirs, but taken upon Trust from the aforesaid Authors. So that though we find Heresie often mentioned in *Lucian*, and other Heathen Authors, yet we shall not find in any of them *Hæreticus* for a Heretick. And this Disorder among the Philosophers continued a long time in *Greece*, and Infecting also the *Romans*, was at the greatest in the times of the Apostles, and in the Primitive Church, till the time of the Nicene Council, and somewhat after. But at last the Authority of the *Stoicks* and *Epicureans* was not much Esteemed, only *Plato's* and *Aristotle's* Philosophy were much in Credit; *Plato's* with the better fort, that founded their Doctrine upon the Conceptions and Ideas of things, and *Aristotle's* with those that reasoned only from the names of Things, according to the Scale of the *Categories*: Nevertheless there were always, though not New Sects of Philosophy, yet New Opinions continually arising. |

La. But how came the word Heretick to be a Reproach?

Ph. Stay a little. After the Death of our Saviour his Apostles, and his
(129) Disciples, as you know, dispersed themselves into several parts
of the World to Preach the Gospel, and converted much People,
especially in *Asia* the less, in *Greece* and *Italy*, where they Constituted many Churches; and as they Travelled from place to
place, left Bishops to Teach and Direct those their Converts, and
to appoint Presbyters under them to Assist them therein, and to
Confirm them by setting forth the Life, and Miracles of our
Saviour, as they had receiv'd it from the Writings of the Apostles
and Evangelists; whereby (and not by the Authority of *Plato*, or
Aristotle, or any other Philosopher) they were to be Instructed.
Now you cannot doubt but that among so many Heathens, converted in the time of the Apostles, there were Men of all Pro-
fessions, and Dispositions, and some that had never thought of
Philosophy at all, but were intent upon their Fortunes, or their
Pleasures; and some that had a greater, some a lesser use of
Reason; and some that had studied Philosophy, but professed it
not, which were commonly the Men of the better Rank; and some
had Professed it only for their better Abstinence,[2] and had it not |
(130) farther, than readily to talk and wrangle; and some were Christians in good earnest, and others but Counterfeit, intending to
make use of the Charity of those that were sincere Christians,
which in those times was very great. Tell[3] me now of these sorts
of Christians which was the most likely to afford the fittest Men
to propagate the Faith by Preaching, and Writing, or Publick or
private Disputation; that is to say, who were fittest to be made
Presbyters and Bishops?

La. Certainly those who (*cæteris paribus*) could make the best use of
Aristotle's Rhetorick, and Logick.

Ph. And who were the most prone to Innovation?

La. They that were most confident of *Aristotle*'s, and *Plato*'s (their
former Masters) Natural Philosophy: For they would be the
aptest to wrest the Writings of the Apostles, and all Scriptures to
the Doctrine in which their Reputation was engag'd.

Ph. And from such Bishops and Priests, and other Sectaries it was,
that Heresie, amongst the Christians, first came to be a Reproach:
For no sooner had one of them Preached, or Published any

---

2. *Sic.*

3. This sentence and the following three speeches should be compared with
Locke's preface to his (posthumously published) interpretations and paraphrases of five of the Epistles.

Doctrine that displeased, either the most, or the most Leading Men of the rest, but it became such a Quarrel as not to be decided, but (131) by a | Council of the Bishops in the Province where they Lived; wherein he that would not submit to the General Decree, was called an Heretick, as one that would not relinquish the Philosophy of his Sect; the rest of the Council gave themselves the name of Catholicks, and to their Church, the name of Catholick Church. And thus came up the opposite Terms of Catholick and Heretick.

La. I understand how it came to be a Reproach, but not how it follows that every Opinion condemned by a Church that is, or calls it self Catholick, must needs be an Error, or a Sin. The Church of *England* denies that Consequence, and that Doctrine as they hold cannot be proved to be Erroneous, but by the Scripture, which cannot Err; but the Church, being but men, may both Err, and Sin.

Ph. In this Case we must consider also that Error, in it's own Nature, is no Sin: For it is Impossible for a Man to Err on purpose, he cannot have an Intention to Err; and nothing is Sin, unless there be a sinful Intention; much less are such Errors Sins, as neither hurt the Common-wealth, nor any private Man, nor are against any Law Positive, or Natural; such Errors as were those for which Men were burnt in the time when the Pope had the Government of this Church. |

La. Since you have told me how Heresie came to be a name, tell me (132) also how it came to be a Crime? And what were the Heresies that first were made Crimes?

Ph. Since the Christian Church could declare, and none else, what Doctrine were Heresies, but had no power to make Statutes for the punishment of Hereticks before they had a Christian King; it is manifest that Heresie could not be made a Crime before the first Christian Emperor, which was *Constantine* the Great. In his time one *Arius* a Priest of *Alexandria* in Dispute with his Bishop, Publickly denied the Divinity of Christ, and Maintained it afterwards in the Pulpit, which was the Cause of a Sedition, and much Blood shed, both of Citizens, and Souldiers in that City. For the preventing of the like for the time to come, the Emperor called a General Council of Bishops to the City of *Nice*, who being met, he exhorted them to agree upon a Confession of the Christian Faith, promising whatsoever they agreed on he would cause to be observed.

La. By the way, the Emperor (I think) was here a little too Indifferent.

Ph. In this Council was Established so much of the Creed we now use, and call the *Nicene* Creed, as reacheth to the words, *I believe* (133) *in the Holy Ghost.* The rest was E-|stablished by the 3 General Councils next succeeding. By the words of which Creed almost all the Heresies then in being, and especially the Doctrine of *Arius*, were Condemn'd: So that now all Doctrines Published by Writing, or by Word, and repugnant to this Confession of the first four General Councils, and contained in the *Nicene* Creed were, by the Imperial Law forbidding them, made Crimes; such as are that of *Arius* denying the Divinity of Christ; that of *Eutiches* denying the 2 Natures of Christ; that of the *Nestorians* denying the Divinity of the Holy Ghost; that of the *Anthropomorphites*, that of the *Manichees*, that of the *Anabaptists*, and many other.

La. What Punishment had *Arius*?

Ph. At the first for refusing to Subscribe, he was deprived and Banished; but afterwards having satisfied the Emperor concerning his future Obedience (for the Emperor caused this Confession to be made, not for the regard of Truth of Doctrine, but for the preserving of the Peace, especially among his Christian Souldiers, by whose valour he had gotten the Empire, and by the same was to preserve it) he was received again into Grace, but dyed before he could repossess his Benefice. But after the time of those Councils, the Imperial Law made the Punishment for Heresie to (134) be Capital, though | the manner of the Death was left to the *Præfects* in their several Jurisdictions; and thus it continued till somewhat after the time of the Emperor *Frederick Barbarossa*, and the Papacy having gotten the upper hand of the Emperor, brought in the use of Burning both Hereticks, and Apostates; and the Popes from time to time made Heresie of many other points of Doctrine, (as they saw it conduce to the setting up of the Chair above the Throne) besides those determined in the *Nicene* Creed, and brought in the use of Burning; and according to this Papal-Law there was an Apostate Burnt at *Oxford* in the time of *William* the Conqueror for turning *Jew*. But of a Heretick Burnt in *England* there is no mention made till after the Statute of 2 *Hen.* 4. Whereby some followers of *Wiclif* (called *Lollards*) were afterwards Burned, and that for such Doctrines, as by the Church of *England*, ever since the first year of Queen *El.* have been approved for Godly Doctrines, and no doubt were Godly then; and so you see how many have been Burnt for Godliness.

La. 'Twas not well done; but 'tis no wonder we read of no Hereticks before the time of *H*. 4. For in the Preamble to that Statute it is intimated, that before those *Lollards* there never was any Heresie in *England*. |

Ph. I think so too; for we have been the tamest Nation to the Pope of
(135) all the World. But what Statutes concerning Heresie have there been made since?

La. The Statute of 2 *H*. 5. *c*. 7. which adds to the Burning the Forfeiture of Lands, and Goods, and then no more till the 25 *H*. 8. *c*. 14. which confirms the two former and giveth some new Rules concerning how they shall be Proceeded with. But by the Statute of 1 *Ed*. 6. *cap*. 12. All Acts of Parliament formerly made to punish any manner of Doctrine concerning Religion are repeal'd. For therein it is ordain'd, after divers Acts specified; that all and every other Act, or Acts of Parliament concerning Doctrine, or matters of Religion, and all, and every Branch, Article, Sentence and Matter, Pains and Forfeitures contained, mentioned, or any wise declared in the same Acts of Parliament or Statutes shall be from henceforth Repealed, utterly void, and of none effect. So that in the time of King *Ed*. 6. not only all Punishments of Heresie were taken away, but also the Nature of it was changed, to what Originally it was, a Private Opinion. Again in [1 and 2][4] *Phil*. and *Ma*. those former Statutes of 2 *H*. 4. *cap*. 15. 2 *H*. 5. *Cap*. [7][5]. 25. *H*. 8, *cap*. 14.[6] are Revived, and the Branch of 1 *Ed*. 6. *cap*. 12.
(136) touching Doctrine (though not specially | named) [repealed; but another effect][7] seemeth to be this, that the same Statute confirmeth the Statute of 25 *Ed*. 3. concerning Treasons. Lastly, in

---

4. ⟨12⟩   5. ⟨17⟩

6. 1 & 2 Phil. & M. c. 6 revived 5 Rich. 2 St. 2 c. 5 and 2 Hen. 4 c. 15 and 2 Hen. 5 c. 7; but 25 Hen. 8 c. 14 does not appear.

7. The words "and the Branch of 1 Ed. 6. cap 12 . . . 25 Ed. 3 concerning Treasons" are confused, presumably through printing error. The words cannot mean that the part of 1 Edw. 6 touching heresy was among the statutes revived by 1 & 2 Phil. & M. c. 6, partly because there was no need to "revive" it, but more emphatically because it was in fact repealed by 1 & 2 Phil. & M. c. 6 through that Act's revival of law repealed by 1 Edw. 6. It is further true that in the section of 1 Edw. 6. c. 12 preceding the section on doctrine and heresy, the legislation on treason was returned to the state in which it had been put by 25 Edw. 3, which enables us to understand Hobbes to mean 1 Edw. 6 c. 12 when he uses the words "the same Statute" in the expression "the same Statute confirmeth the Statute of 25 Ed. 3 concerning Treasons." The suggested emendation of the text is based on these considerations.

the first year of Queen *Eliz. cap.* 1. the aforesaid Statutes of Queen *Mary* are taken away, and thereby the Statute of 1 *Ed.* [6] *cap.* 12. Revived; so as there was no Statute left for the Punishment of Hereticks. But Queen *Eliz.* by the Advice of her Parliament gave a Commission (which was called the High-Commission) to certain Persons (amongst whom were very many of the Bishops) to Declare what should be Heresie for the future; but with a Restraint, that they should Judge nothing to be Heresie, but what had been so declared in the first four General Councils.

Ph. From this which you have shewed me, I think we may proceed to the Examination of the Learned Sir *Edw. Coke* concerning Heresie. In his Chapter of Heresie, 3 *Inst.* p. 40. he himself confesseth, that no Statute against Heresie stood then in force: when in the 9th year of King *James*, *Bartholomew Legat* was Burnt for *Arianism*, and that from the Authority of the Act of 2 *Hen.* 4. *cap.* 15. and other Acts cited in the Margin, it may be gather'd, that the Diocesan hath the Jurisdiction of Heresie. This I say is not true: For as to Acts of Parliament it is manifest, that from Acts

(137) Repea-|led; that is to say, from things that have no being, there can be gathered nothing. And as to the other Authorities in the Margin, *Fitzherbert*, and the Doctor and Student, they say no more than what was Law in the time when they writ; that is, when the Popes Usurped Authority was here obeyed: But if they had Written this in the time of King *Ed.* 6. or Queen *Elizabeth*, Sir *Edw. Coke* might as well have citied his own Authority, as theirs; for their Opinions had no more the force of Laws than his. Then he cites this Precedent of *Legat*, and another of *Hammond* in the time of Queen *Elizabeth*; but Precedents prove only what was done, and not what was well done. What Jurisdiction could the Diocesan then have of Heresie, when by the Statute of *Ed.* 6. *cap.* 12. then in force, there was no Heresie, and all Punishment for Opinions forbidden: For Heresie is a Doctrine contrary to the Determination of the Church, but then the Church had not Determined any thing at all concerning Heresie.

La. But seeing the High Commissioners had Power to Correct, and Amend Heresies, they must have Power to cite such as were Accused of Heresie, to appear before them, or else they could not execute their Commission. |

Ph. If they had first made, and published a Declaration of what
(138) Articles they made Heresie, that when one Man heard another speak against their Declaration, he might thereof inform the

Commissioners, then indeed they had Power to cite, and imprison the Person accus'd; but before they had known what should be Heresie; how was it possible that one Man should accuse another? And before he be accused, how can he be cited?

La. Perhaps it was taken for granted, that whatsoever was contrary to any of the 4 first General Councils, was to be judged Heresie.

Ph. That granted, yet I see not how one Man might accuse another 'ere the better for those Councils. For not one Man of ten thousand had ever read them, nor were they ever Published in *English*, that a Man might avoid Offending against them, nor perhaps are they extant; nor if those that we have Printed in *Latin* are the very Acts of the Councils (which is yet much disputed amongst Divines) do I think it fit they were put in the Vulgar Tongues. But it is not likely that the makers of the Statutes had any purpose to make Heresie of whatsoever was repugnant to those 4 General Councils: For if they had, I believe the Anabaptists, of which (139) there was great plen-|ty in those times, would one time or other have been question'd upon this Article of the Nicene Creed, *I believe one Baptism for the Remission of sins*; nor was the Commission it self for a long time after Registred, that Men might in such uncertainty take heed and abstain (for their better safety) from speaking of Religion any thing at all. But by what Law was this Heretick *Legat* burnt? I grant he was an *Arian*, and his Heresie contrary to the Determination of the Church of *England*, in the Highest Points of Christianity; but seeing there was no Statute-Law to burn him, and [the][8] Penalty forbidden, by what Law, by what Authority was he burn't?

La. That this *Legat* was accused of Heresie, was no fault of the High Commissioners, but when he was accused, it had been a fault in them not to have examin'd him, or having examin'd him, and found him an *Arian*, not to have judged him so, or not to have certified him so. All this they did, and this was all that belonged unto them; they medled not with his Burning, but left him to the Secular Power to do with him what they pleased.

Ph. Your Justification of the Commissioners is nothing to the Question; the Question is by what Law he was burn't, the Spiritual- (140) Law gives no Sentence of Tem-|poral Punishment, and Sir *Edw. Coke* confesseth that, he could not be burned, and Burning forbidden by Statute-Law. By what Law then was he burned?

---

8. ⟨no⟩

La. By the Common-Law.

Ph. What's that? It is not Custom; for before the time of *Henry* the 4th, there was no such Custom in *England*; for if there had, yet those Laws that came after were but Confirmations of the Customs, and therefore the Repealing of those Laws was a Repealing of the Custom. For when King *Ed.* the 6th, and Queen *Eliz.* abolished those Statutes, they abolished all Pains, and consequently, Burning, or else they had abolished nothing. And if you will say he was burn't by the Law of Reason, you must tell me how there can be Proportion between Doctrine and Burning; there can be no Equality, nor Majority, nor Minority Assigned between them. The Proportion that is between them, is the Proportion of the Mischief which the Doctrine maketh, to the Mischief to be Inflicted on the Doctor; and this is to be measur'd only by him that hath the charge of Governing the People, and consequently, the Punishing of Offences can be determined by none but by the King, and that, if it extend to life or member, with the Assent of Parliament. |

La. He does not draw any Argument for it from Reason, but alledgeth
(141) for it this Judgment executed upon *Legat*, and a story out of *Hollingshed*, and *Stow*: But I know that neither History, nor Precedent will pass with you for Law. And though there be a Writ *de hæretico comburendo* in the Register (as you may Read in *Fitzherbert*)[9] grounded upon the Statutes of 2 *H.* 4. *cap.* 15. and 2 *H.* 5. *cap.* 7. yet seeing those Statutes are void, you will say the Writ is also void.

Ph. Yes indeed will I. Besides this, I understand not how that is true that he saith; that the Diocesan hath Jurisdiction of Heresie, and that so it was put in ure in all Queen *Elizabeths* Reign; whereas by the Statute[10] it is manifest, that all Jurisdiction spiritual, was given under the Queen, to the High Commissioners, how then could any one Diocesan have any part thereof without deputation from them, which by their Letters Patents they could not grant, nor was it reasonable they should: For the Trust was not committed to the Bishops only, but also to divers Lay-Persons, who might have an Eye upon their Proceedings, lest they should Incroach upon the power Temporal. But at this day there is neither Statute, nor any Law to Punish Doctrine, but the ordinary Power Ecclesiastical, and that | according to the Canons of the Church of

---

9. *Nat. Brev.*, § de haeretico comburendo.   10. 1 Eliz. c. 1 (36).

England, only Authorized by the King, the High Commission being long since abolished. Therefore let us come now to such Causes Criminal, as are not Capital.

Of Præmunire.

La. THE GREATEST OFFENCE NOT CAPITAL IS THAT WHICH is done against the Statute of Proviso[r]¹s.

Ph. You have need to expound this.

La. This Crime is not unlike to that for which a Man is outlawed, when he will not come in and submit himself to the Law; saving that in Outlawries there is a long Process to precede it; and he that is outlawed, is put out of the Protection of the Law. But for the Offence against the Statute of Provisors (which is called *Præmunire facias* from the words in the Original Writ) if the Offender submit not himself to the Law within the space of 2 Months after notice, he is presently an Outlaw: and this Punishment (if not Capital) is equivalent to Capital: For he lives secretly at the Mercy of those that know where he is, and cannot without the like Peril to themselves, but discover him. And it has been much disputed before the time of Queen *Elizabeth,* whether he
(143) might not be lawful-|ly killed by any Man that would, as one might kill a Wolf: It is like the Punishment amongst the old *Romans* of being barred the use of Fire and Water, and like the great Excommunication in the Papacy, when a Man might not eat, or drink with the Offender without incurring the like Penalty.

Ph. Certainly the Offence for which this Punishment was first Ordained, was some abominable Crime, or of extraordinary Mischief.

La. So it was: For the Pope, you know, from long before the Conquest, incroached every day upon the Power Temporal. Whatsoever could be made to seem to be *in ordine ad Spiritualia* was in every Commonwealth claimed, and haled to the Jurisdiction of the *Pope*: And for that end in every Country he had his Court Ecclesiastical, and there was scarce any cause Temporal, which he could not, by one shift or other, hook into his Jurisdiction, in such sort as to have it tryed in his own Courts at *Rome*, or in *France*, or in *England* it self. By which means the Kings Laws were

1. ⟨e⟩

not regarded, Judgments given in the Kings Courts were avoided, and presentations to Bishopricks, Abbies, and other Benefices (founded, and endowed by the Kings, and Nobility of *England*)
(144) were bestowed by the *Pope* upon | strangers, or such (as with Money in their Purses) could travel to *Rome*, to provide themselves of such Benefices. And suitably hereunto, when there was a Question about a Tythe, or a Will, though the point were meerly Temporal, yet the Popes Court here would fetch them in, or else one of the Parties would appeal to *Rome*. Against these Injuries of the *Roman* Church, and to maintain the Right and Dignity of the Crown of *England*, *Ed.* [3][2] made a Statute concerning Provisors (that is, such as provide themselves with Benefices here from *Rome*) for in the 25th year of his Reign he ordained in a full Parliament that the Right of Election of Bishops, and Right of Advowsans, and Presentations belonged to himself, and to the Nobility that were the founders of such Bishopricks, Abbies, and other Benefices. And he enacted farther, that if any Clerk, which he, or any of his Subjects should present, should be disturbed by any such Provisor that such Provisor, or Disturber should be attached by his Body, and if Convicted, lye in Prison till he were Ransomed at the Kings Will, and had satisfied the Party griev'd, renounced his Title, and found sureties not to sue for it any farther; and that if they could not be found, then Exigents should go forth to Outlawrie, and the Profits of the Benefice in the mean
(145) time be taken into the | Kings hands. And the same Statute is confirmed in the 27th year of King *Ed.* the 3d, which Statute alloweth to these Provisors six weeks Day to appear, but if they appear before they be outlaw'd, they shall be received to make Answer, but if they render not themselves, they shall forfeit all their Lands, Goods, and Chattels, besides that they stand outlaw'd. The same Law is confirmed again by 16 *Rich.* 2d. *cap.* 5. in which is added (because these Provisors obtained sometimes from the *Pope*, that such *English* Bishops as according to the Law were instituted, and inducted by the Kings Presentees should be excommunicated) that for this also both they, and the Receivers and Publishers of such Papal Process, and the Procurers should have the same Punishment.

Ph. Let me see the Statute it self of 27 *Ed.* 3.

---

2. ⟨1⟩ The Statute of Provisors, 25 Edw. 3, refers in its preamble to 35 Edw. 1, the so-called Statute of Carlisle, which regulated the contact of the English church with the church abroad.

La. It lies there before you set down *verbatim* by Sir *Edw. Coke* himself,[3] both in *English*, and *French*.

Ph. 'Tis well, we are now to consider what it means, and whether it be well, or ill interpreted by Sir *Edw. Coke*. And first it appeareth by the Preamble (which Sir *Edw. Coke* acknowledgeth[4] to be the best Interpreter of the Statute) that this Statute was made against (146) the Incroachments only | of the Church of *Rome*, upon the Right of the King, and other Patrons to collate Bishopricks and other Benefices within the Realm of *England*, and against the power of the Courts Spiritual, to hold Plea of Controversies determinable in any of the Courts of the King, or to reverse any Judgment there given, as being things that tend to the Disherison of the King, and Destruction of the Common-Law of the Realm always used. Put the case now that a Man had procur'd the *Pope* to reverse a Decree in Chancery, had he been within the danger of Premunire?

La. Yes certainly; or if the Judgment had been given in the Court of the Lord Admiral, or in any other Kings Court whatsoever, either of Law, or Equity; for Courts of Equity are most properly Courts of the Common-Law of *England*, because Equity, and Common-Law (as Sir *Ed. Coke* says) are all one.[5]

Ph. Then the word Common-Law is not in this Preamble restrained to such Courts only where the Tryal is by Juries, but comprehends all the Kings Temporal Courts, if not also the Courts of those Subjects that are Lords of great Mannors.

La. 'Tis very likely, yet I think it will not by every Man be granted. |

Ph. The Statute also says; That they who draw Men out of the Realm (147) in Plea, whereof the Cognizance pertaineth to the Kings Court, or of things whereof Judgment is given in the Kings Court, are within the Cases of Premunire. But what if one Man draw another to *Lambeth* in Plea, whereof Judgment is already given at *Westminster*. Is he by this Clause involv'd in a Premunire?

La. Yes: For though it be not out of the Realm, yet it is within the meaning of the Statute, because the *Popes* Court, not the Kings Court, was then perhaps at *Lambeth*.

Ph. But in Sir *Edw. Coke*'s time the Kings Court was at *Lambeth*, and not the Popes.

La. You know well enough, that the Spiritual-Court has no power to hold Pleas of Common-Law.

---

3. 3 *Inst.* chap. 54.   4. 1 *Inst.* fol. 19b.   5. 1 *Inst.* fol. 97b.

Ph. I do so; but I know not for what cause any simple Man that mistakes his right Court, should be out of the Kings Protection, lose his Inheritance, and all his Goods Personal, and Real; and if taken, be kept in Prison all his Life. This Statute cannot be by Sir *Edw. Cokes* Torture made to say it. Besides, such Men are ignorant in what Courts they are to seek their Remedy: And it is a Custom

(148) confirmed by perpetual usage, that such ignorant Men should | be guided by their Council at Law. It is manifest therefore, that the makers of the Statute intended not to prohibit Men from their suing for their Right, neither in the Chancery, nor in the Admiralty, nor in any other Court, except the Ecclesiastical Courts, which had their Jurisdiction from the Church of *Rome*. Again, where the Statute says, "which do sue in any other Court, or defeat a Judgment in the Kings Court," what is the meaning of another Court? Another Court than what? Is it here meant the Kings-Bench, or Court of Common-Pleas? Does a Premunire lye for every Man that sues in Chancery, for that which might be remedied in the Court of Common-Pleas? Or can a Premunire lye by this Statute against the Lord Chancellor?[6] The Statute lays it only on the Party that sueth, not upon the Judge which holdeth the Plea. Nor could it be laid neither by this Statute, nor by the Statute of 16 *Rich.* 2. upon the Judges, which were then punishable only by the Popes Authority. Seeing then the Party Suing has a just excuse upon the Council of his Lawyer; and the Temporal Judge, and the Lawyer both are out of the Statute, the punishment of the Premunire can light upon no body.

La. But Sir *Edw. Coke* in this same Chapter bringeth two Precedents
(149) to prove, that | though the Spiritual-Courts in *England* be now the Kings Courts, yet whosoever sueth in them for any thing tryable by the Common-Law, shall fall into a Premunire. One is, that whereas in the 22d of *Hen.* 8. all the Clergy of *England* in a Convocation by publick Instrument acknowledged the King to be Supream Head of the Church of *England*; yet after this, *viz.* 24 of *H.* 8. this Statute was in force.

Ph. Why not? A Convocation of the Clergy could not alter the Right of Supremacie; their Courts were still the *Popes* Courts. The other Precedent in the 25th of *Hen.* 8. of the Bishop of *Norwich* may have the same Answer, for the King was not declared Head of the

---

6. For an account of the very concrete matter to which Hobbes is referring here, see Bacon's letter (no. 128) to James I, dated 21 February 1615, in Bacon's *Works* (1740), 4:610 ff.; also Introd. p. 39 above.

Church by Act of Parliament, till the 26th year of his Reign. If he had not mistrusted his own Law, he would not have laid hold on so weak a Proof as these Precedents. And as to the Sentence of Premunire upon the Bishop of *Norwich*, neither doth this Statute, nor that other of R. 2. warrant it; he was sentenced for threatning to excommunicate a Man which had sued another before the Mayor: But this Statute forbids not that, but forbids the bringing in, or publishing of Excommunications, or other Process from *Rome*, or any other Place. Before the 26 *Hen.* 8. there is no Ques-
(150) tion, but that for a Suit in the | Spiritual Court here in a Temporal Cause, there lay a Premunire; and if perhaps some Judge or other hath since that time judged otherwise, his Judgment was erroneous.

La. Nay but by the Statute of 16 *Rich.* 2. *cap.* 5. it appeareth to the contrary, as Sir *Edw. Coke* here will shew you. The effect (saith he) of the Statute of *Rich.* 2. is; That if any Pursue, or cause to be Pursued in the Court of *Rome*, or elsewhere any thing which toucheth the King, against him, his Crown, or Regality, or his Realm, they, their Notaries, *&c.* shall be out of the Kings Protection.

Ph. I pray you let me know the very words of the Statutes as they ly.

La. Presently. The words are, *If any Man Purchase, or Pursue, or cause to be Purchased, or Pursued in the Court of* Rome, *or elsewhere, any such Translations, Processes and Sentences of Excommunication, Bulls, Instruments, or any other things whatsoever, which touch the King, against him, his Crown, and his Regality, or his Realm, as is aforesaid,* &c.

Ph. If a Man bring a Plea of Common-Law into the Spiritual Court, which is now the Kings Court, and the Judge of this Spiritual Court hold Plea thereof: By what Construction can you draw it
(151) within the | compass of the words you have now read. To sue for my Right in the Kings Court, is no pursuing of Translations of Bishopricks made, or procur'd in the Court of *Rome*, or any place else, but only in the Court of the King, nor is this the suit against the King, nor his Crown, nor his Regality, nor his Realm, but the contrary. Why then is it a Premunire? No. He that brings in, or setteth out a Writing in any place whatsoever, wherein is contained, that the King hath so given away his Jurisdiction, as that if a Subject be condemned falsly, his Submission to the Kings Judgment is of none effect; or that the King upon no necessity whatsoever can, out of Parliament time raise Money for the defence of the Kingdom, is, in my opinion, much more within the Statute of Provisors, than they which begin suit for a Tem-

poral Matter in a Court Spiritual. But what Argument has he for this Law of his (since the Statute Law fails him) from the Law of Reason.

La. He says they are called [other] Courts, either because they proceed by the Rules of other Laws, as by the Canon, or Civil Law, or by other Tryals than the Common Law doth Warrant: For the Tryals Warranted by the Law of *England* for matter of Fact, is by verdict of 12 Men before the Judges of the Common Law, in matters

(152) pertaining | to the Common Law, and not upon Examination of Witnesses, as in the Court of Equity; so that *Alia Curia* is either that which is govern'd *per aliam Legem*, or which draweth the Party *ad aliud Examen*. For if————

Ph. Stop there. Let us consider of this you have read, for the Tryal warranted by the Law of *England,* is by Verdict of 12 Men. What means he here by the Law of *England*? Does it not warrant the Tryals in Chancery, and in the Court of Admiralty by Witnesses?

La. By the Law of *England* he means the Law used in the Kings Bench; that is to say, the Common-Law.

Ph. This is just as if he had said, that these two Courts did warrant their own way of Tryal; but other Courts not so, but were warranted by the King only, the Courts of Common Law were Warrants to themselves: You see that *alia Curia* is this way ill expounded. In the Courts of Common Law all Tryals are by 12 Men, who are Judges of the Fact; and the Fact known and prov'd, the Judges are to pronounce the Law; but in the Spiritual Court, the Admiralty, and in all the Courts of Equity there is but one Judge, both of Fact, and of Law; this is all the difference. If this

(153) difference be intended by the Statute by *alia* | *Curia*, there would be a Premunire for suing in a Court, being[7] the Kings Court: The Kings Bench, and Court of Common Pleas may also be different kinds of Courts, because the Process is different; but 'tis plain that this Statute doth not distinguish Courts otherwise than into the Courts of the King, and into the Courts of the Forraign States, and Princes. And seeing you stand upon the name of a Jury for the distinguishing of Courts, what difference do you find between

---

7. ⟨not⟩ The Philosopher's argument is that if trial warranted by the law of England means trial by jury, then trial before a judge without jury would be trial warranted only by the king. Premunire for suing out of a jury jurisdiction would then be premunire for suing into the jurisdiction of the king. But premunire is the penalty for suing out of the jurisdiction of the king. For this reason, the deletion of "not" is suggested.

the Tryals at the Common-Law, and the Tryals in other Courts? You know that in Tryals of Fact naturally, and through all the World the Witnesses are Judges, and it is impossible to be otherwise. What then in *England* can a Jury judge of, except it be of the sufficiency of the Testimony. The Justices have nothing to judge of, nor do, but after the Fact is proved, to declare the Law, which is not Judgment, but Jurisdiction. Again, though the Tryal be in Chancery, or in the Court of Civil Law, 1.[8] The Witnesses are still Judges of the Fact, and he that hath the Commission to hear the Cause hath both the parts; that is to say, of a Jury to judge of the Testimony, and of a Justice to declare the Law. In this, I say, lyes all the difference, which is indeed enough
(154) to make a Dispute (as the World goes) about Jurisdiction: | But seeing it tends neither to the Disherison of the King, nor of the People, nor to the subversion of the Law of Reason, *i. e.* of Common-Law, nor to the subversion of Justice, nor to any harm of the Realm, without some of which these Statutes are not broken, it cannot be a Premunire.

La. Let me read on.[9] For if the Freehold Inheritances, Goods and Chattels, Debts and Duties, wherein the King and Subject have Right and Property by the Common-Law, should be judged *per aliam Legem*, or be drawn *ad aliud Examen*, the 3 Mischiefs afore exprest, would follow; *viz.* the [disherison][10] of the King, and his Crown, the Disherison of his People, and the undoing and destruction of the Common-Law always used.

Ph. That is to say, of the Law of Reason. From hence it follows, that where there are no Juries, and where there are different Laws from ours; that is to say, in all the World besides, neither King, nor People have any Inheritance, nor Goods, nor any Law of Reason. I will examine his Doctrine concerning Cases Criminal no farther. He no where defineth a Crime, that we may know what it is: An odious name sufficeth him to make a Crime of any thing. He hath put Heresie among the most odious Crimes, not knowing what it
(155) signifies; and | upon no other Cause, but because the Church of *Rome* (to make their usurped Power the more terrible) had made it by long Preaching against it, and Cruelty shown towards many Godly, and learned Men of this, and other Reformed Churches, appear to common People a thing detestable. He puts it in as a Plea of the Crown in the time of Queen *Elizabeth*, whereas in her

---

8. No "2" appears.   9. Continued from the interruption, p. (152) above.
10. ⟨destruction⟩

time there was no Doctrine Heresie; but Justice *Stamford* leaves it out,[11] because when Heresie was a Crime, it was a Plea of the *Mitre*. I see also in this Catalogue of Causes Criminal, he inserteth costly Feeding, costly Apparel, and costly Building, though they were contrary to no Statute.[12] 'Tis true, that by evil Circumstances they become sins; but these sins belong to the Judgement of the Pastors Spiritual. A Justice of the Temporal Law (seeing the Intention only makes them sins) cannot judge whether they be sins or no, unless he have power to take Confessions. Also he makes flattery of the King to be a Crime.[13] How could he know when one Man had flattered another? He meant therefore that it was a Crime to please the King: And accordingly he citeth divers Calamities of such as had been in times past in great favour of the Kings they serv'd; as the Favourites of *Hen*. 3. *Ed*. 2. *Rich*. 2.

(156) *Hen*. 6. which Favourites were some | imprisoned, some banished, and some put to death by the same Rebels that imprisoned, banished, and put to death the same King, upon no better ground than the Earl of *Strafford*, the Arch-Bishop of *Canterbury*, and King *Charles* the first by the Rebels of that time. *Empson*, and *Dudley* were no Favourites of *Hen*. the 7th, but Spunges, which King *Hen*. the 8th did well squeeze. Cardinal *Woolsey* was indeed for divers years a favourite of *Hen*. the 8th, but fell into disgrace, not for flattering the King, but for not flattering him in the business of Divorce from Queen *Katharine*. You see his Reasoning here, see also his Passion in the words following. We will for some Causes descend no lower, *Qui eorum vestigiis insistunt, eorum exitus perhorrescant*, this is put in for the Favourite (that then was) of King *James*.[14] But let us give over this, and speak of the legal Punishments to these Crimes belonging.

11. Sir William Stanford (1509–58), *Pleas of the Crown*.
12. 3 *Inst*. chaps. 96, 95, 97.   13. 3 *Inst*. chap. 99.
14. Let those who stand in their footsteps dread their fate (3 *Inst*. p. 208; also 4 *Inst*. p. 41). At the former place, Coke includes a passage relating Henry VIII's praise of his "favorite,'" Suffolk, for never traducing any other great man to the king. In the latter place, Coke is denouncing Empson and Dudley for making use of an act that dispensed with jury trial in certain situations. This departure from the common law procedure, and the baneful end of those who meddled with it, are held up as a caution to royal favorites who derogate from the common law. Since Bacon surely commented to James on Coke as a public servant (how fairly can be seen, e.g., in his letter of 21 February 1615 to the king), and since Bacon inclined toward chancery and prerogative and away from the independence of the common-lawyers, it is reasonable to suppose that Hobbes means Bacon in referring to the "favorite" of King James.

Of Punishments.[1]

AND IN THE FIRST PLACE I DESIRE TO KNOW WHO IT IS that hath the power, for an Offence committed to define, and appoint the special manner of Punishment; for suppose you are not of the Opinion of the *Stoicks* in old time, that all faults are (157) equal, and | that there ought to be the same Punishment for killing a Man, and for killing a Hen.

La. The manner of Punishment in all Crimes whatsoever is to be determined by the Common-Law. That is to say, if it be a Statute that determins it, then the Judgment must be according to the Statute; if it be not specified by the Statute, then the Custome in such Cases is to be followed: But if the Case be new, I know not why the Judge may not determine it according to Reason.

Ph. But according to whose reason? If you mean the natural Reason of this, or that Judge authorized by the King to have cognisance of the Cause, there being as many several Reasons, as there are several Men, the punishment of all Crimes will be uncertain, and none of them ever grow up to make a Custome. Therefore a Punishment certain can never be assigned, if it have its beginning from the natural Reasons of deputed Judges, no, nor from the natural [reason] of the Supream Judge: For if the Law of Reason did determine Punishments, then for the same Offences there should be through all the World, and in all times the same Punishments; because the Law of Reason is Immutable and Eternal.

La. If the natural Reason neither of the King, nor of any else be able (158) to prescribe a | Punishment, how can there be any lawful Punishment at all?

Ph. Why not? For I think that in this very difference between the rational Faculties of particular Men, lyeth the true and perfect reason that maketh every Punishment certain. For, but give the authority of defining Punishments to any Man whatsoever, and let that Man define them, and right Reason has defin'd them[, s]²uppose the Definition be both made, and made known before the Offence committed: For such authority is to trump in Card-playing, save that in matter of Government, when nothing else is turn'd up, Clubs are Trump. Therefore seeing every Man

---

1. 3 *Inst.* chap. 101 passim.   2. ⟨. S⟩ (Molesworth's emendation.)

knoweth by his own Reason what Actions are against the Law of
Reason, and knoweth what Punishments are by this authority for
every evil action ordained; it is manifest Reason, that for breaking the known Laws, he should suffer the known Punishments.
Now the Person to whom this authority of defining Punishments
is given, can be no other in any place of the World, but the same
Person that hath the Soveraign Power, be it one Man, or one
assembly of Men: For it were in vain to give it to any Person that
had not the power of the Militia to cause it to be executed; for
(159) no less power can do it, when many Offenders be united | and
combin'd to defend one another. There was a Case put to King
David by *Nathan*,[3] of a rich Man that had many Sheep, and of a
poor Man that had but one, which was a tame Lamb: The rich
Man had a stranger in his House, for whose entertainment (to
spare his own Sheep) he took away the poor Mans Lamb. Upon
this Case the King gave Judgment, surely the Man that hath done
this shall die. What think you of this? Was it a Royal, or Tyrannical Judgment?

La. I will not contradict the Canons of the Church of *England*, which
acknowledgeth the King of *England*, within his own Dominions
hath the same Rights, which the good Kings of *Israel* had in theirs,
nor deny King *David* to have been one of those good Kings: But
to punish with death without a precedent Law, will seem but a
harsh proceeding with us, who unwillingly hear of Arbitrary
Laws, much less of Arbitrary Punishments, unless we were sure
that all our Kings would be as good as *David*. I will only ask you by
what Authority the Clergy may take upon them to determine, or
make a Canon concerning the power of their own King, or to
distinguish between the Right of a good, and an evil King.

Ph. It is not the Clergy that maketh their Canons to be Law, but it is
(160) the King that doth it by the Great Seal of *England*; and | it is the
King that giveth them power to teach their Doctrines, in that,[4]
he authoriseth them publickly to teach and preach the Doctrine
of Christ and his Apostles, according to the Scriptures, wherein
this Doctrine is perspicuously contained. But if they had dero-
gated from the Royal Power in any of their Doctrines published,
then certainly they had been [to][5] blame; nay, I believe that had
been more within the Statute of Premunire of 16 *Rich.* 2. *c.* 5.
than any Judge of a Court of Equity for holding Pleas of Common

---

3. 2 Sam. 12:1–6. See above, p. (35).   4. ⟨that⟩   5. ⟨too⟩

Law. I cite not this Precedent of King *David*, as approving the breach of the great Charter, or justifying the Punishment with loss of Life, or Member of every Man that shall offend the King; but to shew you that before the Charter was granted, in all Cases where the Punishments were not prescribed, it was the King only that could prescribe them; and that no deputed Judge could punish an Offender, but by force of some Statute, or by the words of some Commission, and not *ex officio*. They might for a contempt of their Courts, because it is a contempt of the King, imprison a Man, during the Kings pleasure, or fine him to the King, according to the greatness of the Offence: But all this amounteth to no more, than to leave him to the Kings Judgment.

(161) As for cutting off of Ears, | and for the Pillory, and the like corporal Punishments usually inflicted heretofore in the Star-Chamber, they were warranted by the Statute of [3] *Hen.* 7. that giveth them power to punish sometimes by discretion. And generally it is a rule of Reason, that every Judge of Crimes, in case the positive Law appoint no Punishment, and he have no other Command from the King; then to consult the King before he pronounce Sentence of any irreparable dammage on the Offender: For otherwise he doth not pronounce the Law, which is his Office to do, but makes the Law, which is the Office of the King. And from this you may collect, that the Custome of punishing such and such a Crime, in such and such a manner, hath not the force of Law in it self, but from an assured presumption, that the Original of the Custome was the Judgment of some former King. And for this Cause the Judges ought not to run up for the Customs by which they are warranted to the time of the *Saxon* Kings, nor to the time of the Conquest: For the most immediate, antecedent precedents are the fairest warrants of their Judgments, as the most recent Laws have commonly the greatest vigor, as being fresh in the memory of all Men, and tacitly confirmed (because not disapprov'd) by the Soveraign Legislator. What can be said [against][6] this? |

La. Sir *Edw. Coke* 3 *Inst.* p. 210. in the Chapter of Judgments and
(162) Executions saith, that of Judgments some are by the Common-Law, some by Statute-Law, and some by Custome; wherein he distinguisheth Common-Law, both from Statute-Law and from Custome.

---

6. ⟨a–aginst⟩

Ph. But you know, that in other places[7] he makes the Common-Law, and the Law of Reason to be all one, as indeed they are, when by it is meant the Kings Reason; and then his meaning in this distinction must be, that there be Judgments by Reason without Statute-Law, and Judgments neither by Statute-Law, nor by Reason, but by Custome without Reason; for if a Custome be Reasonable, then, both he, and other Learned Lawyers say, it is Common-Law; and if unreasonable, no Law at all.

La. I believe Sir *Edw. Coke's* meaning was no other than yours in this point, but that he inserted the word Custom, because there be not many that can distinguish between Customs reasonable and unreasonable.

Ph. But Custom, so far forth as it hath the force of a Law, hath more of the nature of a Statute, than of the Law of Reason, especially where the question is not of Lands, and Goods, but of Punishments, which are to be defined only by authority. Now to come (163) to particulars: What Pu-|nishment is due by Law for High Treason?

La. To be drawn upon a Hurdle from the Prison to the Gallows, and there to be hanged by the Neck, and laid upon the ground alive, and have his Bowels taken out, and burnt, whilst he is yet living; to have his Head cut off, his Body to be divided into four parts, and his Head, and Quarters to be placed as the King shall assign.

Ph. Seeing a Judge ought to give Judgment according to the Law, and that this Judgment is not appointed by any Statute, how does Sir *Edw. Coke* warrant it by Reason, or how by Custom?

La. Only thus, Reason it is, that his Body, Lands, Goods, Posterity, *&c.* should be torn, pulled asunder, and destroy'd, that intended to destroy the Majesty of Government.

Ph. See how he avoids the saying the Majesty of the King. But does not this Reason make as much for punishing a Traytor as *Metius Suffetius*, in old time, was executed by *Tullus Hostilius* King of *Rome*, or as *Ravillac*, not many years ago in *France*, who were torn in pieces by four Horses, as it does for Drawing, Hanging, and Quartering?

La. I think it does. But he confirms it also in the same Chapter, by (164) holy Scripture. | Thus *Joab* for Treason, 1 *Kings* 2. 28. was drawn from the horns of the Altar; that's proof for drawing upon a Hurdle. *Esth.* 2. 22. *Bithan* for Treason was Hang'd; there's for

---

7. E. g., 1 *Inst.* fol. 97b.

hanging. *Acts.* 1. 18. *Judas* hanged himself, and his Bowels were poured out; there's for hanging, and embowelling alive. 2 *Sam.* 18. 14. *Joab* pierced *Absalom*'s heart; that's proof for pulling out a Traytors heart. 2 *Sam.* 20. 22. *Sheba* the Son of *Bichri* had his Head cut off; which is proof that a Traytors Head ought to be cut off. 2 *Sam.* 4. 12. They slew *Baanah* and *Rechab*, and hung up their Heads over the Pool of *Hebron*; this is for setting up of Quarters. And Lastly for forfeiture of Lands, and Goods, *Psal.* 109. *v.* 9. 10. *&c.* "Let their Children be driven out, and beg, and other Men make spoil of their labours, and let their Memory be blotted out of the Land."

Ph. Learnedly said; and no Record is to be kept of the Judgment.[8] Also the Punishments divided between those Traytors must be joyn'd in one Judgment for a Traytor here.

La. He meant none of this, but intended (his Hand being in) to shew his Reading, or his Chaplains in the Bible.

Ph. Seeing then for the specifying of the Punishment in Case of
(165) Treason, he brings no argument from natural Reason; that is | to say, from the Common Law; and that it is manifest that it is not the general Custom of the Land, the same being rarely, or never executed upon any Peer of the Realm, and that the King may remit the whole Penalty, if he will; it follows, that the specifying of the Punishment depends meerly upon the authority of the King. But this is certain, that no Judge ought to give other Judgment, than has been usually given, and approv'd either by a Statute, or by Consent express or implyed, of the Soveraign Power; for otherwise it is not the Judgment of the Law, but of a Man subject to the Law.

La. In Petit Treason the Judgment is, to be drawn to the place of execution, and hang'd by the Neck, or if it be a Woman, to be drawn and burnt.

---

8. This remark implies that Coke's piety in respecting the scriptural prescriptions for treason should lead him also to favor blotting out the sentence from the record of the court, i.e., not attaching importance to the record keeping or record status of the court. But in what seems to be a tacit depreciation of Chancery, Coke writes, "Nota, the legall proceedings of this court [Chancery] be not inrolled in rolls, but remaine *in filaciis* being filed up in the office of the pety-bag" (4 *Inst.* p. 80); and "This court of equity proceeding by English bill is no court of record . . ." (ibid., p. 84). If Hobbes understood these remarks to be incidents in Coke's campaign in defense of the common law against equity, the Philosopher's remark may be construed as having a counteracting intention.

Ph. Can you imagine that this so nice a distinction can have any other foundation than the wit of a private Man?

La. Sir *Edw. Coke* upon this place says, that she ought not to be beheaded, or hanged.

Ph. No, not by the Judge, who ought to give no other Judgment than the Statute, or the King appoints, nor the Sheriff to make other execution than the Judge pronounceth; unless he have a special warrant from the King. And this I should have thought he had
(166) meant, had he not said before, that | the King had given away all his Right of Judicature to his Courts of Justice.

La. The Judgment for Felony is———

Ph. Heresie is before Felony in the Catalogue of the Pleas of the Crown.

La. He has omitted the Judgment against a Heretick, because (I think) no Jury [can find]⁹ Heresie, nor no Judge Temporal did ever pronounce Judgment upon it: For the Statute of 2 *H.* 5. *c.* 7. was, that the Bishop having convicted any Man of Heresie, should deliver him to the Sheriff, and that the Sheriff should believe the Bishop. The Sheriff therefore was bound by the Statute of 2. *H.* 4. after he was delivered to him, to burn him; but that Statute being repeal'd, the Sheriff could not burn him, without a Writ *de Heretico comburendo*, and therefore the Sheriff burnt *Legat* 9. King *James* by that Writ, which was granted by the Judges of the Common-Law at that time, and in that Writ the Judgment is expressed.

Ph. This is strange reasoning; when Sir *Edw. Coke* knew, and confessed, that the Statutes upon which the Writ *de Heretico comburendo* was grounded, were all repeal'd, how could he think the Writ it self could be in force? Or that the Statute which repealeth the Statutes for burning Hereticks was not made with an intent
(167) to forbid such | burning? It is manifest he understood not his Books of Common-Law: For in the time of *Hen.* 4. and *Hen.* 5. the word of the Bishop was the Sheriff's warrant, and there was need of no such Writ; nor could he till the 25 *Hen.* 8. when those Statutes were repeal'd, and a Writ made for that purpose, and put into the Register, which Writ *Fitzherbert* cites in the end of his *natura brevium*. Again, in the later end of the Reign of Queen *Elizabeth* was published a correct Register of Original and

---

9. ⟨confin'd⟩ This error, seen at least as early as 1750 (*Works*), points to Hobbes's amanuensis rather than to a compositor.

Judicial Writs, and the Writ *de Hæretico comburendo* left out, because that Statute of 25 *H*. 8. and all Statutes against Hereticks were repeal'd, and burning forbidden. And whereas he citeth[10] for the granting of this Writ, 9. *Jac*. the Lord Chief Justice, the Lord Chief Baron, and two Justices of the Common-Pleas, it is, as to all, but the Lord Chief [Justice] against the Law; for neither the Judges of Common-Pleas, nor of the Exchequer can hold Pleas of the Crown (without special Commission) and if they cannot hold Plea, they cannot condemn.

La. The Punishment for Felony is, that the Felon be hang'd by the Neck till he be dead. And to prove that it ought to be so, he cites a Sentence (from whence I know not) *Quod non licet Felonem pro Felonia decollare*.[11] |

Ph. It is not indeed lawful for the Sheriff of his own Head to do it, or (168) to do otherwise than is commanded in the Judgement, nor for the Judge to give any other Judgment, than according to Statute-Law, or the usage consented to by the King, but this hinders not the King from altering his Law concerning Judgments, if he see good cause.

La. The King may do so, if he please: And Sir *Edw. Coke* tells you how he altered particular Judgments in case of Felony, and sheweth, that Judgment being given upon a Lord in Parliament, that he should be hang'd, he was nevertheless beheaded; and that another Lord had the like Judgment for another Felony, and was not hang'd, but beheaded; and withal he shews you the inconveniency of such proceeding, because (saith he) if hanging might be altered to beheading, by the same reason it might be altered to burning, stoning to Death, *&c*.

Ph. Perhaps there might be inconveniency in it; but 'tis more than I see, or he shews, nor did there happen any inconveniency from the execution he citeth: Besides he granteth, that death being *ultimum supplicium* is a satisfaction to the Law. But what is all this to the purpose, when it belongeth not to consider such incon-(169) venien-|cies of Government but to the King and Parliament? Or who from the authority of a deputed Judge can derive a power to censure the actions of a King that hath deputed him?

La. For the death of a Man by misfortune, there is (he saith) no express Judgment, nor for killing a Man in ones own defence; but he

---

10. 3 *Inst*. p. 40.
11. It is not lawful to decapitate the felon for felony (3 *Inst*. p. 217).

saith, that the Law hath in both Cases given judgment, that he that so killeth a Man shall forfeit all his Goods and Chattels, Debts and Duties.

Ph. If we consider what Sir *Edw. Coke* saith, 1 *Inst. Sect.* 745. at the word *Felony*, these Judgments are very favourable: For there he saith, that killing of a Man by *Chance-medley*, or *se defendendo* is *Felony*. His words are; wherefore by the Law at this day, under the word *Felony* in Commissions, *&c.* is included Petit Treason, Murder, Homicide, burning of Houses, Burglary, Robbery, Rape, *&c. Chance-medley*, and *se defendendo*. But if we consider only the intent of him that killeth a Man by misfortune, or in his own defence, the same judgments will be thought both cruel, and sinful Judgments. And how they can be *Felony* at this day cannot be understood, unless there be a Statute to make them so. For the Statute of [52]¹² *H.* 3. *cap.* 25. [t]¹³he words whereof, Murder

(170) from henceforth shall not | be judged before our Justices, where it is found Misfortune only; but it shall take place in such as are slain by *Felony*, and not otherwise, make it manifest, if they be *Felonies*, they must also be Murders, unless they have been made *Felonies* by some latter Statute.

La. There is no such latter Statute, nor is it to say in Commission; nor can a Commission, or any thing but another Statute make a thing *Felony*, that was not so before.

Ph. See what it is for a Man to distinguish *Felony* into several sorts, before he understands the general name of *Felony* what it meaneth; but that a Man, for killing another Man by misfortune only, without any evil purpose, should forfeit all his Goods and Chattels, Debts and Duties, is a very hard Judgment, unless perhaps they were to be given to the Kindred of the Man slain, by way of amends for dammage. But the Law is not that. Is it the Common-Law (which is the Law of Reason) that justifies this Judgment, or the Statute-Law? It cannot be the Law of Reason, if the Case be meer misfortune. If a Man be upon his Apple-tree, to gather his Apples, and by ill fortune fall down, and lighting on the Head of another Man kill him, and by good fortune saves himself; shall

(171) he for this | mischance be punished with the forfeiture of his Goods to the King? Does the Law of Reason warrant this? He should (you'l say) have look'd to his Feet; that's true, but so should he that was under have look'd up to the Tree. Therefore

---

12. ⟨25⟩   13. ⟨T⟩

in this Case the Law of Reason (as I think) dictates, that they ought each of them to bear his own misfortune.

La. In this Case I agree with you.

Ph. But this Case is the true Case of meer misfortune, and a sufficient reprehension of the Opinion of Sir *Edw. Coke.*

La. But what if this had hapned to be done by one that had been stealing Apples upon the Tree of another Man? Then (as Sir *Edw. Coke* says, 3 *Inst.* p. 56.) it had been Murder.

Ph. There is indeed great need of good distinction in a Case of killing by misfortune; but in this Case the unlawfulness of stealing Apples cannot make it Murder, unless the falling it self be unlawful. It must be a voluntary unlawful Act that causeth the death, or else it is no Murder by the Law of Reason: Now the death of the Man that was under the Tree proceeded not from that, that the Apples were not his that fell, but from the fall. But if a Man shoot with a Bow or a Gun at another Man's Deer, and by misfortune kill a (172) Man, such shooting be-|ing both voluntary, and unlawful, and also the immediate Cause of the Mans death, may be drawn perhaps well enough sometimes to Murder by a Judge of the Common-Law. So likewise if a Man shoot an Arrow over a House, and by chance kill a Man in the Street, there is no doubt but by the Law of Reason it is Murder, for though he meant no malice to the Man slain, yet it is manifest, that he cared not whom he slew. In this difficulty of finding out what it is that the Law of Reason dictates, who is it that must decide the Question?

La. In the Case of misfortune, I think it belongs to the Jury; for it is matter of Fact only: But when it is doubtful whether the action from which the misfortune came, were Lawful, or Unlawful, it is to be judged by the Judge.

Ph. But if the unlawfulness of the action (as the stealing of the Apples) did not cause the death of the Man, then the stealing, be it, Trespass, or *Felony*, ought to be punished alone, as the Law requireth.

La. But for killing of a Man *se defendendo,* the Jury (as Sir *Edw. Coke* here says)[14] shall not in their Verdict say it was *se defendendo*, but shall declare the manner of the Fact in special, and clear it to the Judge, to consider how it is to be called, whether *se defendendo*, Manslaughter, or Murder. |

Ph. One would think so; for it is not often within the capacity of a

---

14. 3 *Inst.* p. 220.

(173) Jury to distinguish the signification of the different and hard names which are given by Lawyers to the killing of a Man; as Murder and Felony, which neither the Laws, nor the makers of the Laws have yet defined. The Witnesses say, that thus and thus the Person did, but not that it was Murder or *Felony*; no more can the Jury say, who ought to say nothing but what they hear from the Witnesses, or from the Prisoner. Nor ought the Judge to ground his Sentence upon any thing else, besides the special matter found, which according as it is contrary, or not contrary to the Statute, ought to be pronounced.

La. But I have told you, that when the Jury has found misfortune, or *se defendendo*, there is no judgment at all to be given, and the Party is to be pardoned of course, saving that he shall forfeit his Goods and Chattells, Debts and Duties to the King.

Ph. But I understand not how there can be a Crime for which there is no Judgment, nor how any Punishment can be inflicted without a precedent Judgment, nor upon what ground the Sheriff can seize the Goods of any Man, till it be judged that they be forfeited. I know that Sir *Edw. Coke* saith, that in the Judgment of hanging,

(174) the Judg-|ment of forfeiture is implyed, which I understand not; though I understand well enough, that the Sheriff by his Office may seize the Goods of a *Felon* convicted; much less do I conceive how the forfeiture of Goods can be implyed in a no-judgment, nor do I conceive, that when the Jury has found the special manner of the Fact to be such, as is really no other than *se defendendo*, and consequently, no fault at all, why he should have any Punishment at all. Can you shew me any Reason for it?

La. The Reason lies in the Custom.[15]

---

15. Cf. Bacon's reflection on the legal maxim that "necessity carries a privilege": "This rule admitteth an exception when the law doth intend some fault or wrong in the party that hath brought himself into the necessity; so that is *necessitas culpabilis*. This I take to be the chief reason why *seipsum defendendo* is not matter of justification, because the law intends it hath a commencement upon an unlawful cause, because quarrels are not presumed to grow without some wrongs either in words or deeds on either part, and the law that thinketh it a thing hardly triable in whose default the quarrel began, supposeth the party that kills another in his own defence not to be without malice; and therefore as it doth not touch him in the highest degree, so it putteth him to sue out his pardon of course, and punisheth him by forfeiture of goods: for where there cannot be any malice nor wrong presumed, as where a man assails me to rob me, and I kill him that assaileth me; or if a women kill him that assaileth her to ravish her, it is justifiable without any pardon" (*The Elements of the Common Law of England, Works* [1740], 4:30).

Ph. You know that unreasonable Customs are not Law, but ought to be abolished; and what Custom is there more unreasonable than that a Man should be punished without a fault?

La. Then see the Statute of 24 *Hen.* 8. *cap.* 5.

Ph. I find here, that at the making of this Statute there was a Question amongst the Lawyers, in case one Man should kill another that attempted feloniously to Rob, or Murder him in, or near any Common High-way, Court-way, Horse-way, or Foot-way, or in his Mansion, Messuage, or Dwelling-place; whether for the death of such a Man one shall forfeit his Goods and Chattells, as a Man should do for killing another by Chance-medley, or in his own

(175) de-|fence. This is the Preamble, and penned as well as Sir *Edw. Coke* could have wished; but this Statute does not determine that a Man should forfeit his Goods for killing a Man *se defendendo*, or for killing him by misfortune; but supposeth it only upon the opinion of the Lawyers that then were. The body of the Statute is, that if a Man be indicted, or appealed for the death of such Person so attempting as aforesaid, and the same by verdict be so found and tryed, he shall not forfeit any thing, but shall be discharged as if he had been found *not Guilty*. You see the Statute, now consider thereby in the case of killing *se defendendo*. F[i]rst, if a Man kill another in his own defence, it is manifest, that the Man slain did either attempt to Rob, or to Kill, or to Wound him; for else it was not done in his own defence. If then it were done in the Street, or near the Street as in a Tavern, he forfeits nothing because the Street is a High-way. So likewise it is to be said of all other Common-ways. In what place therefore can a Man kill another in his own defence, but that this Statute will discharge him of the forfeiture?

La. But the Statute says the attempt must be felonious.

Ph. When a Man assaults me with a Knife, Sword, Club, or other

(176) mortal Wea-|pon; does any Law forbid me to defend my self, or command me to stay so long as to know whether he have a felonious intent, or no? Therefore by this Statute, in case it be found *se defendendo*, the forfeiture is discharged, if it be found otherwise, it is Capital. If we read the Statute of *Glocester*,[16] *cap.* 9. I think it will take away the difficulty: For by that Statute, in case it be found by the Countrey, that he did it in his own defence, or by misfortune, then by the report of the Justices to the King, the

---

16. 6 Edw. 1.

King shall take him to his Grace, if it please him. From whence it followeth; first, that it was then thought Law, that the Jury may give the general verdict of *se defendendo*, which Sir *Edw. Coke* denies. Secondly, that the Judge ought to report especial matter to the King. Thirdly, that the King may take him to his Grace, if he please, and consequently, that his Goods are not to be seiz'd, till the King (after the report of the Judge heard) give the Sheriff command to do it. Fourthly, that the general verdict of the [jury][17] hinders not the King, but that he may Judge of it upon the special matter, for it often happens that an ill-disposed Person provokes a Man with words, or otherwise on purpose to make him draw his Sword, that he may kill him, and pretend it

(177) done in his own defence; which ap-|pearing, the King may, without any offence to God, punish him as the cause shall require. Lastly (contrary to the Doctrine of Sir *Edw. Coke*) he may in his own Person be Judge in the case, and annul the Verdict of the Jury, which a deputed Judge cannot do.

La. There be some cases wherein a Man, though by the Jury he be found *not Guilty*, shall nevertheless forfeit his Goods and Chattells to the King. For example; a Man is slain, and one *A.* hating *B.* giveth out that it was *B.* that slew him: *B.* hearing thereof, fearing if he be tryed for it, that through the great power of *A.* and others that seek his hurt, he should be condemned, flieth, and afterwards is taken, and tryed; and upon sufficient evidence is by the Jury found *Not Guilty*; yet because he fled he shall forfeit his Goods and Chattels, notwithstanding there be no such Judgment given by the Judge, nor appointed by any Statute, but the Law it self authoriseth the Sheriff to seize them to the use of the King.[18]

Ph. I see no reason (which is Common-Law) for it, and am sure it is grounded upon no Statute.

La. See Sir *Edw. Coke, Inst.* 1. *Sect.* 709. and read. |

Ph. If a Man that is Innocent be accus'd of *Felony*, and for fear flieth
(178) for the same; albeit that he be judicially acquitted of the *Felony*, yet if it be found that he fled for the same, he shall (notwithstanding his Innocence) forfeit all his Goods and Chattells, Debts and Duties.[19] O unchristian, and abominable Doctrine! which also he in his own words following contradicteth: For (saith he) as to the forfeiture of them, the Law will admit no proof against the

---

17. ⟨King⟩   18. Cf. *Leviathan*, chap. 26.   19. 1 *Inst.* fol. 373b.

presumption of the Law grounded upon his flight, and so it is in many other cases: But that the general Rule is, *Quod stabitur præsumptioni, donec probetur in contrarium*, but you see it hath many exceptions.[20] This general Rule contradicts what he said before; for there can be no exceptions to a general Rule in Law, that is not expresly made an exception by some Statute, and to a general Rule of equity there can be no exception at all. From the power of Punishing, let us proceed to the power of Pardoning.

La. Touching the power of Pardoning,[21] Sir *Edw. Coke* says, 3 *Inst.* p. 236. That no Man shall obtain Charter of pardon out of Parliament, and cites for it the Statute of 2 *Ed.* 3. *cap.* 2. and says farther, that accordingly in a Parliament Roll it is said, that for the peace
(179) of the Land it would help, | that no pardon were granted but by Parliament.

Ph. What lawful power would he have left to the King, that thus disableth him to practice Mercy? In the Statute which he citeth, to prove that the King ought not to grant Charters of Pardon, but in Parliament there are no such words, as any Man may see; for that Statute is in Print; and that which he says is in the Parliament Roll, is but a wish of he tells not whom, and not a Law; and 'tis strange that a private wish should be inroll'd amongst Acts of Parliament. If a Man do you an injury, to whom (think you) belongeth the Right of pardoning it?

La. Doubtless to me alone, if to me alone be done that injury; and to the King alone, if to him alone be done the injury; and to both together, if the injury be done to both.

Ph. What part then has any Man in the granting of a pardon, but the King and the party wrong'd. If you offend no Member of either House, why should you ask their pardon. It is possible that a Man may deserve a pardon; or he may be such a one sometimes as the defence of the Kingdom hath need of; may not the King pardon him, though there be no Parliament then sitting? Sir *Edw. Coke's*
(180) Law is too general in this | point, and I believe, if he had thought on't, he would have excepted some Persons, if not all the Kings Children, and his Heir apparent; and yet they are all his Subjects, and subject to the Law as other Men.

La. But if the King shall grant pardons of Murder and Felony, of his own head, there would be very little safety for any Man, either

---

20. The presumptive stands until the contrary is proved (ibid).
21. 3 *Inst.* chap 105 passim.

out of his House, or in it, either by Night, or by Day: And for that very cause there have been many good Statutes provided, which forbid the Justices to allow of such pardons as do not specially name the Crime.

Ph. Those Statutes, I confess, are reasonable, and very profitable, which forbid the Judge to pardon Murders, but what Statute is there that forbids the King to do it? There is a Statute of 13 *Rich.* 2. *c.* 1. wherein the King promiseth not to pardon Murder, but there is in it a clause for the saving of the Kings Regality. From which may be inferr'd, that the King did not grant away that power, when he thought good to use it for the Commonwealth. Such Statutes are not Laws to the King, but to his Judges, and though the Judges be commanded by the King not to allow pardons in many cases, yet if the King by writing command the Judges to allow them, they ought to do it. I think, if the King

(181) think | in his conscience it be for the good of the Common-wealth, he sinneth not in it; but I hold not that the King may pardon him without sin, if any other Man be damnified by the Crime committed, unless he cause reparation to be made, as far as the party offending can do it:[22] And howsoever be it sin, or not sin, there is no power in *England* that may resist him, or speak evil of him lawfully.

La. Sir *Edw. Coke* denies not that; and upon that ground it is that the King, he says, may pardon high Treason; for there can be no high Treason, but against the King.

Ph. That's well; therefore he confesseth, that whatsoever the offence be, the King may pardon so much of it as is an injury to himself, and that by his own right, without breach of any Law positive, or natural, or of any grant, if his Conscience tell him that it be not to the dammage of the Common-wealth; and you know that to judge of what is good or evil to the Common-wealth, belongeth to the King only. Now tell me what it is which is said to be pardoned?

La. What can it be but only the offence? If a Man hath done a Murder and be pardoned for the same, is it not the Murder that is pardoned? |

Ph. Nay, by your favour, if a Man be pardon for Murder or any other

(182) offence, it is the Man that is pardoned, the Murder still remains Murder. But what is pardon?

---

22. Cf. Bracton, fol. 132b.

La. Pardon (as Sir *Edw. Coke* says, 3 *Inst.* p. 233) is deriv'd of *per* and *dono*, and signifies throughly to remit.

Ph. If the King remit the Murder and not pardon the Man that did it, what does the remission serve for?

La. You know well enough that when we say a Murder, or any thing else is pardoned, all *English-men* understand thereby, that the punishment due to the offence is the thing remitted.

Ph. But for our understanding of one another, you ought to have said so at first. I understand now, that to pardon Murder or Felony is throughly to save the offender from all the punishment due unto him by the Law for his offence.

La. Not so; for Sir *Edw. Coke* in the same Chapter, p. 238. saith thus: A Man commits Felony, and is attainted thereof, or is abjur'd; the King pardoneth the Felony without any mention of the attainder or abjuration, the pardon is void.

Ph. What is it to be attainted?

La. To be attainted is, that his Blood be held in Law as stained and (183) corrupted; so | that no inheritance can descend from him to his Children, or to any that make claim by him.

Ph. Is this attaint a part of the Crime, or of the Punishment?

La. It cannot be a part of the Crime, because it is none of his own Act; 'tis therefore a part of the Punishment, *viz.* a disherison of the offender.

Ph. If it be a part of the Punishment due, and yet not pardoned together with the rest; then a pardon is not a through remitting of the Punishment as Sir *Edw. Coke* says it is. And what is Abjuration?

La. When a Clerk heretofore was convicted of Felony, he might have saved his life by abjuring the Realm; that is, by departing the Realm within a certain time appointed, and taking an Oath never to return. But at this day all Statutes for Abjuration are repeal'd.

Ph. That also is a Punishment, and by a pardon of the Felony pardoned unless a Statute be in force to the contrary. There is also somewhat in the Statute of 13 *Rich.* 2. *c.* 1. concerning the allowance of Charters of pardons, which I understand not well. The words are these; No Charter of pardon for henceforth shall be allowed before our Justices for Murder, or for the death of a Man by (184) awayt, or malice prepens'd, | Treason, or Rape of a Woman, unless the same be specified in the same Charter, for I think it follows thence, that if the King say in his Charter, that he pardoneth the Murder, then he breaketh not the Statute, because he specifies the offence; or if he saith, he pardoneth the killing by awayt, or of malice prepensed, he breaketh not the Statute, he specifies the offence. Also if he say so much as that the Judge cannot doubt of the Kings meaning to pardon him, I think the Judge ought to allow it, because the Statute saveth the Kings liberty and regality in that point; that is to say, the power to pardon him, such as are these words, notwithstanding any Statute to the contrary, are sufficient to cause the Charter to be allowed: For these words make it manifest, that the Charter was not granted upon surprise, but to maintain and claim the Kings liberty and power to shew mercy, when he seeth cause. The like meaning have these words *Perdonavimus omnimodam interfectionem*; that is to say, we have pardoned the killing in what manner soever it was done. But here we must remember that the King cannot pardon, without sin, any dammage thereby done to another Man, unless he causes satisfaction to be made, as far as possibly the offender can, but is not bound to satisfie Mens thirst of revenge; for all revenge |

(185) ought to proceed from God, and under God from the King. Now (besides in Charters) how are these offences specified?

La. They are specified by their names, as Treason, Petit Treason, Murder, Rape, Felony, and the like.

Ph. Petit Treason is Felony, Murder is Felony, so is Rape, Robbery and Theft, and (as Sir *Edw. Coke* says) Petit Larceny is Felony;[23] now if in a Parliament-pardon, or in a Coronation-pardon all Felonies be pardoned; whether is Petit Larceny pardoned, or not?

La. Yes certainly it is pardoned.

---

23. It is not clear that Coke says, or in what sense he says, that petty larceny is felony. At 3 *Inst.* p. 109, he reports the ancient distinction between grand and petty larceny according to the value of the thing stolen, the penalty for petty larceny being forfeiture of goods and corporal punishment such as whipping, which is not the penalty for felony. At p. 110, he reports Hain's case, tenth year of James I, in which he himself deliberated on the nature of the offense, which was the stealing of the winding sheets from buried cadavers. Coke concurred in a decision that led to Hain's indictment of felony; "but the jury found it but petit larceny, for which he was whipped, as he well deserved." It appears that Coke regarded the theft as a felony rather than a petty larceny while the jury, perhaps on a different reckoning of the value of the sheets, regarded it as a petty larceny rather than a felony. Hobbes seems to understand Coke as having taken the theft to be petty larceny and *therefore* felony, which is a construction that does not emerge from the passage. See further 3 *Inst.* p. 213: "If a man be attainted of petit larceny, he may be after attainted of a felony, for the which he shall have judgment of death, because it is an higher offence, and is to have an other judgment."

Ph. And yet you see it is not specified, and yet it is a Crime that hath less in it of the nature of Felony, than there is in Robbery. Do not therefore Rape, Robbery, Theft, pass under the pardon of all Felonies?

La. I think they are all pardoned by the words of the Statute, but those that are by the same Statute excepted; so that specification is needful only in Charters of pardon, but in general pardons not so. For the Statute 13 *Rich. 2. cap.* 1. forbids not the allowance of Parliament-pardons, or Coronation-pardons, and therefore the offences pardoned need not be specified, but may pass under the general word of all Felonies. Nor is it likely that the members of

(186) the Parliament | who drew up their own pardons, did not mean to make them as comprehensive as they could: And yet Sir *Edw. Coke,* [1]²⁴ *Inst. Sect.* 745. at the word *Felony*, seemeth to be of another mind; for *Piracy* is one species of *Felony*, and yet when certain *English-men* had committed *Piracy* in the last year of Queen *Elizabeth*, and came home into *England*, in the beginning of the Reign of King *James*, trusting to his Coronation-pardon of all *Felonies*; they were indicted (Sir *Edw. Coke* was then Attorney General) of the *Piracy* before Commissioners according to the Statute of 28 *H.* 8. and being found *Guilty* were hang'd. The reason he alledgeth for it is, that it ought to have been specified by the name of *Piracy* in the pardon, and therefore the pardon was not to be allowed.

Ph. Why ought it to have been specified more than any other *Felony*? He should therefore have drawn his argument from the Law of reason.

La. Also he does that; for the Tryal (he says)²⁵ was by the Common-Law, and before Commissioners[,] not in the Court of the Lord Admiral, by the Civil-Law, therefore he says it was an offence whereof the Common-Law could not take notice because it could not be Tryed by twelve Men. |

Ph. If the Common-Law could not, or ought not to take notice of

(187) such offences, how could the offenders be Tryed by twelve Men, and found *Guilty*, and hang'd, as they were? If the Common-Law take no notice of *Piracy*, what other offence was it for which they were hang'd? Is *Piracy* two *Felonies*, for one of which a Man shall be hang'd by the Civil-Law, and for the other by the Common-Law? Truly I never read weaker reasoning in any Author of the

---

24. ⟨2⟩   25. 1 *Inst.* fol. 391a; cf. 3 *Inst.* chaps. 49, 105.

Law of *England*, than in Sir *Edw. Coke*'s Institutes, how well soever he could plead.

La. Though I have heard him much reprehended by others, as well as by you; yet there be many excellent things, both for subtility, and for truth in these his Institutes.

Ph. No better things than other Lawyers have that write of the Law, as of a Science: His citing of *Aristotle*, and of *Homer*, and of other Books which are commonly read to Gown-men, do, in my opinion, but weaken his Authority, for any Man may do it by a Servant; but seeing the whole scene of that time is gone and past, let us proceed to somewhat else. Wherein doth an Act of *Oblivion* differ from a Parliament-pardon?[26]

La. This word *Act of Oblivion* was never in our Law-Books before the (188) 12 *Car.* 2. | *c.* 11. and I wish it may never come again; but from whence it came you may better know perhaps than I.

Ph. The first, and only *Act of Oblivion* that ever passed into a Law, in any State that I have read of, was that *Amnestia*, or *Oblivion* of all Quarrels between any of the Citizens of *Athens*, at any time before that Act, without all exception of Crime, or Person. The occasion whereof was this. The *Lacedemonians* having totally subdued the *Athenians*, entred into the City of *Athens*, and ordained that the People should choose thirty Men of their own City to have the Soveraign Power over them. These being chosen behav'd themselves so outragiously, as caused a Sedition, in which the Citizens on both sides were daily slain. There was then a discreet Person that propounded to each of the parties this proposition, that every Man should return to his own, and forget all that was past; which proposition was made, by consent on both sides, into a publick Act, which for that cause was called an *Oblivion*. Upon the like disorder hapning in *Rome* by the Murder of *Julius Cæsar,* the like Act was propounded by *Cicero,* and indeed passed, but was within few days after broken again by *Marcus Antonius.* In imitation of this Act was made the Act of 12 *Car.* 2. *c.* 11. |

La. By this it seems, that the Act of *Oblivion* made by King *Charles*, (189) was no other than a Parliament-pardon, because it containeth a great number of exceptions, as the other Parliament-pardons do, and the Act of *Athens* did not.

Ph. But yet there is a difference between the late Act of *Oblivion* made here, and an ordinary Parliament-pardon: For concerning a fault

---

26. Cf. pp. (43)–(45) above.

pardoned in Parliament by a general word, a suit in Law may arise about this, whether the offender be signified by the word, or not, as whether the pardon of all *Felonies*, be a pardon of *Piracy*, or not: For you see by Sir *Edw. Coke*'s reports, that notwithstanding a pardon of *Felony*, a Sea-*Felony* (when he was Attourney General) was not pardoned. But by the late Act of *Oblivion*, which pardoned all manner of offences committed in the late Civil War, no question could arise concerning Crimes excepted. First, because no Man can by Law accuse another Man of a Fact, which by Law is to be forgotten. Secondly, because all Crimes may be alledged, as proceeding from the Licentiousness of the time, and from the silence of the Law occasion'd by the Civil War, and consequently (unless the offenders Person also were excepted, or unless the Crime were committed before the War began) are within the Pardon. |

La. Truly I think you say right: For if nothing had been pardoned,
(190) but what was done by occasion of the War, the raising of the War it self had not been pardoned.

Ph. I have done with Crimes and Punishments, let us come now to the Laws of *Meum* and *Tuum*.

La. We must then examine the Statutes.

Ph. We must so, what they command and forbid, but not dispute of their Justice: For the Law of Reason commands that every one observe the Law which he hath assented to, and obey the Person to whom he hath promised obedience and fidelity.

[*La.*]²⁷ Then let us consider next the Commentaries of Sir *Edw. Coke* upon *Magna Charta*, and other Statutes.²⁸

Ph. For the understanding of *Magna Charta*, it will be very necessary to run up into Antient times, as far as History will give us leave, and consider not only the Customs of our Ancestors the *Saxons*, but also the Law of nature (the most Antient of all Laws) concerning the original of Government, and acquisition of Property, and concerning Courts of Judicature. And first, it is evident, that Dominion, Government, and Laws, are far more Antient than

---

27. The first edition attributes two consecutive speeches to the Philosopher, one beginning "We must so" and the other, which is the next paragraph, beginning "For the understanding of *Magna Charta*." Molesworth makes of them a single speech by the Philosopher. The attribution suggested here shows the Lawyer as proposing that they examine the statutes and augmenting that proposal with the suggestion that they next consider Coke's commentaries on the statutes.   28. 2 *Inst.*

History, or any other writing, and that the beginning of all
(191) Dominion amongst Men was in | Families; in which, first, the
Father of the Family by the Law of nature was absolute Lord of
his Wife and Children. Secondly, made what Laws amongst them
he pleased. Thirdly, was Judge of all their Controversies.
Fourthly, was not obliged by any Law of Man to follow any
Counsel, but his own. Fifthly, What Land soever the Lord
sat down upon, and made use of for his own, and his Families
benefit, was his Propriety by the Law of First-Possession, in case
it was void of Inhabitants before, or by the Law of War, in case
they conquer'd it. In this Conquest what Enemies they took and
saved were their Servants: Also such Men as wanting Possessions
of Lands, but furnished with Arts necessary for Mans life, came
to dwell in the Family for Protection, became their Subjects, and
submitted themselves to the Laws of the Family: And all this is
consonant, not only to the Law of nature, but also to the practice
of Mankind set forth in History Sacred, and Pr[o][29]phane.

La. Do you think it lawful for a Lord that is the Soveraign Ruler of
his Family, to make War upon another like Soveraign Lord, and
dispossess him of his Lands?

Ph. It is Lawful, or not Lawful according to the intention of him that
(192) does it. For, First, being a Soveraign Ruler, he is | not subject to
any Law of Man; and as to the Law of God, where the intention
is justifiable, the action is so also. The intention may be Lawful
in divers Cases by the right of nature; one of those Cases is, when
he is constrained to it by the necessity of subsisting. So the
Children of *Israel*, besides that their leaders, *Moses* and *Joshua* had
an immediate command from God to dispossess the *Canaanites*,
had also a just pretence to do what they did from the right of
nature, which they had to preserve their lives, being unable otherwise to subsist. And as their preservation, so also is their security
a just pretence of invading those whom they have just cause to
fear, unless sufficient caution be given to take away their fear,
which Caution (for any thing I can yet conceive) is utterly impossible. Necessity, and Security are the principal justifications,
before God, of beginning War. Injuries receiv'd justifie a War
defensive; but for reparable injuries, if Reparation be tendred,
all invasion upon that Title is Iniquity. If you need examples,
either from Scripture, or other History concerning this right of

29. ⟨a⟩

nature in making War, you are able enough from your own reading, to find them out at your leisure.

La. Whereas you say, that the Lands so won by the Soveraign Lord
(193) of a Family, are | his in propriety, you deny (methinks) all property to the Subjects, how much soever any of them hath contributed to the Victory.

Ph. I do so, nor do I see any reason to the contrary: For the Subjects, whether they come into the Family, have no title at all to demand any part of the Land, or any thing else but security, to which also they are bound to contribute their whole strength, and, if need be, their whole fortunes: For it cannot be supposed that any one Man can protect all the rest with his own single strength: And for the Practice, it is manifest in all Conquests, the Land of the vanquished is in the sole power of the Victor, and at his disposal. Did not *Joshua* and the high-Priest divide the Land of *Canaan* in such sort among the Tribes of *Israel*, as they pleased? Did not the *Roman* and *Grœcian* Princes and States according to their own discretion, send out the Colonies to inhabit such Provinces as they had Conquered? Is there at this day among the *Turks* any inheritor of Land, besides the *Sultan*? And was not all the Land in *England* once in the hands of *William* the Conqueror? Sir *Edw. Coke* himself confesses it; therefore it is an universal truth, that all Conquer'd Lands, presently after Victory are the Lands of him that Conquer'd them. |

La. But you know that all Soveraigns are said to have a double
(194) Capacity; *viz.* a natural Capacity, as he is a Man, and a politick Capacity, as a King. In his politick Capacity I grant you, that King *William* the Conqueror was the proper, and only owner once of all the Land in *England*, but not in his natural Capacity.

Ph. If he had them in his politick Capacity, then they were so his own as not to dispose of any part thereof, but only to the benefit of his People, and that must be either by his own, or by the Peoples discretion; that is, by Act of Parliament. But where do you find that the Conqueror disposed of his Lands (as he did some to *Englishmen*, some to *French-men*, and some to *Normans*) to be holden by divers Tenures, as Knight-service, Soccage, &c. by Act of Parliament? Or that he ever called a Parliament to have the assent of the Lords and Commons of *England* in disposing of those Lands he had taken from them? Or for retaining of such and such Lands in his own hands by the name of Forrests for his own Recreation,

or Magnificence? You have heard perhaps that some Lawyers,
or other Men reputed wise and good Patriots have given out, that
all the Lands which the Kings of *England* have possessed, have
(195) been given them by the People, to the end that | they should there-
with defray the Charges of their Wars, and pay the wages of their
Ministers, and that those Lands were gained by the Peoples
Money; for that was pretended in the late Civil War, when they
took from the King his Town of *Kingston* upon *Hull*; but I know
you do not think that the pretence was just. It cannot therefore
be denied but that Land which King *William* the Conqueror
gave away to *English-men* and others, and which they now hold
by his Letters Patents, and other conveyances, were properly, and
really his own, or else the Titles of them that now hold them must
be invalid.

La. I assent. As you have shewed me the beginning of Monarchies,
so let me hear your opinion concerning their growth.

Ph. Great Monarchies have proceeded from small Families. First, by
War, wherein the Victor not only enlarged his Territory, but also
the number and riches of his Subjects. As for other forms of
Common-wealths, they have been enlarged otherways. First, by
a voluntary conjunction of many Lords of Families into one great
Aristocracie. Secondly, by Rebellion proceeded first, *Anarchy*,
and from *Anarchy* proceeded any form that the Calamities of them
that lived therein did prompt them to; whether it were that they
(196) chose an Hereditary King, or | an elective King for life, or that
they agreed upon a Council of certain Persons (which is *Aristocracy*) or a Council of the whole People to have the Soveraign
Power, which is *Democracy*.

After the first manner which is by War, grew up all the greatest
Kingdoms in the World, *viz.* the *Ægyptian*, *Assyrian*, *Persian* and
the *Macedonian Monarchy*; and so did the great Kingdoms of
England, *France*, and *Spain*.

The second manner was the original of the *Venetian Aristocracy*[. B][30]y the third way which is Rebellion, grew up[31] divers
great Monarchies, perpetually changing from one form to
another; as in *Rome* rebellion against Kings produced *Democracy*,
upon which the Senate usurped under *Sylla*, and the People again
upon the Senate under *Marius*, and the Emperor usurped upon
the People under *Cæsar* and his Successors.

---

30. ⟨, b⟩   31. ⟨in⟩

La. Do you think the distinction between natural and politick Capacity is insignificant?[32]

Ph. No; If the Soveraign power be in an assembly of Men, that Assembly, whether it be *Aristocratical*, or *Democratical*, may possess Lands, but it is in their politick Capacity, because no natural Man has any right to those Lands, or any part of them[;][33] (197) in the same manner they can command an | Act by plurality of Commands, but the Command of any one of them is of no effect. But when the Soveraign power is in one Man, the Natural and Politick Capacity are in the same Person, and as to possession of Lands undistinguishable: But as to the Acts and Commands, they may be well distinguished in this manner. Whatsoever a Monarch does Command, or do by consent of the People of his Kingdom, may properly be said to be done in his politick Capacity; and whatsoever he Commands by word of Mouth only, or by Letters Signed with his hand, or Sealed with any of his private Seals is done in his natural Capacity: Nevertheless, his publick Commands, though they be made in his politick Capacity, have their original from his natural Capacity. For in the making of Laws (which necessarily requires his assent) his assent is natural: Also those Acts which are done by the King previously to the passing of them under the Great Seal of *England*, either by word of Mouth, or warrant under his Signet, or privy Seal, are done in his natural Capacity; but when they have past the Seal of *England*, they are to be taken as done in his politick Capacity.

La. I think verily your distinction is good: For natural Capacity, and (198) politick Capacity signifie no more than private and | publick right. Therefore leaving this argument let us consider in the next place, as far as History will permit, what were the Laws and Customs of our Ancestors.

Ph. The *Saxons*, as also all the rest of *Germany* not Conquer'd by the *Roman* Emperors, nor compelled to use the imperial Laws, were a Savage and Heathen People, living only by War and Rapine; and as some learned Men in the *Roman* Antiquities affirm, had their name of *Germans* from that their ancient trade of life, as if *Germans* and *Hommes de guerre* were all one. Their rule over their Family, Servants and Subjects was absolute, their Laws no other than natural Equity; written Law they had little, or none, and very few there were in the time of the *Cæsars* that could write, or

---

32. Cf. *Leviathan*, chap. 24.   33. ⟨,⟩

read. The right to the Government was either Paternal, or by Conquest, or by Marriages. Their succession to Lands was determined by the pleasure of the Master of the Family, by Gift, or Deed in his life time; and what Land they disposed not of in their life time, descended after their death to their Heirs. The Heir was the Eldest Son; The issue of the Eldest Son failing, they descended to the younger Sons in their order, and for want of Sons, to the Daughters joyntly, as to one Heir, or to be divided amongst

(199) them, and so to descend to their Heirs in the same man-|ner: And Children failing, the Uncle by the Fathers, or Mothers side (according as the Lands had been the Fathers or the Mothers) succeeded to the inheritance, and so continually to the next of blood. And this was a natural descent, because naturally the nearer in Blood, the nearer in kindness, and was held for the Law of nature, not only amongst the *Germans*, but also in most Nations before they had a written Law.

The right of Government, which is called *Jus Regni* descended in the same manner, except only that after the Sons, it came to the eldest Daughter first, and her Heirs; the reason whereof was, that Government is indivisible. And this Law continues still in *England*.

La. Seeing all the Land which any Soveraign Lord possessed, was his own in propriety; how came a Subject to have a propriety in their Lands?

Ph. There be two sorts of Propriety. One is, when a Man holds his Land from the gift of God only, which Lands *Civilians* call *Allodial* which in a Kingdom no Man can have but the King. The other is when a Man holds his Land from another Man as given him, in respect of service and obedience to that Man, as a Fee. The first kind of propriety is absolute, the other is in a manner

(200) conditional, because given for some | service to be done unto the giver. The first kind of propriety excludes the right of all others; the second excludes the right of all other Subjects to the same Land, but not the right of the Soveraign, when the common good of the People shall require the use thereof.

La. When those Kings had thus parted with their Lands, what was left them for the maintenance of their Wars, either offensive, or defensive; or for the maintenance of the Royal Family in such manner as not only becomes the dignity of a Soveraign King, but is also necessary to keep his Person and People from contempt[?][34]

---

34. ⟨.⟩

Ph. They have means enough; and besides what they gave their Subjects, had much Land remaining in their own hands afforrested for their recreation: For you know very well that a great part of the Land of *England* was given for Military service to the great Men of the Realm, who were for the most part of the Kings kindred, or great Favourites, much more Land than they had need of for their own Maintenance; but so charged with one, or many Souldiers, according to the quantity of Land given, as there could be no want of Souldiers, at all times, ready to resist an invading Enemy: Which Souldiers those Lords were bound to

(201) furnish, for a time certain, at their own | Charges. You know also, that the whole Land was divided into Hundreds, and those again into Decennaries; in which Decennaries all Men even to Children of 12 years of age, were bound to take the Oath of Allegiance: And you are to believe, that those Men that hold their Land by the service of Husbandry, were all bound with their Bodies, and Fortunes to defend the Kingdom against invaders by the Law of nature: And so also such as they called Villains, and held their Land by baser drudgery, were obliged to defend the Kingdom to the utmost of their power. Nay, Women, and Children in such a necessity are bound to do such service as they can, that is to say, to bring Weapons and Victuals to them that fight, and to Dig: But those that hold their Land by service Military, have lying upon them a greater obligation: For read and observe the form of doing homage, according as it is set down in the Statute of 17 *Edw.* 2. which you doubt not, was in use before that time, and before the Conquest.

La. I become your Man for Life, for Member and for worldly Honour, and shall owe you my faith for the Lands that I hold of you.

Ph. I pray you expound it.

La. I think it is as much, as if you should say, I promise you to be at

(202) your Command; | to perform with the hazard of my Life, Limbs and all my Fortune, as I have charged my self to the reception of the Lands you have given me, and to be ever faithful to you. This is the form of Homage done to the King immediately; but when one Subject holdeth Land of another by the like Military service, then there is an exception added; *viz.* saving the faith I owe to the King.

Ph. Did he not also take an Oath?

La. Yes; which is called the Oath of *Fealty*; I shall be to you both faithful, and lawfully shall do such customs and services, as my duty is to you at the terms assigned; so help me God, and all his Saints. But both these services, and the services of Husbandry were quickly after turned into Rents, payable either in Money, as in *England*; or in Corn, or other Victuals, as in *Scotland* and *France*. When the service was Military, the Tenant was for the most part bound to serve the King in his Wars with one, or more Persons, according to the yearly value of the Land he held.

Ph. Were they bound to find Horse-men, or Foot-men?

La. I do not find any Law that requires any Man, in respect of his Tenancie, to serve on Horseback.

Ph. Was the Tenant bound, in case he were called, to serve in Person? |

La. I think he was so in the beginning: For when Lands were given
(203) for service Military, and the Tenant dying left his Son and Heir, the Lord had the custody both of Body and Lands till the Heir was twenty one years old; and the reason thereof was, that the Heir till that Age of twenty one years, was presum'd to be unable to serve the King in his Wars, which reason had been insufficient, if the Heir had been bound to go to the Wars in Person. Which (methinks) should ever hold for Law, unless by some other Law it come to be altered. These services together with other Rights, as Wardships[, first][35] possession of his Tenants inheritance, Licenses for Alienation, Felons Goods, Felons Lands, if they were holden of the King, and the first years profit of the Lands, of whomsoever they were holden, Forfeitures, Amercements, and many other aids could not but amount to a very great yearly Revenue. Add to this all that which the King might reasonably have imposed upon Artificers and Tradesmen (for all Men, whom the King protecteth, ought to contribute towards their own protection) and consider then whether the Kings of those times had not means enough, and to spare (if God were not their Enemy) to defend their People against Forreign Enemies, and also to compell them to keep the Peace amongst themselves. |

Ph. And so had had the succeeding Kings, if they had never given
(204) their rights away, and their Subjects always kept their Oaths, and promises. In what manner proceeded those Ancient *Saxons*, and other Nations of *Germany*, especially the Northern parts, to the making of their Laws?

La. Sir *Edw. Coke* out of divers *Saxon* Laws gathered and published in *Saxon* and *Latine* by Mr. *Lambert*, inferreth,[36] that the *Saxon*

---

35. ⟨first,⟩   36. 1 *Inst.* fol. 110a. See also 4 *Inst.* chap. 1.

Kings, for the making of their Laws, called together the Lords and Commons, in such manner as is used at this day in *England*. But by those Laws of the *Saxons* published by Mr. *Lambert*, it appeareth, that the Kings called together the Bishops, and a great part of the wisest and discreetest Men of the Realm, and made Laws by their advice.

Ph. I think so; for there is no King in the World, being of ripe years and sound mind, that made any Law otherwise; for it concerns them in their own interest to make such Laws as the people can endure, and may keep them without impatience, and live in strength and courage to defend their King and Countrey, against their potent neighbours. But how was it discerned, and by whom was it determined, who were those wisest and discreetest Men? It is a hard matter to know who is wisest in our times. We know
(205) well enough who choo-|seth a Knight of the Shire, and what Towns are to send Burgesses to the Parliament, therefore if it were determined also in those dayes [as it has been since], who those wise Men should be, then, I confess, that the Parliaments of the old *Saxons*, and the Parliaments of *England* since are the same thing, and Sir *Edw. Coke* is in the right. Tell me therefore, if you can, when those Towns which now send Burgesses to the Parliament, began to do so, and upon what cause one Town had this priviledge, and another Town, though much more populous, had not.

La. At what time began this custom I cannot tell; but I am sure it is more ancient than the City of *Salisbury*; because there come two Burgesses to Parliament for a place near to it, called *Old Sarum*, which (as I Rid in sight of it) if I should tell a stranger that knew not what the word *Burgess* meant, he would think were a couple of Rabbets, the place looketh so like a long Cony-Borough. And yet a good Argument may be drawn from thence, that the Towns-men of every Town were the Electors of their own Burgesses, and Judges of their discretion; and that the Law, whether they be discreet or not, will suppose them to be discreet till the contrary be apparent. Therefore where it is said, that the King called
(206) together the more discreet Men of his Realm; | it must be understood of such Elections as are now in use: By which it is manifest, that those great and general Moots assembled by the old *Saxon* Kings, were of the same nature with the Parliaments assembled since the Conquest.

Ph. I think your reason is good: For I cannot conceive, how the

King, or any other but the inhabitants of the Boroughs themselves, can take notice of the discretion, or sufficiency of those they were to send to the Parliament. And for the Antiquity of the Burgess-Towns, since it is not mentioned in any History, or certain Record now extant, it is free for any Man to propound his conjecture. You know, that this Land was invaded by the *Saxons* at several times, and conquered by pieces in several Wars; so that there were in *England* many Kings at once, and every of them had his Parliament, and therefore according as there were more, or fewer walled Towns within each Kings Dominion, his Parliament had the more, or fewer Burgesses: But when all these lesser Kingdoms were joyned into one, then to that one Parliament came Burgesses from all the Burroughs of *England*. And this perhaps may be the reason, why there be so many more such Burroughs in the West, than in any other part of the Kingdom;

(207) the West being more populous, and also more | obnoxious to invaders, and for that cause having greater store of Towns Fortified. This I think may be the original of that priviledge which some Towns have to send Burgesses to the Parliament, and others have not.

La. The Conjecture is not improbable, and for want of greater certainty, may be allowed. But seeing it is commonly receiv'd, that for the making of a Law, there ought to be had the assent of the Lords Spiritual and Temporal; whom do you account in the Parliaments of the old *Saxons* for Lords Temporal, and whom for Lords Spiritual? For the Book called *The mode of holding Parliaments*, agreeth punctually with the manner of holding them at this day, and was written (as Sir *Edw. Coke* says) in the time of the *Saxons*, and before the Conquest.

Ph. Mr. *Selden* (a greater Antiquary than Sir *Edw. Coke*) in the last Edition of his Book of Titles of *Honour* says, that that Book called the *Mode, &c.* was not written till about the time of *Rich.* 2. and seems to me to prove it.[37] But howsoever that be, it is apparent by the *Saxon* Laws set forth by Mr. *Lambert*, that there were always called to the Parliament, certain great Persons called Aldermen, *alias* Earls; and so you have a House of Lords, and a House of Commons. Also you will find in the same place, that

(208) after the *Saxons* had received the Faith of Christ, | those Bishops

---

37. John Selden, *Titles of Honor*, 3d ed. (1672), pt. 2, chap. 5, sect. 26, pp. 613-15.

that were amongst them, were always at the great Mootes, in which they made their Laws.

Thus you have a perfect *English* Parliament, saving that the name of Barons was not amongst them, as being a *French* Title, which came in with the Conqueror.

FINIS.